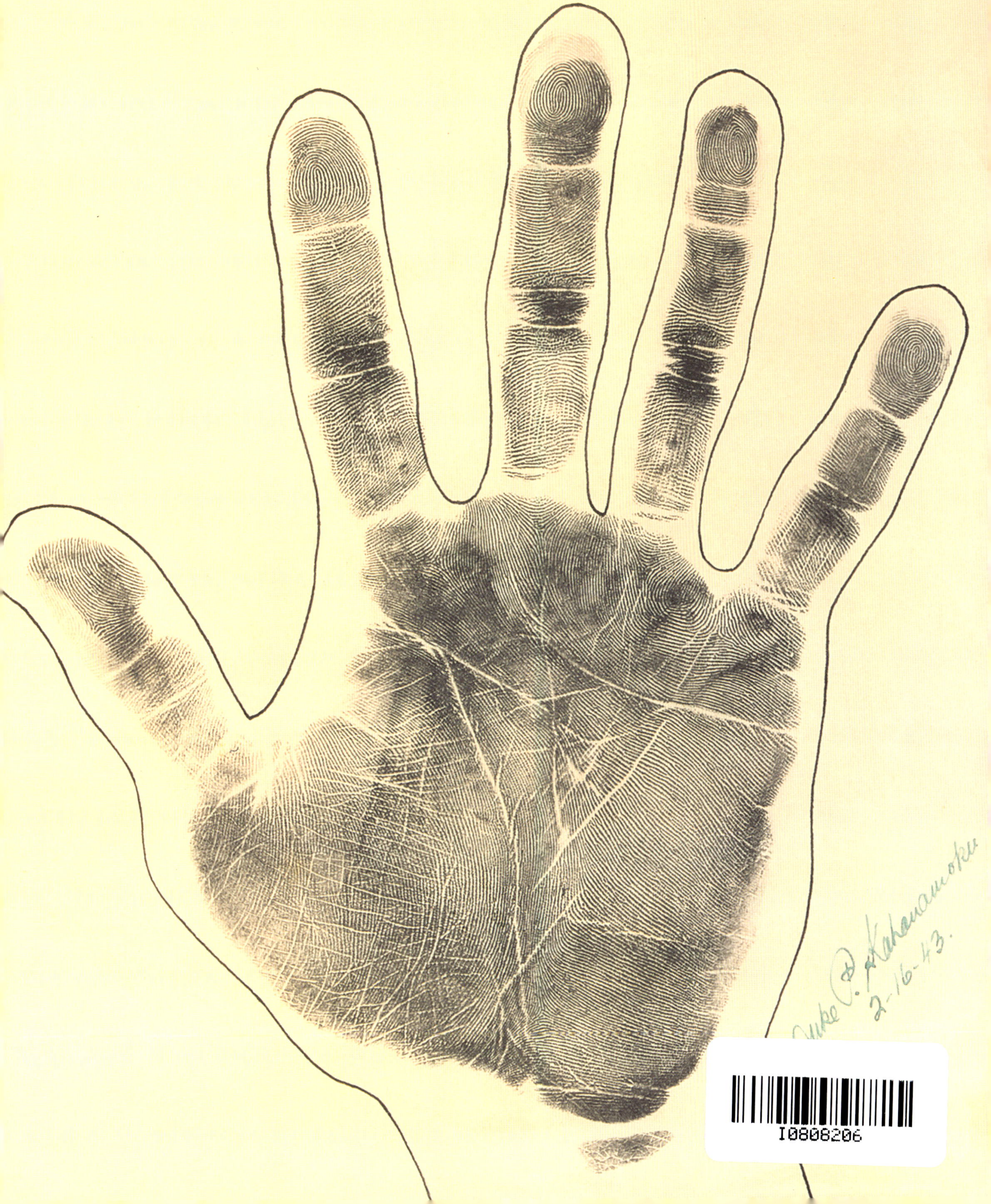
uke P. Kahanamoku
2-16-43.

Surf's Up

Collecting the Longboard Era

Mark A. Blackburn

Schiffer Publishing Ltd®
4880 Lower Valley Road, Atglen, PA 19310 USA

Dedication

This book is dedicated to my good friend Ken Wainwright, whose soul is surfing and who shared with me the secrets of Honolii.

Acknowledgements

I thank the following people for their help in making this book possible: Ken Wainwright, Buck Labadie, Pete Noble, Mark Fragale, Dick Metz, Ben Finney, Alan Seymour, Walter and Flippy Hoffman, Spencer Croul, Peter and Nancy Schiffer, and my manager at WholesaleRug.com, Kelly Glouner.

Author's Note

In the case of Hawaiian words, the absence of the glottal stop and the macron in my text is a deliberate omission and not due to an oversight. During the time period of the items covered in this book, correct pronunciations were universally known, making diacritical marks totally unnecessary and, therefore, not used.

Notes on the Pricing

Magazines & Books- All prices listed are for good condition with their original covers attached. Add 100% for mint condition copies. The listings end with magazine issues dated 1969, due to the arrival of the shortboard.

Posters, Ephemera, Artwork & Curios- add 50% for autographed items.

Library of Congress Cataloging-in-Publication Data

Blackburn, Mark (Mark A.)
Surfs up: collecting the longboard era / Mark A. Blackburn.
p. cm.
ISBN 0-7643-1355-X
1. Surfing--Collectibles. 2. Surfing--History. 3. Surfing--Bibliography. 4. Surfboards. I. Title.
GV840.S8 B495 2001
797.3'2--dc21
2001001212

Endsheets: **Duke Kahanamoku's Handprints and Signature.**

Title page: **Vintage Advertisement** and **United Airlines** ***Surfs Up*** **Poster.** Circa 1960. Scarce 'Bring your own board' version. Mauna Kea Galleries, Kamuela, Hawaii. $800-1200

Back jacket flap: **Redwood Plank Board, 11'2".** Circa 1920s. Rare and historic, this is one of Duke Kahanamoku's personal boards. **Canoe Paddle, 5'9".** This canoe paddle was presented to Duke Kahanamoku in 1931 by Dad Center of the Outrigger Canoe Club. It weighs nearly 8 pounds. The board and paddle show Duke's great strength and endurance. Both descended directly from the Kahanamoku family. Mauna Kea Galleries, Kamuela, Hawaii.

Layout by Bonnie M. Hensley
Cover design by Bruce M. Waters
Type set in Impress BT/Aldine721 BT
ISBN: 0-7643-1355-X
Printed in China
1 2 3 4

Published by Schiffer Publishing Ltd.
4880 Lower Valley Road
Atglen, PA 19310
Phone: (610) 593-1777; Fax: (610) 593-2002
E-mail: Schifferbk@aol.com
Please visit our web site catalog at
www.schifferbooks.com

This book may be purchased from the publisher.
Include $3.95 for shipping. Please try your bookstore first.
We are always looking for people to write books on new and related subjects. If you have an idea for a book please contact us at the above address.
You may write for a free catalog.

In Europe, Schiffer books are distributed by
Bushwood Books
6 Marksbury Avenue
Kew Gardens
Surrey TW9 4JF England
Phone: 44 (0) 20-8392-8585; Fax: 44 (0) 20-8392-9876
E-mail: Bushwd@aol.com
Free postage in the UK. Europe: air mail at cost.

Contents

Going My Wave. A John Severson film, circa 1962. Mauna Kea Galleries, Kamuela, Hawaii. $150-250

Original Engraving by John Webber - ***A View of Karakakooa, in Owyhee.*** From Captain Cook's Third Voyage Atlas, London 1784. This superb panorama of Kealekekua Bay, Hawaii, is looking towards Ka'awaloa from Napo'opo'o. The Kikiau heiau or Hawaiian temple is on the right; Captain Cook's ships are in the foreground. This is a nearly exact representation of what it looked like in 1779 when Cook arrived in the bay. What makes this engraving so important is that it is the first known depiction of a man paddling out on a surfboard (lower left) with other Hawaiians to meet Cook's ships. Lt. James King published the account of the voyage in 1784, and this was the first published account of surfing; the following is an excerpt:
The boldness and address with which I saw them perform these difficult and dangerous manoeuvers was altogether astonishing and is scarcely believed. Mauna Kea Galleries, Kamuela, Hawaii. $1,200-1,800

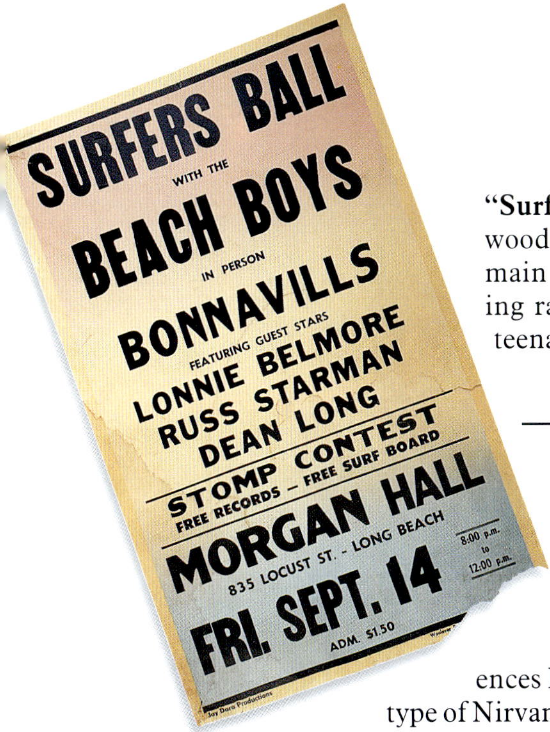

Introduction

"**Surfing** A water sport in which the participant stands on a floating slab of wood resembling an ironing board in both size and shape and attempts to remain perpendicular while being hurled towards the shore at a rather frightening rate of speed on the crest of a huge wave. (Especially recommended for teenagers and all others without the slightest regard for either life or limb.)"

The Beach Boys, "Surfin' U.S.A." note on record album, 1963

This book is a project I have taken on with great enthusiasm so that the readers hopefully will find it enjoyable and informative. Surfing to me is one of the most pleasurable and spiritual experiences I have encountered and represents a type of Nirvana and lifestyle not encountered anywhere else. The simple act of "paddling out" seems to relieve the everyday stress and strain of life and frees one's mind; once you are on a wave you are taken to another dimension – a harmonious adventure of being one with nature...

Surfing has its soul and origins in Ancient Polynesia where, on several islands, it was mainly a children's pastime using small bodyboards. In the islands of Tahiti it may have advanced to a somewhat more serious level as early visitors in the 18th century cite Tahitians riding boards in a kneeling position. From here, if current Pacific voyaging theories are correct, it probably spread to the islands of Hawaii and New Zealand, with the Maori people in a prone position riding short boards of up to six feet in length and eight to nine inches in width.

In Hawaii, the sport seems to have blossomed early into a recreational activity primarily reserved for Hawaiian nobility where riders rode boards of up to 24 feet in length and approximately 2 feet in width and weighing up to 200 pounds. These large boards provided the necessary flotation to support the rider in sitting, kneeling and standing positions. The three principal types of boards ridden according to size were the *paipo* or bodyboard usually measuring up to four feet in length; the *alaia*, measuring from approximately seven to twelve feet; and the *olo*, which was the largest and most regal board, measuring from sixteen to twenty-four feet and reserved only for Hawaiian *al'i*, or chiefs.

Early explorers and missionaries to the islands all recorded the sport of surfing on all the islands, although with the advent of the missionaries in the 1820s the sport seemed to decrease in activity; in the 1890s it was recorded by some visitors as being a thing of the past. With the advance of tourism to the islands around the turn of the century, surfing took on a whole new meaning. A renaissance in the sport took place under the likes of Alexander Ford Hume, George Freeth, and Duke Kahanamoku. By the 1920s, surfing was firmly established in California and Hawaii, with Waikiki being the center of the sport.

Above: **Surfers Ball with the Beach Boys in Person.** Circa early 1960s. Rare. Courtesy of Buck Labadie/Artstuff. $600-900

Right: **Kou Wood Surf Board, Olo Type, 8'4".** Collected by a Mr. Arning in 1887 in Hilo, Hawaii, this board may be one of the earliest boards of its type collected in Hawaii. This is the first time this board has ever been published. Staatliche Mussen zu Berlin–PreuBischer Kulturbesitz Ethnologisches Museum. Photographer: Martin Franken

In the 1930s and '40s, it was watermen like Tom Blake, Joe Quigg, Doc Ball, and others who helped popularize the sport and promote it as a 'lifestyle.'

With the onset of the 1950s, surfing was well entrenched. The explosion of surfing as popular culture happened in the late 1950s with the advent of *Gidget* (book and movie) and the popular music of Dick Dale, followed soon by the Beach Boys and an endless series of Hollywood surf movies. With the development of the foam board at this time, surfing became available to the masses; the assistance of board makers like Dale Velzy, among others, made the new lighter-weight boards affordable to the waiting public. By the mid-1960s, I estimate that over 20,000 boards were being produced each year– just at the onset of the Viet Nam conflict. This war took its toll in many ways, including surfing, when many a GI left his board back home, never to return. By 1969 the popularity of surfing had somewhat faded as new shorter boards were introduced. For this book, I conclude with the end of the longboard era in 1969.

Today, "longboarding" is making a revival as many older surfers return to the waves–often searching for a happier and healthier time. I find myself in this category–searching, in my way, for a time of lost innocence and freedom from daily challenges we all face. To me, surfing is a lifestyle and a sport unlike any other–"The Sport of Kings." May you experience some of its joy and Nirvana through the following pages.

Mark Blackburn
Kamuela, Hawaii
January 2001

Original Engraving from the French Voyage of the *Uranie*. Published in the official Atlas from the French voyage of the *Uranie*, the original drawing was done by Alphonse Pellion in 1819 at the residence of Chief Kalanimoku at Kailua, Kona. This is one of the earliest known depictions of a surfboard. The author had the privilege of buying the original Hawaiian drawings from this voyage directly from the Freycinet family in France. They are now housed in the Honolulu Academy of Arts, with the exception of three. Mauna Kea Galleries, Kamuela, Hawaii. $80-120

Surf's Up
Collecting the Longboard Era

And I have loved thee, Ocean! and my joy
Of youthful sports was on thy breast to be
Borne like thy bubbles, onward; from a boy
I wantoned with thy breakers, - They to me
Were a delight; and if the freshening sea
Made them a terror, 'twas a pleasing fear;
For I was as it were a child of thee,
And trusted to thy billows far and near,
And laid my hand upon thy mane, -
As I do here.
Lord Byron, from "Childe Harold," 1812

Original Engraving – *Hawaiian Sport of Surf Playing*. From William Ellis' tour of Hawaii, 1827. Mauna Kea Galleries, Kamuela, Hawaii. $80-120

Souvenir China. Circa 1890s. A fine china demitasse cup and saucer with an early image of a surfer and grass hut. Cup is entitled *Native with Surf Board, Honolulu, H.I.*, and saucer is entitled *Native Grass House, Honolulu, H.I.* Made in Karlsbad, Austria. Mauna Kea Galleries, Kamuela, Hawaii. $400-600

Postcard. Circa 1905. Entitled "Famous Surf Riders, Hawaiian Islands." Mauna Kea Galleries, Kamuela, Hawaii. $30-50

Redwood, 10'0". A solid redwood board made in 1908 by the Outrigger Canoe Club. Dick Metz, Dana Point, California. $6,000-9,000

George Freeth

Born in 1883 in Honolulu, this Irish-Hawaiian was the first to introduce surfing to Southern California in 1907. He was brought to California from Honolulu by Henry Huntington, whose Pacific Electric Railroad was in need of promotion along with his new salt water plunge. A close friend of Alexander Hume Ford and Duke Kahanamoku, he was one of the charter members of the Outrigger Canoe Club.

Original Photograph of Members of the Hui Nalu Club. Circa 1915, Waikiki Beach. Mauna Kea Galleries, Kamuela, Hawaii. $500-700

Trophy, Indoor Yacht Club, Pacific Coast Swimming Championships, July 4-18, 1913. Won by Hui Nalu, Honolulu. A rare and historic bit of Hawaiian surfing and swimming history. Allan Seymour, Pacific Coast Vintage Surf Auctions. $4,000-6,000

Hui Nalu Club

Informally founded by native Hawaiians as a surf club in 1905, it was officially organized by John D. Kaupiko in 1911 as a response to the Outrigger Canoe Club that, several years earlier, had been started by Alexander Ford Hume and the local haole population of Honolulu. Besides giving Hawaiian's their rightful place on the beach, it provided friendly rivalry among the two clubs with considerable competition in canoes, swimming and paddle boards. Duke Kahanamoku and his brothers were early members, winning many races for the club during Kamehameha Day celebrations and other competitions.

Alexander Hume Ford 1868-1945

Born of a Southern family in Charleston, South Carolina, he attended Porter Military Academy. After graduating, he began working as a writer of plays and articles for newspapers and magazines. On a research trip to Hawaii in 1907, this adventurous mainlander became so enamoured with the sport of surfing that he took it upon himself to boost its revival and popularity. This one-week research trip turned into a lifetime of passion and enthusiasm for the sport. In this same year, he began conducting surfing classes for children on the beach at Waikiki. It was at this time that the famous author Jack London was visiting Hawaii on his famous cruise of "The Snark." London was so impressed with the sport that he asked Hume to teach him, and so, on a hot June afternoon, the two of them, along with George Freeth, paddled out at Waikiki, forming a friendship that lasted a lifetime.

With the development of Waikiki Beach, hotels and bungalows began blocking off beach access. Hume founded the famous Outrigger Canoe Club on May 1, 1908, for the purpose of "preserving surfing on boards and in Hawaiian outrigger canoes." Being the first organization of its type in the world, the club offered facilities for dressing and a grass hut for board storage right on the beach, giving surfers easy access. (When Jack London returned to Hawaii in 1915, he was amazed to find the Club had over 1,200 members.)

A close friend of George Freeth and Duke Kahanamoku, Hume also organized a "Hands-Around-the-Pacific Club" and held a Pan-Pacific Conference in Honolulu in 1911. An avid outdoorsman, he also was the founder of the Hawaiian Trail and Mountain Club and the Boy Scouts of Hawaii. Without a doubt, it was Alexander Ford Hume, with his close friendship with Jack London, who exposed surfing to the rest of the world and in so-doing made Waikiki a major tourist destination. Surfing was recognized as an invigorating and healthy pastime.

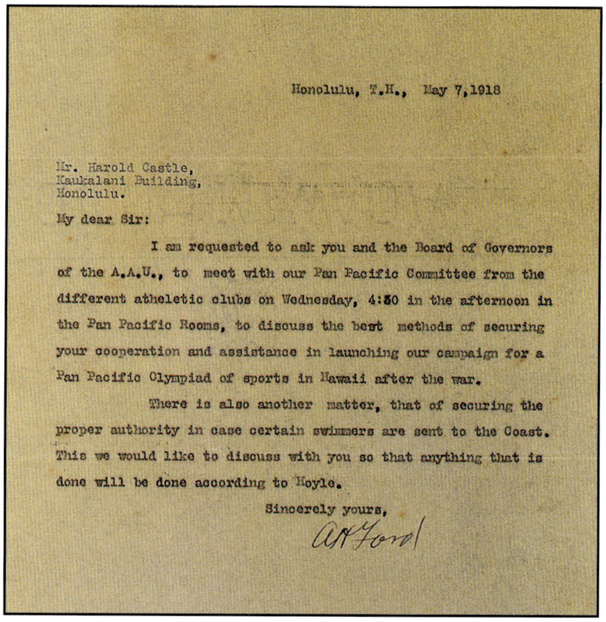

Honolulu, T.H., May 7,1918

Mr. Harold Castle,
Kaukalani Building,
Honolulu.

My dear Sir:

I am requested to ask you and the Board of Governors of the A.A.U., to meet with our Pan Pacific Committee from the different atheletic clubs on Wednesday, 4:30 in the afternoon in the Pan Pacific Rooms, to discuss the best methods of securing your cooperation and assistance in launching our campaign for a Pan Pacific Olympiad of sports in Hawaii after the war.

There is also another matter, that of securing the proper authority in case certain swimmers are sent to the Coast. This we would like to discuss with you so that anything that is done will be done according to Hoyle.

Sincerely yours,

AHFord

Letter from Alexander Hume Ford, May 7, 1918, relating to the A. A. U. discussing plans for a possible Pan Pacific Olympiad in Hawaii. Rare. Mauna Kea Galleries, Kamuela, Hawaii. $1,200-1,800

Booklet – *A Trip to Hawaii*. Published in 1894 by the Union Photo and Engraving Company in San Francisco. This is one of the earliest known tourist booklets promoting the Islands. Mauna Kea Galleries, Kamuela, Hawaii. $300-500

Original Photograph of Jack London by Ray Jerome Baker. Circa 1915. Here the Londons are sitting on the beach in front of the Outrigger Canoe Club, along with an unidentified woman and young girl, and, to the right, Alexander Hume Ford, who taught Jack London to surf. This photograph is reproduced in *Our Hawaii* by Charmain London, p. 246. Mauna Kea Galleries, Kamuela, Hawaii. $500-700

Jack London 1876-1916

Born John Griffith London in San Francisco, California, London earned a reputation as an adventurer and popular author. Mr. and Mrs. Jack London arrived at Pearl Harbor from San Francisco on May 20, 1907, aboard their 43-foot yacht the *Snark* (named after the imaginary creature in Lewis Carroll's fantasy poem *The Hunting of the Snark*).

This was his second trip to Hawaii and the first for his wife, spending five months on the islands of Oahu, Molokai, Maui and Hawaii, before embarking on a two-year cruise of the South Seas. It was during this time that London was the world's highest paid writer, having considerable success with his many popular stories, including *The Call of the Wild*, *The Sea Wolf* and *White Fang*. While in Hawaii, he was entertained by Hawaiian Royalty, including the deposed Queen. It was during this time that he had his first encounter with the sport of surfing, after being taught to surf by Alexander Ford Hume. In his powerful essay *A Royal Sport*, he describes his personal experiences when first learning to ride a surfboard at Waikiki Beach. This, along with Hume's promotion of the sport, exposed this relatively unknown pastime to a worldwide audience. With the publication of *The Cruise of the Snark* in 1911, the acclaimed author placed Waikiki on the map as the center of the sport. London's second wife Charmain Kittredge (1871-1955), whom he married not long before the voyage, was also an enthusiast, although there is no apparent reference to her surfing. An author herself, she wrote many books, including *Our Hawaii*, which was based upon her five months in the Islands in 1907 as well as their second and third trips in 1915 and 1916.

Often troubled by physical ailments, London developed kidney disease of unknown origin during his thirties. Jack London died at his Beauty Ranch in Glen Ellen, California, in 1916, of renal failure. Upon his death, the deposed Queen Liliuokalani stated, *By the point of his pen his genius conquered all prejudice and gave out to the world at large true facts concerning the Hawaiian people...*

Original Signed Passport Photo of Jack London by Arnold Genthe. A rare photo given by Jack London who tore off his passport photo from the *Cruise of the Snark* and gave it to Edith B. Williams, who was the sister of Claire (Mrs. Bruce Cartwright) of Honolulu. Very rare. Mauna Kea Galleries, Kamuela, Hawaii. $6,000-9,000

Booklet - *Jack London – Learning Hawaiian Surfing*. Privately published in Honolulu in 1983 by Scott Burlington. This small booklet contains London's published essay entitled "A Royal Sport." What makes this copy extremely important is that noted surf historian Gary Lynch sent this copy to Tom Blake with accompanying letter asking him to make notations in his handwriting of any similar conditions he found in Hawaii while visiting there for the first time. Rare. Mauna Kea Galleries, Kamuela, Hawaii. $1,200-1,800 Booklet alone: $40-60

Real Photo Postcard Depicting Jack London Surfing. Circa 1910. Here Jack London is seen surfing at Canoes, Waikiki, in a standing position on his board. Possibly the only existing photo of Jack London surfing. Mauna Kea Galleries, Kamuela, Hawaii. $800-1,200

Comic Postcard by Boisse. Circa 1915. Mauna Kea Galleries, Kamuela, Hawaii. $30-50

Original Signed and Dated Photograph of Jack and Charmain London. Waikiki Beach, 1915. This is the only known signed photo of the Londons during their stay in Hawaii. This previously unpublished photograph was taken by Ray Jerome Baker in front of the Outrigger Canoe Club and was found in Baker's personal effects at the time of his death. Mauna Kea Galleries, Kamuela, Hawaii. $8,000-12,000

Excerpts From *A Royal Sport: Surfing at Waikiki*

By Jack London

That is what it is, a royal sport for the natural kings of earth. The grass grows right down to the water at Waikiki Beach, and within fifty feet of the everlasting sea. The trees also grow down to the salty edge of things, and one sits in their shade and looks seaward at a majestic surf thundering in on the beach to one's very feet. Half a mile out, where is the reef, the white-headed combers thrust suddenly skyward out of the placid turquoise-blue and come rolling into shore. One after another they come, a mile long, with smoking crests, the white battalions of the infinite army of the sea. And one sits and listens to the perpetual roar, and watches the unending procession, and feels tiny and fragile before this tremendous force expressing itself in fury and foam and sound. Indeed, one feels microscopically small, and the thought that one may wrestle with this sea raises in one's imagination a thrill of apprehension, almost of fear. Why, they are a mile long, these bull-mouthed monsters, and they weight a thousand tons, and they charge in to shore faster than a man can run. What chance? No chance at all, is the verdict of the shrinking ego; and one sits, and looks and listens, and thinks the grass and the shade are a pretty good place in which to be.

And suddenly, out there where a big smoker lifts skyward, rising like a sea-god from out of the welter of spume and churning white, on the giddy, toppling, overhanging and downfalling, precarious crest appears the dark head of a man. Swiftly he rises through the rushing white. His black shoulders, his chest, his loins, his limbs—all is abruptly projected on one's vision. Where but the moment before was only the wide desolation and invincible roar, is now a man, erect, full-statured, not struggling frantically in that wild movement, not buried and crushed and buffeted by those mighty monsters, but standing above them all, calm and superb, poised on the giddy summit, his feet buried in the churning foam, the salt smoke rising to his knees, and all the rest of him in the free air and flashing sunlight, and he is flying through the air, flying forward, flying fast as the surge on which he stands. He is a Mercury—a brown Mercury. His heels are winged, and in them is the swiftness of the sea. In truth, from out of the sea he has leaped upon the back of the sea, and he is riding the sea that roars and bellows and cannot shake him from its back. But no frantic outreaching and balancing is his. He is impassive, motionless as a statue carved suddenly by some miracle out the sea's depth from which he rose. And straight on toward shore he flies on his winged heels and the white crest of the breaker. There is a wild burst of foam, a long tumultuous rushing sound as the breaker falls futile and spent on the beach at your feet; and there, at your feet, steps calmly ashore a Kanaka, burnt golden and brown by the tropic sun. Several minutes ago he was a speck a quarter of a mile away. He has "bitted the bull-mouthed breaker" and ridden it in, and the pride in the feat shows in the carriage of his magnificent body as he glances for a moment carelessly at you who sit in the shade of the shore. He is a Kanaka—and more, he is a man, a member of the kingly species that has mastered matter and the brutes and lorded it over creation.

Original Photograph of Jack and Charmain London by Ray Jerome Baker. Taken in front of the Outrigger Canoe Club in 1915. Mauna Kea Galleries, Kamuela, Hawaii. $600-900

And one sits and thinks of Tristram's last wrestle with the sea on that fatal morning; and one thinks further to the fact that Kanaka has done what Tristram never did, and that he knows a joy of the sea that Tristram never knew. And still further one thinks. It is all very well, sitting here in cool shade of the beach, but you are a man, one of the kingly species, and what that Kanaka can do, you can do yourself. Go to. Strip off your clothes that are a nuisance in this mellow clime. Get in and wrestle with the sea; wing your heels with the skill and power that reside in you; bite the sea's breakers, master them, and ride upon their backs as a king should.

And that is how it came about that I tackled surf-riding. And now that I have tackled it, more than ever do I hold it to be a royal sport. But first let me explain the physics of it. A wave is a communicated agitation. The water that composes the body of a wave does not move. If it did, when a stone is thrown into a pond and the ripples spread away in an ever widening circle, there would appear at the center an ever increasing hole. No, the water that composes the body of a wave is stationary. Thus, you may watch a particular portion of the ocean's surface and you will see the same water rise and fall a thousand times to the agitation communicated by a thousand successive waves. Now imagine this communicated agitation moving shoreward. As the bottom shoals, the lower portion of the wave strikes land first and is stopped. But water is fluid, and the upper portion has not struck anything, wherefore it keeps on communicating its agitation, keeps on going. And when the top of the wave keeps on going, while the bottom it if lags behind, something is bound to happen. The bottom of the wave drops out from under and the top of the wave falls over, forward, and down, curling and cresting and roaring as it does so. It is the bottom of a wave striking against the top of the land that is the cause of all surfs.

But the transformation from a smooth undulation to a breaker is not abrupt except where the bottom shoals abruptly. Say the bottom shoals gradually for from quarter of a mile to a mile, then an equal distance will be occupied by the transformation. Such a bottom is that off the beach of Waikiki, and it produces a splendid surf-riding surf. One leaps upon the back of a breaker just as it begins to break, and stays on as it continues to break all the way in to shore.

And now to the particular physics of surf-riding. Get out on a flat board, six feet long, two feet wide, and roughly oval in shape. Lie down upon it like a small boy on a coaster and paddle with your hands out to deep water, where the waves begin to crest. Lie out there quietly on the board. Sea after sea breaks before, behind, and under and over you, and rushes in to shore, leaving you behind. When a wave crests, it gets steeper. Imagine yourself, on your board, on the face of that steep slope. If it stood still, you would slide down just as a boy slides down a hill on his coaster. "But," you object, "the wave doesn't stand still." Very true, but the water composing the wave stands still, and there you have the secret. If ever you start sliding down the face of that wave, you'll keep on sliding and you'll never reach the bottom. Please don't laugh. The face of that wave may be only six feet, yet you can slide down it a quarter of a mile, or half a mile, and not reach the bottom. For, see, since a wave is only a communicated agitation of impetus, and since the water that composes a wave is changing every instant, new water is rising into the wave as fast as the wave travels. You slide down this new water, and yet remain in your old position on the wave, sliding down the still newer water that is rising and forming the wave. You slide precisely as fast as the wave travels. If it travels fifteen miles an hour, you slide fifteen miles an hour. As the wave travels, this water obligingly heaps itself into the wave, gravity does the rest, and down you go, sliding the whole length of it. If you still cherish the notion, while sliding, that the water is moving with you, thrust your arms into it and attempt to paddle; you will find that you have to be remarkably quick to get a stroke, for that water is dropping astern just as fast as you are rushing ahead.

And now for another phase of the physics of surf-riding. All rules have their exceptions. It is true that the water in a wave does not travel forward. But there is what may be called the send of the sea. The water in the overtoppling crest does move forward, as you will speedily realize if you are slapped in the face by it, or if you are caught under it and are pounded by one mighty blow down under the surface panting and gasping for half a minute. The water in the top of a wave rests upon the water in the bottom of the wave. But when the bottom of the wave strikes the land, it stops, while the top goes on. It no longer has the bottom of the wave to hold it up. Where was solid water beneath it, is now air, and for the first time it feels the grip of gravity, and down it falls, at the same time being torn asunder from the lagging bottom of the wave and flung forward. And it is because of this that riding a surfboard is something more than a mere placid sliding down a hill. In truth, one is caught up and hurled shoreward as by some Titan's hand.

I deserted the cool shade, put on a swimming suit, and got hold of a surfboard. It was too small a board. But I didn't know, and nobody told me. I joined some little Kanaka boys in shallow water, where the breakers were well spent and small—a regular kindergarten school. I watched the little Kanaka boys. When a likely-looking breaker came along, they flopped upon their stomachs on their boards, kicked like mad with their feet, and rode the breaker in to the beach. I tried to emulate them. I watched them, tried to do everything that they did, and failed utterly. The breaker swept past, and I was not on it. I tried again and again. I kicked twice as madly as they did, and failed. Half a dozen would be around. We would all leap on our boards in front of a good breaker. Away our feet would churn like the stern-wheels of river steamboats, and away the little rascals would scoot while I remained in disgrace behind.

I tried for a solid hour, and not one wave could I persuade to boost me shoreward. And then arrived a friend, Alexander Hume Ford, a globe-trotter by profession, bent ever on the pursuit of sensation. And he had found it at Waikiki. Heading for Australia, he had stopped off for a week to find out if there were any thrills of surf-riding, and he had become wedded to it. He had been at it every day for a month and could not yet see any symptoms of the fascination lessening on him. He spoke with authority.

"Get off the board," he said. "Chuck it away at once. Look at the way you're trying to ride it. If ever the nose of that board hits bottom, you'll be disemboweled. Here, take my board. It's a man's size."

I am always humble when confronted by knowledge. Ford knew. He showed me how properly to mount his board. Then he waited for a good breaker, gave me a shove at the right moment, and started me in. Ah, delicious moment when I felt that breaker grip and fling me! On I dashed, a hundred and fifty feet, and subsided with the breaker on the sand. From that moment I was lost. I waded back to Ford with his board. It was a large one, several inches thick, and weighed all of seventy-five pounds. He gave me advice, much of it. He had had no one to teach him, and all that he had laboriously learned in several weeks he communicated to me in half and hour. I really learned by proxy. And inside of half an hour I was able to start myself and ride in. I did it time after time, and Ford applauded and advised. For instance, he told me to get just so far forward on the board and no farther. But I must have got some farther, for as I came charging in to land, that miserable board poked its nose down to bottom, stopped abruptly, and turned a somersault, at the same time violently severing our relations. I was tossed through the air like a chip and buried ignominiously under the downfalling breaker. And I realized that if it hadn't been for Ford, I'd have been disemboweled. That particular risk is part of the sport, Ford says. Maybe he'll have it happen to him before he leaves Waikiki, and then, I feel confident, his yearning for sensation will be satisfied for a time...

...The water that rolls in on Waikiki Beach is just the same as the water that laves on the shores of all the Hawaiian Islands; and in ways, especially from the swimmer's standpoint, it is wonderful water. It is cool enough to be comfortable, while it is warm enough to permit a swimmer to stay in all day without experiencing a chill. Under the sun or the stars, at high noon or at midnight, in midwinter or in midsummer, it does not matter when, it is always the same temperature—not too warm, not too cold, just right. It is wonderful water, salt as old ocean itself, pure and crystal-clear. When the nature of the water is considered, it is not so remarkable after all that the Kanakas are one of the most expert of swimming races.

So it was, next morning, when Ford came along, that I plunged into the wonderful water for a swim of indeterminate length. Astride of our surfboards, or, rather, flat down upon them on our stomachs, we paddled out through the kindergarten where the little Kanaka boys were at play. Soon we were out in deep water where the big smokers came roaring in. The mere struggle with them, facing them, and paddling seaward over them and through them, was sport enough in itself. One had to have his wits about him, for it was a battle in which mighty blows were struck, on one side, and in which cunning was used on the other side—a struggle between insensate force and intelligence. I soon learned a bit. When a breaker curled over my head, for a swift instant I could see the light of day through its emerald body; then down would go my head, and I would clutch the board with all my strength. Then would come the blow, and to the onlooker on shore I would be blotted out. In reality the board and I have passed through the crest and emerged in the respite of the other side. I should not recommend those smashing blows to an invalid or delicate person. There is weight behind them, and the impact of the driven water is like a sandblast. Sometimes one passes through half a dozen combers in quick succession, and it is just about that time that he is liable to discover new merits in the stable land and new reasons for being on shore.

Out there in the midst of such a succession of big smoky ones, a third man was added to our part, one Freeth. Shaking the water from my eyes as I emerged from one wave and peered ahead to see what the next one looked like, I saw him tearing in on the back of it, standing upright on his board, carelessly poised, a young god bronzed with sunburn. We went through the wave on the back of which he rode. Ford called to him. He turned an airspring from his wave, rescued his board

Original Photograph of Jack London by Ray Jerome Baker. Taken in front of Jack's bungalow on Waikiki Beach in 1915. Mauna Kea Galleries, Kamuela, Hawaii. $400-600

from its maw, paddled over to us and joined Ford in showing me things. One thing in particular I learned from Freeth, namely, how to encounter the occasional breaker of exceptional size that rolled in. Such breakers were really ferocious, and it was unsafe to meet them on top of the board. But Freeth showed me, so that whenever I saw one of that caliber rolling down on me, I slid off the rear end of the board and dropped down beneath the surface, my arms over my head and holding the board. Thus, if the wave ripped the board out of my hands and tried to strike me with it (a common trick of such waves), there would be a cushion of water a foot or more in depth, between my head and the blow. When the wave passed, I climbed upon the board and paddled on. Many men have been terribly injured, I learn, by being struck by their boards...

...The man who wants to learn surf-riding must be a strong swimmer, and he must be used to going under the water. After that, fair strength and common sense are all that is required. The force of the big comber is rather unexpected. There are mix-ups in which board and rider are torn apart and separated by several hundred feet. The surf-rider must take care of himself. No matter how many riders swim out with him, he cannot depend upon any of them for aid. The fancied security I had in the presence of Ford and Freeth made me forget that it was my first swim out in deep water among the big ones. I recollected, however, and rather suddenly, for a big wave came in, and away went the two men on its back all the way to shore. I could have been drowned a dozen different ways before they got back to me.

One slides down the face of a breaker on his surfboard, but he has to get started to sliding. Board and rider must be moving shoreward at a good rate before the wave overtakes them. When you see the wave coming that you want to ride in, you turn tail to it and paddle shoreward with all your strength, using what is called the windmill stroke. This is a sort of spurt performed immediately in front of the wave. If the board is going fast enough, the wave accelerates it, and the board begins its quarter-of-a-mile slide.

I shall never forget the first big wave I caught out there in the deep water. I saw it coming, turned my back on it, and paddled for dear life. Faster and faster my board went, till it seemed my arms would drop off. What was happening behind me I could not tell. One cannot look behind and paddle the windmill stroke. I heard the crest of the wave hissing and churning, and then by board was lifted and flung forward. I scarcely knew what happened the first half-minute. Though I kept my eyes open, I could not see anything, for I was buried in the rushing white of the crest. But I did not mind. I was chiefly conscious of ecstatic bliss at having caught the wave. At the end of the half-minute, however, I began to see things, and to breathe. I saw that three feet of the nose was clear out of water and riding on the air. I shifted my weight forward, and made the nose come down. Then I lay, quite at rest in the midst of the wild movement, and watched the shore and the bathers on the beach grow distinct. I didn't cover quite

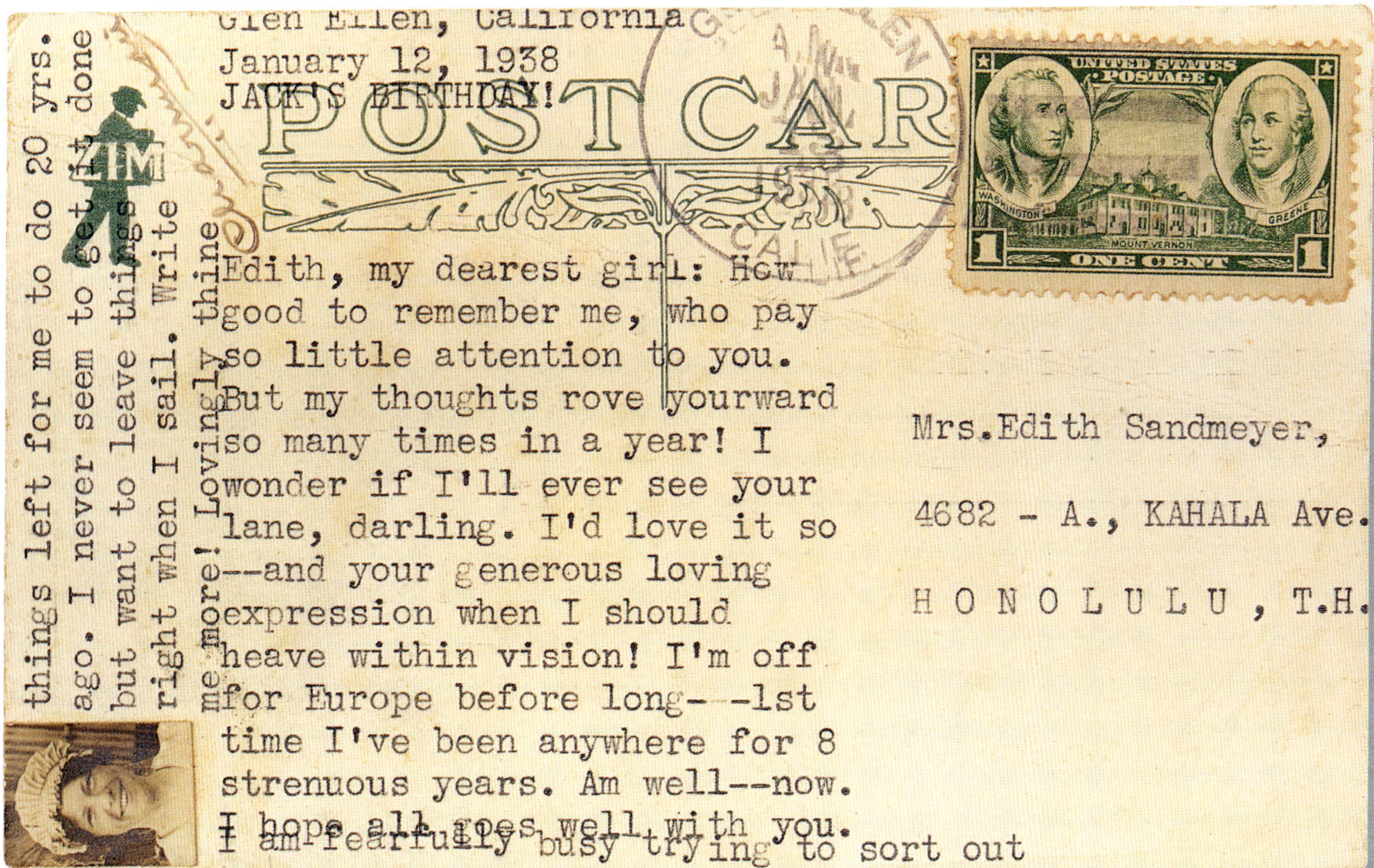

Glen Ellen, California
January 12, 1938
JACK'S BIRTHDAY!

POST CARD

Edith, my dearest girl: How good to remember me, who pay so little attention to you. But my thoughts rove yourward so many times in a year! I wonder if I'll ever see your lane, darling. I'd love it so—and your generous loving expression when I should heave within vision! I'm off for Europe before long——1st time I've been anywhere for 8 strenuous years. Am well—now. I hope all goes well with you. I am fearfully busy trying to sort out things left for me to do 20 yrs. ago. I never seem to get it done but want to leave things right when I sail. Write me more! Lovingly thine

Mrs. Edith Sandmeyer,
4682 - A., KAHALA Ave.
HONOLULU, T.H.

Postcard – *Jack London's 'Snark' on Alameda Estuary*. An unusual personal postcard sent by Charmain London in 1938, with her photograph attached to the reverse. Mauna Kea Galleries, Kamuela, Hawaii. $400-600

a quarter of a mile on that wave, because, to prevent the board from diving, I shifted my weight back, but shifted it too far and fell down the rear slope of the wave.

It was my second day at surf-riding, and I was quite proud of myself. I stayed out there four hours, and when it was over, I was resolved that on the morrow I'd come in standing up. But that resolution paved a distant place. On the morrow I was in bed. I was not sick, but I was very unhappy, and I was in bed. When describing the wonderful water of Hawaii I forgot to describe the wonderful sun of Hawaii. It is a tropic sun, and, furthermore, in the first part of June, it is an overhead sun. It is also an insidious, deceitful sun. For the first time in my life I was sunburned unawares. My arms, shoulders, and back had been burned many times in the past and were tough; but not so my legs. And for four hours I had exposed the tender backs of my legs, at right angles, to that perpendicular Hawaiian sun. It was not until after I got ashore that I discover the sun had touched me. Sunburn at first is merely warm; after that it grows intense and the blisters come out. Also, the joints, where the skin wrinkles, refuse to bend. That is why I spent the next day in bed. I couldn't walk. And that is why, today, I am writing in this bed. It is easier to than not to. But tomorrow, ah, tomorrow, I shall be out in that wonderful water, and I shall come in standing up, even as Ford and Freeth. And if I fail tomorrow, I shall do it on the next day, or the next. Upon one thing I am resolved: the *Snark* shall not sail from Honolulu until I, too, wing my heels with the swiftness of the sea, and become a sunburned, skin-peeling Mercury.

Redwood, 6'0". A solid redwood board with an important history, as this was Roy Blackshear's personal board and was previously used by his father, one of the Shipman's of Hilo, Hawaii. He used this board on the Shipman Estate in Keaau while growing up in the 1920s. This board exhibits the shape and style of all the greatest elements of ancient Polynesian design and influence. Board has old, wood butterfly repairs. Mauna Kea Galleries, Kamuela, Hawaii. $5,000-7,000

Real Photo Postcard of Waikiki Beach. The two children in this photo are shown holding a small wood body board, circa 1915. Mauna Kea Galleries, Kamuela, Hawaii. $120-180

Break The area where the waves are breaking. Synonymous with

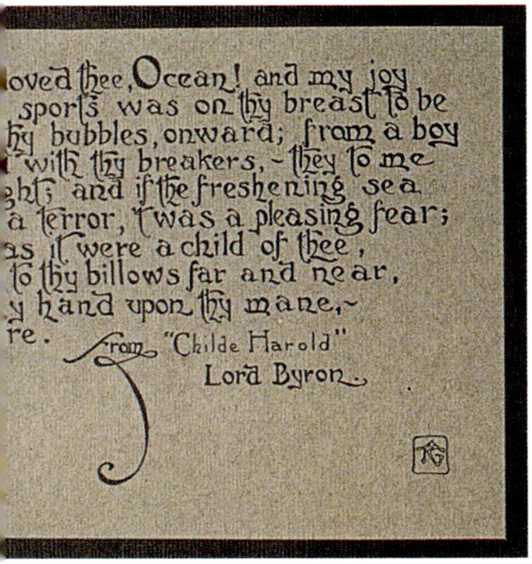
oved thee, Ocean! and my joy
sports was on thy breast to be
hy bubbles, onward; from a boy
with thy breakers, — they to me
ght; and if the freshening sea
a terror, 'twas a pleasing fear;
as it were a child of thee,
to thy billows far and near,
y hand upon thy mane, —
re.
from "Childe Harold"
Lord Byron

***The Surf Riders of Hawaii*.** Published by the noted art dealer A. R. Gurrey of Honolulu, circa 1913. There are seven tipped-in original photographs in this book, the photographs all being taken by his wife, Caroline H. Gurrey, who was a very well known photographer of the day. Fascinated by Hawaii's mixed races, especially children, her portraits gained her an invitation to display her work at the San Francisco exhibition of 1915. Today her rare sets of "Hawaiian Types" can be found housed in the Library of Congress and in the Academy of Arts, Honolulu. This booklet is extremely rare and is the first book ever published devoted entirely to the sport of surfing. Mauna Kea Galleries, Kamuela, Hawaii. $3,000-5,000

"surf break."

***The Mid-Pacific Magazine*, December 1912.** A forerunner to Paradise of the Pacific Magazine, this is the first issue to depict a surfer on the front cover. Edited by Alexander Hume Ford. Very rare. Mauna Kea Galleries, Kamuela, Hawaii. $600-900

Christmas Postcard – *Merry Christmas to You, Honolulu, T.H., Winter Sports*. Published by H. Culman, Fort & Hotel Sts., Honolulu, T.H., circa 1910. Mauna Kea Galleries, Kamuela, Hawaii. $60-90

Redwood, 7'5". A solid redwood Waikiki board, circa 1915. Old koa wood butterfly repairs. Dick Metz, Dana Point, California. $5,000-7,000

Wine Glass from the Pleasanton Hotel, Honolulu. Etched with a surfrider motif. Circa early 20th century. Mauna Kea Galleries, Kamuela, Hawaii. $120-180

Real Photo Postcard ***Native Surf Boats - Honolulu - Hawaii.*** Circa 1915, Mauna Kea Galleries, Kamuela, Hawaii. $120-180

Real Photo Postcard of Duke Kahanamoku. Circa 1915. An unusual postcard depicting the Duke doing a headstand while his tandem partner pulls the board down on the tail. Queen's Surf, Waikiki. Duke was well known for his wide repertoire of stunts, including jumping from one board to another and standing on his head, as shown in this photo. Rare. Mauna Kea Galleries, Kamuela, Hawaii. $200-300

Shore Break Describes small waves breaking close to or directly on the shore.

Real Photo Postcard. Circa 1915. Mauna Kea Galleries, Kamuela, Hawaii. $100-150

Postcard of Duke Kahanamoku. Circa 1912. Entitled "D. Kahanamoku, Hawai." Mauna Kea Galleries, Kamuela, Hawaii. $150-250

Duke Paoa Kahanamoku 1890-1968
The Legendary Father of Surfing

Born in Haleakala on the island of Maui, son of Duke Halapu Kahanamoku and Julia Paoakania Lonokahini Kahanamoku, he had six brothers and three sisters. He grew up in Waikiki, attended the local grammar school, Kaahumanu School, and the Kamehameha School for boys. As a youth, he mastered early the sport of surfing on a 16-foot koa wood board weighing in excess of a hundred pounds. The following is a timeline of his many accomplishments:

1910 Developed what he called "the Hawaiian crawl," a basic swimming stroke used in competition and today known as "the American crawl."
1911 In Honolulu Harbor breaks freestyle world records in his first serious swimming competitions in the 50- and 100-yard sprints.
1912 Enters Stockholm Olympics, sweeping the swimming events and setting a world record for the 100-meter freestyle and wins a silver medal on the 200-meter freestyle relay team. Upon his return to Hawaii, stops and introduces Surfing to the East Coast of the United States.
1916 Due to the cancellation of the Olympics because of World War One, Duke travels to over thirty mainland cities to raise money for Liberty bonds and the Red Cross by demonstrating his swimming skills. Due to this, swimming becomes ever more popular as a sport and recreational activity.
1920 Enters the Antwerp Olympics, winning the 100-meter freestyle by beating his previous record, making the course in one minute flat. Also wins another gold medal in the 200-meter freestyle relay and fourth place in water polo. Recommends that Surfing be made an Olympic event.
1922 Begins a Hollywood film career playing roles as an American Indian, Hindu, etc.– everything but a Hawaiian.
1924 Enters the Paris Olympics losing the 100-meter freestyle by only one second to Johnny Weissmuller of Tarzan fame, but places second receiving a silver medal.
1925 Becomes a national hero when he rescues eight of twelve men from a capsized boat in high surf off Newport Beach, California, on his surfboard and, in so doing, pioneers the use of the surfboard as a life saving tool in the minds of the American public.
1928 Enters the Amsterdam Olympics, but does not compete due to an illness and continues acting in Hollywood until 1929, playing minor parts in a total of 30 movies over a period of 7 years.

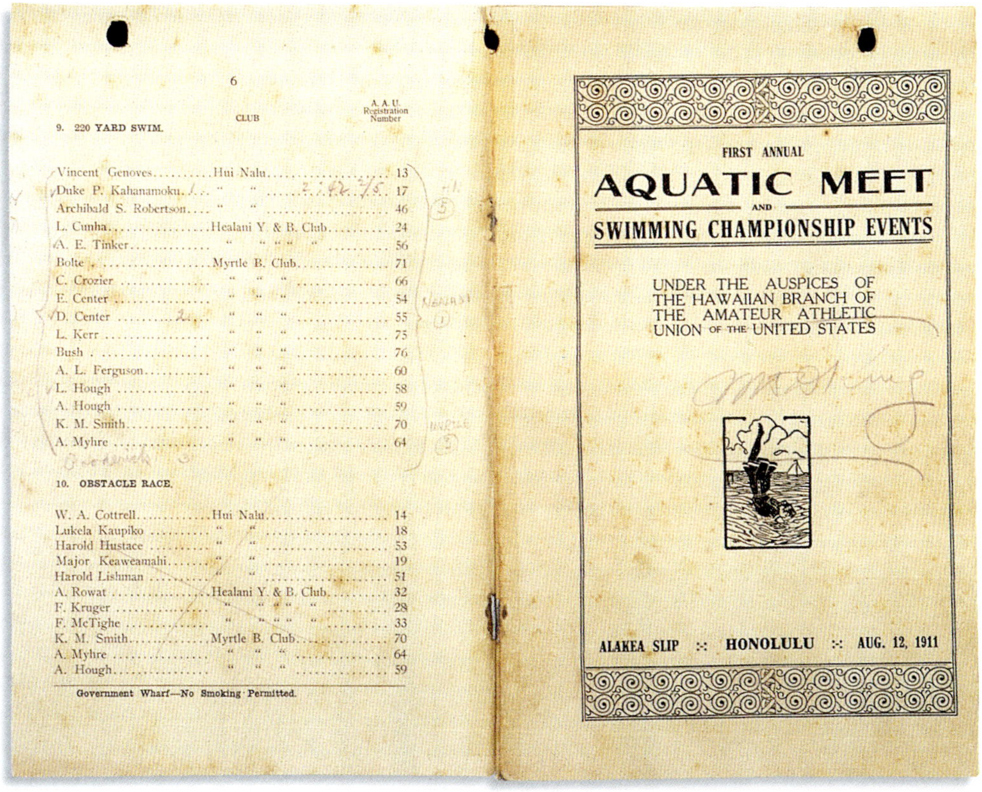

6

9. 220 YARD SWIM.

	CLUB	A. A. U. Registration Number
Vincent Genoves	Hui Nalu	13
Duke P. Kahanamoku	" "	17
Archibald S. Robertson	" "	46
L. Cunha	Healani Y. & B. Club	24
A. E. Tinker	" " " "	56
Bolte	Myrtle B. Club	71
C. Crozier	" " "	66
E. Center	" " "	54
D. Center	" " "	55
L. Kerr	" " "	75
Bush	" " "	76
A. L. Ferguson	" " "	60
L. Hough	" " "	58
A. Hough	" " "	59
K. M. Smith	" " "	70
A. Myhre	" " "	64

10. OBSTACLE RACE.

W. A. Cottrell	Hui Nalu	14
Lukela Kaupiko	" "	18
Harold Hustace	" "	53
Major Keaweamahi	" "	19
Harold Lishman	" "	51
A. Rowat	Healani Y. & B. Club	32
F. Kruger	" " " "	28
F. McTighe	" " " "	33
K. M. Smith	Myrtle B. Club	70
A. Myhre	" " "	64
A. Hough	" " "	59

Government Wharf—No Smoking Permitted.

FIRST ANNUAL

AQUATIC MEET

AND

SWIMMING CHAMPIONSHIP EVENTS

UNDER THE AUSPICES OF THE HAWAIIAN BRANCH OF THE AMATEUR ATHLETIC UNION OF THE UNITED STATES

ALAKEA SLIP :: HONOLULU :: AUG. 12, 1911

Souvenir Program for the First Annual Aquatic Meet and Swimming Championship Events, Honolulu 1911. Rare program and Duke Kahanamoku's first attempt at a serious swimming competition where he set world records in 50- and 100-yard sprints, enabling him to enter the 1912 Olympics in Stockholm. Ed and Randi Economy Collection. $600-900

Souvenir Program for the Swimming Events at Stockholm Olympics, 1912. A very rare program with photographs, etc. of all the contenders in the swimming events. Mauna Kea Galleries, Kamuela, Hawaii. $800-1200

Duke Kahanamoku Rookie Premium Card. Circa 1913.
DUKE KAHANAMOKU
Duke Kahanamoku, who broke all records at the swimming contest in the Stockholm Olympic, is a Hawaiian, and, like all his countrymen, has been used to the water almost from his very birth. Caucasians have little chance against the Hawaiians. This native holds the 50- and 100-yard records in Hawaii, and is credited with having made the century in 54-4/5 seconds, or 1/5 second better than Cecil Haley, of Australia, made. In February, 1911, at Pittsburgh, he made 50 yards in 23-4/5 seconds and 100 in 56-1/5. He made 100 feet in a tank in 14-1/5 seconds, beating the record. His best time for 100 yards in fresh water was 55-2/5 seconds. In the tryout before leaving for Stockholm he made 220 yards, with one turn, in 2 minutes, 40 seconds. At the Olympics he won his heat in the semifinals, 100 meters, in 1 minute 2-2/5 seconds, and the final heat in the race in 1:3-2/5. At Hamburg, a few days later, he still further lowered the world's record to 1:1-1/5.

WORLD'S CHAMPION ATHLETES
Free With
PAN HANDLE SCRAP

We honestly believe we have produced in Pan Handle Scrap the finest chew that has ever been offered.

Factory No. 6—First Dist. Ohio

Mauna Kea Galleries, Kamuela, Hawaii. $2,000-3,000

1929 Rides a monster wave over one mile, making all "sections" in Waikiki, the longest ride ever recorded.
1932 Enters the Los Angeles Olympics but fails to place in the swimming trial. He earns a spot on the water polo team and is awarded a bronze medal.
1934 After holding many odd jobs through the years, including janitor at City Hall, he is elected Sheriff of Honolulu, where he is re-elected 12 times. Mainly a ceremonial post, he continues to operate his Union gasoline service station in Waikiki opened this same year.
1940 Marries Nadine Alexander. A familiar figure at the Outrigger Canoe Club, he is well known by the majority of visitors to the Islands.
1956 Becomes an official representative of the Melbourne Olympics.
1960 One year after statehood, Sheriff position is abolished, but the new Governor and the Hawaii Visitors Bureau now appoint him the "Ambassador of Aloha".
1963 Attends and judges surfing competitions during his third trip to Australia.
1964 Attends Olympics in Tokyo as an official guest.
1965 Charter member elected to both the Swimming and Surfing Hall of Fame. First Annual Duke Kahanamoku Invitational Surf Meet is held at Sunset Beach on the north shore of Oahu.
1967 Becomes one of twenty-six all-time sports champions.
1968 January 22, dies in Honolulu. Massive Waikiki beach boy funeral held.
1984 Posthumously inducted into the U.S. Olympic Hall of Fame.
1990 Statue dedicated and erected in Waikiki upon the centennial of his birth.

Mid-Pacific Carnival Poster Card. Circa 1913. Rare. Mauna Kea Galleries, Kamuela, Hawaii. $600-900

Official Program Mid-Pacific Carnival, February 1914. Featuring Duke Kahanamoku on the cover. Scarce. Mauna Kea Galleries, Kamuela, Hawaii. $300-500

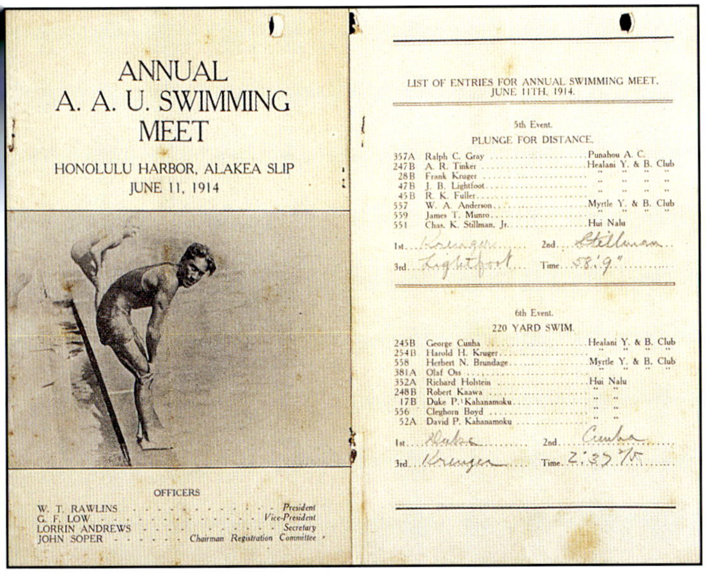
ANNUAL
A. A. U. SWIMMING
MEET

HONOLULU HARBOR, ALAKEA SLIP
JUNE 11, 1914

OFFICERS

W. T. RAWLINS - - - President
G. F. LOW - - - Vice-President
LORRIN ANDREWS - - - Secretary
JOHN SOPER - - - Chairman Registration Committee

LIST OF ENTRIES FOR ANNUAL SWIMMING MEET.
JUNE 11TH, 1914.

5th Event.
PLUNGE FOR DISTANCE.

357A Ralph C. Gray .... Punahou A. C.
247B A. R. Tinker .... Healani Y. & B. Club
28B Frank Kruger .... " " " "
47B J. B. Lightfoot .... " " " "
45B R. K. Fuller .... " " " "
557 W. A. Anderson .... Myrtle Y. & B. Club
559 James T. Munro .... " " " "
551 Chas. K. Stillman, Jr. .... Hui Nalu

1st. .... 2nd. Stillman
3rd. Lightfoot Time. 58'9"

6th Event.
220 YARD SWIM.

245B George Cunha .... Healani Y. & B. Club
254B Harold H. Kruger .... " " " "
558 Herbert N. Brundage .... Myrtle Y. & B. Club
381A Olaf Oss .... " " " "
352A Richard Holstein .... Hui Nalu
248B Robert Kaawa .... " "
17B Duke P. Kahanamoku .... " "
556 Cleghorn Boyd .... " "
52A David P. Kahanamoku .... " "

1st. Duke 2nd. Cunha
3rd. Kruger Time. 2:37 1/5

Souvenir Program for the Annual A.A.U. Swimming Meet, Honolulu 1914. Scarce program with The Duke on the front cover. He finished first in the 220 yard swim. Ed and Randi Economy Collection. $400-600

Mid-Pacific Carnival Poster Card. Circa 1914. Rare. Mauna Kea Galleries, Kamuela, Hawaii. $500-700

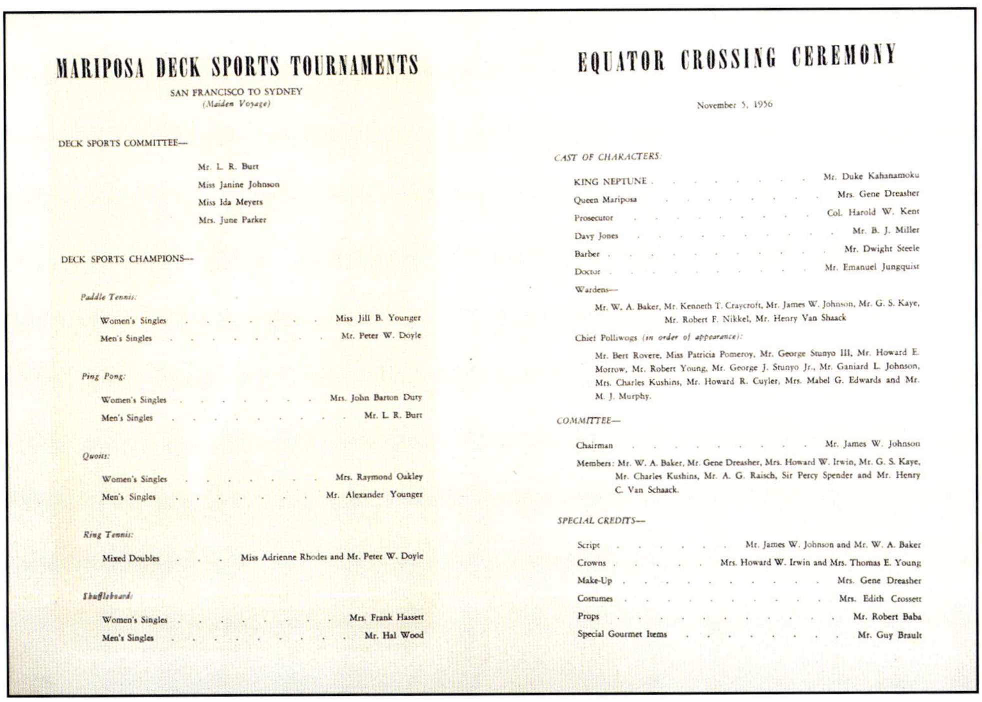
MARIPOSA DECK SPORTS TOURNAMENTS

SAN FRANCISCO TO SYDNEY
(Maiden Voyage)

DECK SPORTS COMMITTEE—

Mr. L. R. Burt
Miss Janine Johnson
Miss Ida Meyers
Mrs. June Parker

DECK SPORTS CHAMPIONS—

Paddle Tennis:

Women's Singles . . . . Miss Jill B. Younger
Men's Singles . . . . Mr. Peter W. Doyle

Ping Pong:

Women's Singles . . . . Mrs. John Barton Duty
Men's Singles . . . . Mr. L. R. Burt

Quoits:

Women's Singles . . . . Mrs. Raymond Oakley
Men's Singles . . . . Mr. Alexander Younger

Ring Tennis:

Mixed Doubles . . . Miss Adrienne Rhodes and Mr. Peter W. Doyle

Shuffleboard:

Women's Singles . . . . Mrs. Frank Hassett
Men's Singles . . . . Mr. Hal Wood

EQUATOR CROSSING CEREMONY

November 5, 1956

CAST OF CHARACTERS:

KING NEPTUNE . . . . Mr. Duke Kahanamoku
Queen Mariposa . . . . Mrs. Gene Dreasher
Prosecutor . . . . Col. Harold W. Kent
Davy Jones . . . . Mr. B. J. Miller
Barber . . . . Mr. Dwight Steele
Doctor . . . . Mr. Emanuel Jungquist

Wardens—

Mr. W. A. Baker, Mr. Kenneth T. Craycroft, Mr. James W. Johnson, Mr. G. S. Kaye, Mr. Robert F. Nikkel, Mr. Henry Van Shaack

Chief Polliwogs *(in order of appearance):*

Mr. Bert Rovere, Miss Patricia Pomeroy, Mr. George Stunyo III, Mr. Howard E. Morrow, Mr. Robert Young, Mr. George J. Stunyo Jr., Mr. Ganiard L. Johnson, Mrs. Charles Kushins, Mr. Howard R. Cuyler, Mrs. Mabel G. Edwards and Mr. M. J. Murphy.

COMMITTEE—

Chairman . . . . Mr. James W. Johnson

Members: Mr. W. A. Baker, Mr. Gene Dreasher, Mrs. Howard W. Irwin, Mr. G. S. Kaye, Mr. Charles Kushins, Mr. A. G. Raisch, Sir Percy Spender and Mr. Henry C. Van Schaack.

SPECIAL CREDITS—

Script . . . . Mr. James W. Johnson and Mr. W. A. Baker
Crowns . . . . Mrs. Howard W. Irwin and Mrs. Thomas E. Young
Make-Up . . . . Mrs. Gene Dreasher
Costumes . . . . Mrs. Edith Crossett
Props . . . . Mr. Robert Baba
Special Gourmet Items . . . . Mr. Guy Brault

Original Photograph of Duke Kahanamoku on the Beach at Waikiki. Circa 1915. Mauna Kea Galleries, Kamuela, Hawaii. $200-300

Original Photograph of Duke Kahanamoku on Board the *U.S.S. Manchuria*. Circa 1915. Mauna Kea Galleries, Kamuela, Hawaii. $300-500

Canoe Surfing The act of riding waves in an outrigger canoe.

Duke Kahanamoku Tourist Brochure. Published by the Hawaii Tourist Bureau, circa 1915, and printed by the Paradise of the Pacific Press. Mauna Kea Galleries, Kamuela, Hawaii. $300-500

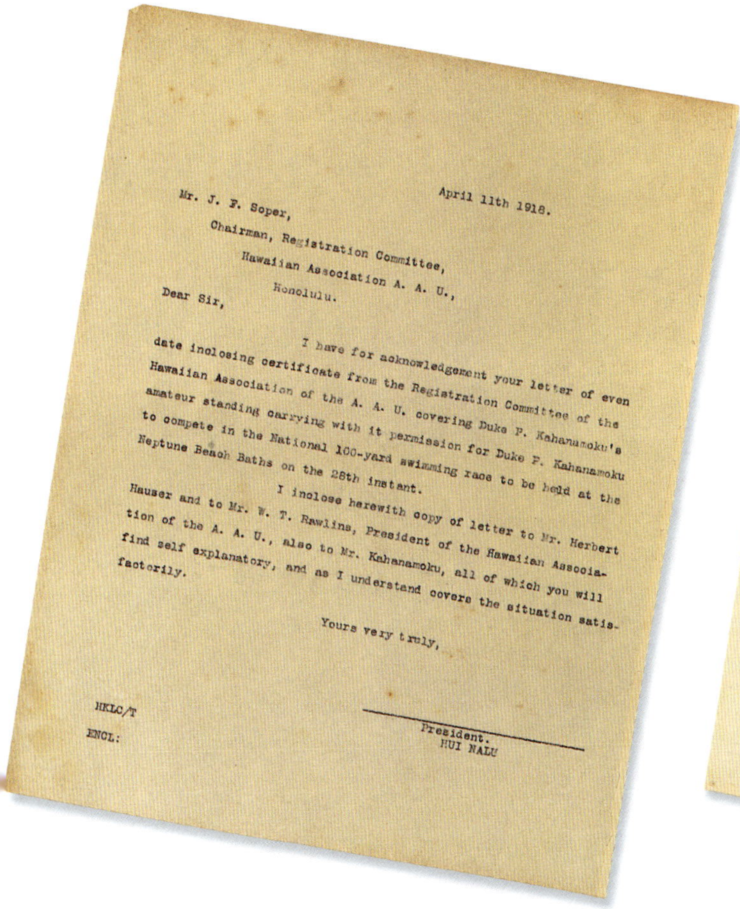

April 11th 1918.

Mr. J. F. Soper,
Chairman, Registration Committee,
Hawaiian Association A. A. U.,
Honolulu.

Dear Sir,

I have for acknowledgement your letter of even date inclosing certificate from the Registration Committee of the Hawaiian Association of the A. A. U. covering Duke P. Kahanamoku's amateur standing carrying with it permission for Duke P. Kahanamoku to compete in the National 100-yard swimming race to be held at the Neptune Beach Baths on the 28th instant.

I inclose herewith copy of letter to Mr. Herbert Hauser and to Mr. W. T. Rawlins, President of the Hawaiian Association of the A. A. U., also to Mr. Kahanamoku, all of which you will find self explanatory, and as I understand covers the situation satisfactorily.

Yours very truly,

President.
HUI NALU

HKLC/T
ENCL:

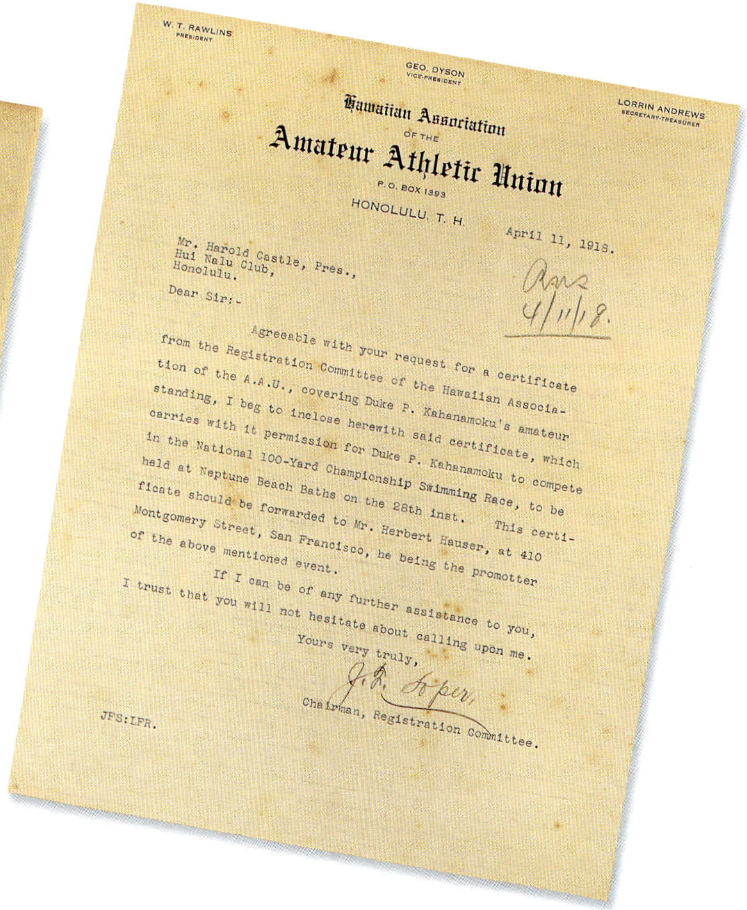

W. T. RAWLINS
PRESIDENT

GEO. DYSON
VICE-PRESIDENT

LORRIN ANDREWS
SECRETARY-TREASURER

Hawaiian Association
of the
Amateur Athletic Union
P. O. BOX 1393
HONOLULU, T. H.

April 11, 1918.

Mr. Harold Castle, Pres.,
Hui Nalu Club,
Honolulu.

Ans
4/11/18.

Dear Sir:-

Agreeable with your request for a certificate from the Registration Committee of the Hawaiian Association of the A.A.U., covering Duke P. Kahanamoku's amateur standing, I beg to inclose herewith said certificate, which carries with it permission for Duke P. Kahanamoku to compete in the National 100-Yard Championship Swimming Race, to be held at Neptune Beach Baths on the 28th inst. This certificate should be forwarded to Mr. Herbert Hauser, at 410 Montgomery Street, San Francisco, he being the promotter of the above mentioned event.

If I can be of any further assistance to you, I trust that you will not hesitate about calling upon me.

Yours very truly,

J. F. Soper,
Chairman, Registration Committee.

JFS:LFR.

Rare Correspondence. Documents dated April 11, 1918, which relate to Duke Kananamoku's participation in the National 100-yard Championship Swimming Race, held at Neptune Beach, Alameda, California, on April 28, 1918. Mauna Kea Galleries, Kamuela, Hawaii. $3,000-5,000

Original Photograph of Duke Kahanamoku on the Beach at Waikiki. Circa 1915. Mauna Kea Galleries, Kamuela, Hawaii. $200-300

Original Photograph of Duke Kahanamoku on Board the *U.S.S. Manchuria*. Circa 1915. Duke Kahanamoku is shown in front of the swimming tank en route home from a swimming competition in California. Mauna Kea Galleries, Kamuela, Hawaii. $300-500

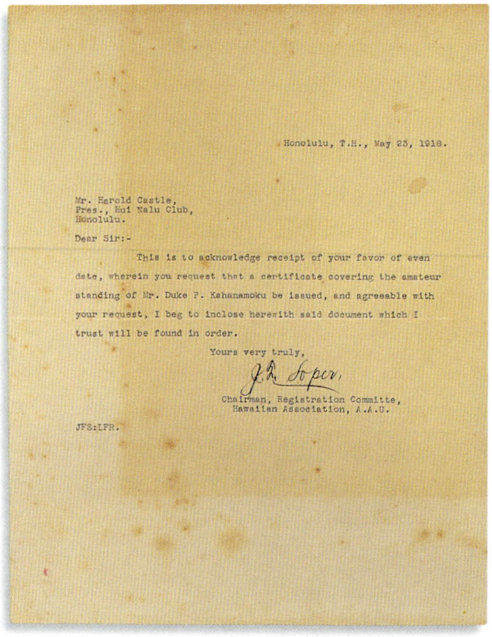

Honolulu, T.H., May 23, 1918.

Mr. Harold Castle,
Pres., Hui Nalu Club,
Honolulu.

Dear Sir:-

This is to acknowledge receipt of your favor of even date, wherein you request that a certificate covering the amateur standing of Mr. Duke P. Kahanamoku be issued, and agreeable with your request, I beg to inclose herewith said document which I trust will be found in order.

Yours very truly,

J.F. Soper,

Chairman, Registration Committe,
Hawaiian Association, A.A.U.

JFS:LFR.

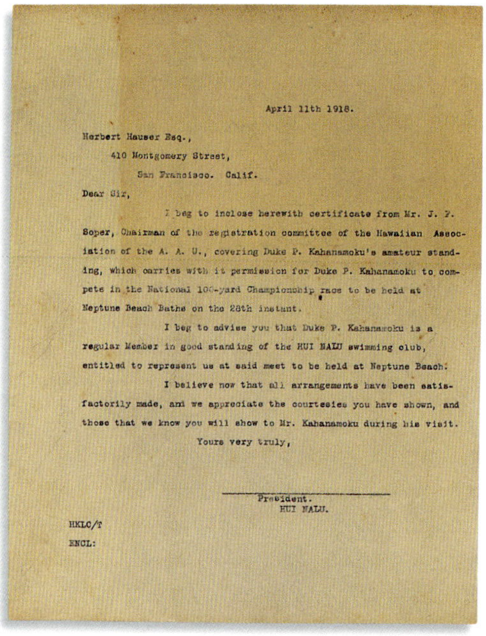

April 11th 1918.

Herbert Hauser Esq.,
410 Montgomery Street,
San Francisco. Calif.

Dear Sir,

I beg to inclose herewith certificate from Mr. J. F. Soper, Chairman of the registration committee of the Hawaiian Association of the A. A. U., covering Duke P. Kahanamoku's amateur standing, which carries with it permission for Duke P. Kahanamoku to compete in the National 100-yard Championship race to be held at Neptune Beach Baths on the 28th instant.

I beg to advise you that Duke P. Kahanamoku is a regular Member in good standing of the HUI NALU swimming club, entitled to represent us at said meet to be held at Neptune Beach.

I believe now that all arrangements have been satisfactorily made, and we appreciate the courtesies you have shown, and those that we know you will show to Mr. Kahanamoku during his visit.

Yours very truly,

President.
HUI NALU.

HKLC/T
ENCL:

Rare Group of Correspondence. Documents dated March 9 through May 23, 1918, some of which relate to Duke Kananamoku's participation in the National 100-yard Championship Swimming Race, held at Neptune Beach, Alameda, California, on April 28, 1918. Other documents include one signed by Alexander Hume Ford that relate to the Pan Pacific Committee and The Hands-Around-The-Pacific Movement. Mauna Kea Galleries, Kamuela, Hawaii. $3,000-5,000

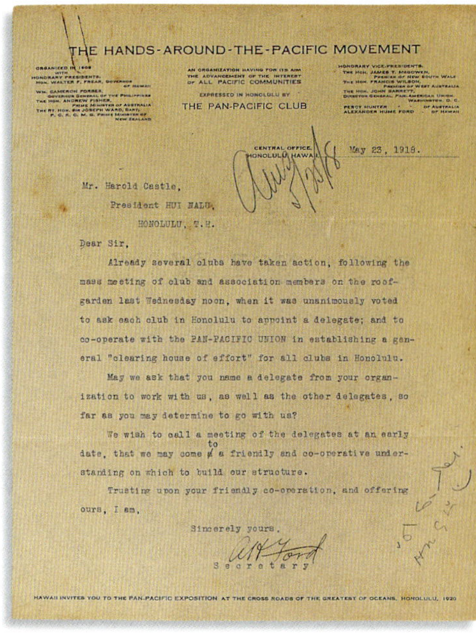

THE HANDS-AROUND-THE-PACIFIC MOVEMENT

AN ORGANIZATION HAVING FOR ITS AIM THE ADVANCEMENT OF THE INTEREST OF ALL PACIFIC COMMUNITIES

EXPRESSED IN HONOLULU BY
THE PAN-PACIFIC CLUB

CENTRAL OFFICE, HONOLULU, HAWAII

May 23, 1918.

Mr. Harold Castle,
President HUI NALU,
HONOLULU, T.H.

Dear Sir,

Already several clubs have taken action, following the mass meeting of club and association members on the roof-garden last Wednesday noon, when it was unanimously voted to ask each club in Honolulu to appoint a delegate; and to co-operate with the PAN-PACIFIC UNION in establishing a general "clearing house of effort" for all clubs in Honolulu.

May we ask that you name a delegate from your organization to work with us, as well as the other delegates, so far as you may determine to go with us?

We wish to call a meeting of the delegates at an early date, that we may come to a friendly and co-operative understanding on which to build our structure.

Trusting upon your friendly co-operation, and offering ours, I am,

Sincerely yours,

AH Ford
Secretary

HAWAII INVITES YOU TO THE PAN-PACIFIC EXPOSITION AT THE CROSS ROADS OF THE GREATEST OF OCEANS, HONOLULU, 1920

Beach Break When the waves are breaking on a sandy bottom, often precariously close to the beach rather than out on a reef.

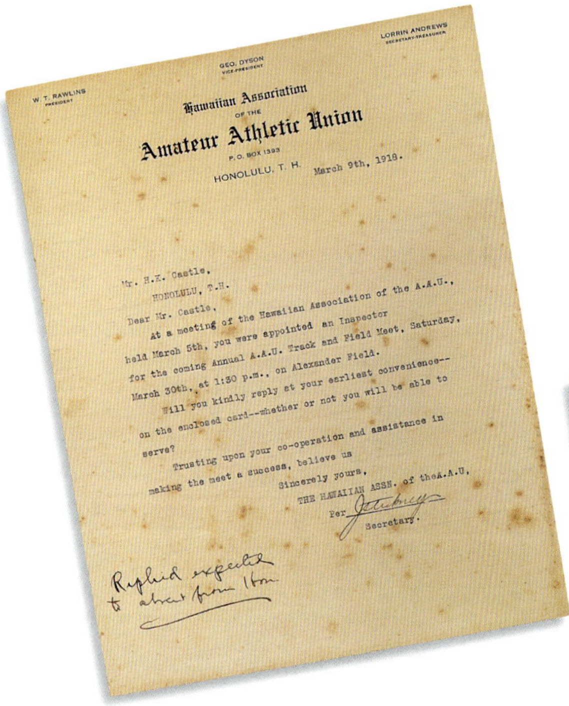

W. T. RAWLINS
PRESIDENT

GEO. DYSON
VICE-PRESIDENT

LORRIN ANDREWS
SECRETARY-TREASURER

Hawaiian Association
OF THE
Amateur Athletic Union
P.O. BOX 1393
HONOLULU, T. H.

March 9th, 1918.

Mr. H.K. Castle,
HONOLULU, T.H.

Dear Mr. Castle,

At a meeting of the Hawaiian Association of the A.A.U., held March 5th, you were appointed an Inspector for the coming Annual A.A.U. Track and Field Meet, Saturday, March 30th, at 1:30 p.m., on Alexander Field.

Will you kindly reply at your earliest convenience--on the enclosed card--whether or not you will be able to serve?

Trusting upon your co-operation and assistance in making the meet a success, believe us

Sincerely yours,
THE HAWAIIAN ASSN. of theA.A.U,
Per
Secretary.

Replied expected to absent from Hon

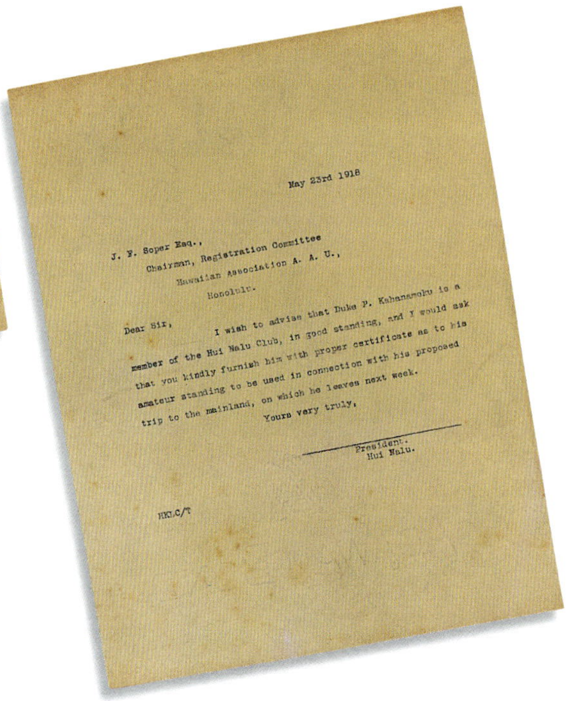

May 23rd 1918

J. F. Soper Esq.,
Chairman, Registration Committee
Hawaiian Association A. A. U.,
Honolulu.

Dear Sir,

I wish to advise that Duke P. Kahanamoku is a member of the Hui Nalu Club, in good standing, and I would ask that you kindly furnish him with proper certificate as to his amateur standing to be used in connection with his proposed trip to the mainland, on which he leaves next week.

Yours very truly,

President.
Hui Nalu.

HKLC/T

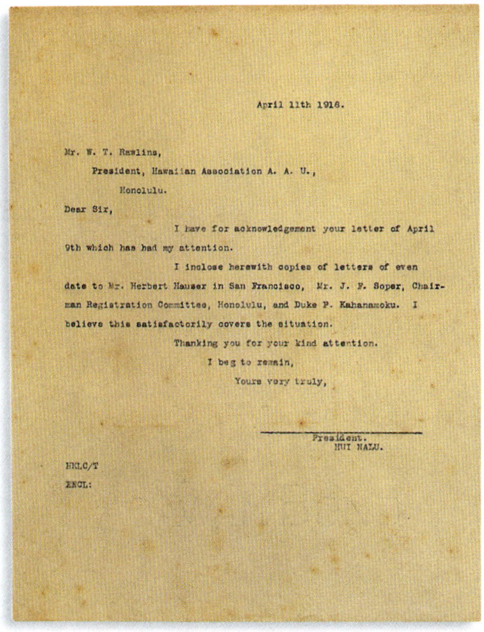

April 11th 1918.

Mr. W. T. Rawlins,
President, Hawaiian Association A. A. U.,
Honolulu.

Dear Sir,

I have for acknowledgement your letter of April 9th which has had my attention.

I inclose herewith copies of letters of even date to Mr. Herbert Hauser in San Francisco, Mr. J. F. Soper, Chairman Registration Committee, Honolulu, and Duke P. Kahanamoku. I believe this satisfactorily covers the situation.

Thanking you for your kind attention.

I beg to remain,

Yours very truly,

President.
HUI NALU.

HKLC/T
ENCL:

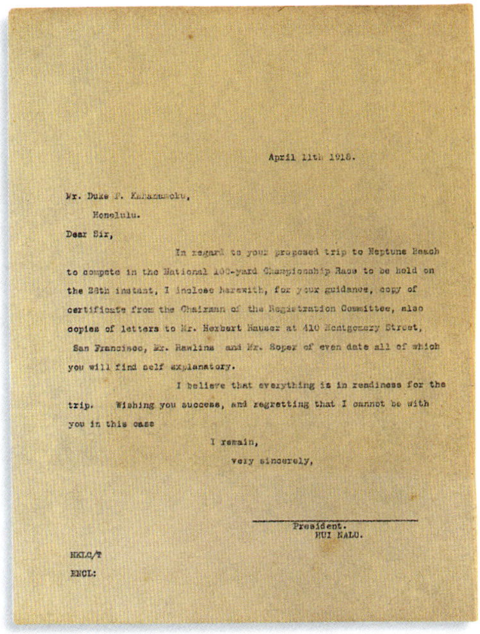

April 11th 1918.

Mr. Duke P. Kahanamoku,
Honolulu.

Dear Sir,

In regard to your proposed trip to Neptune Beach to compete in the National 100-yard Championship Race to be held on the 28th instant, I inclose herewith, for your guidance, copy of certificate from the Chairman of the Registration Committee, also copies of letters to Mr. Herbert Hauser at 410 Montgomery Street, San Francisco, Mr. Rawlins and Mr. Soper of even date all of which you will find self explanatory.

I believe that everything is in readiness for the trip. Wishing you success, and regretting that I cannot be with you in this case

I remain,

very sincerely,

President.
HUI NALU.

HKLC/T
ENCL:

Real Photo Postcard of Duke Kahanamoku. Circa 1915. Rare. Mauna Kea Galleries, Kamuela, Hawaii. $150-250

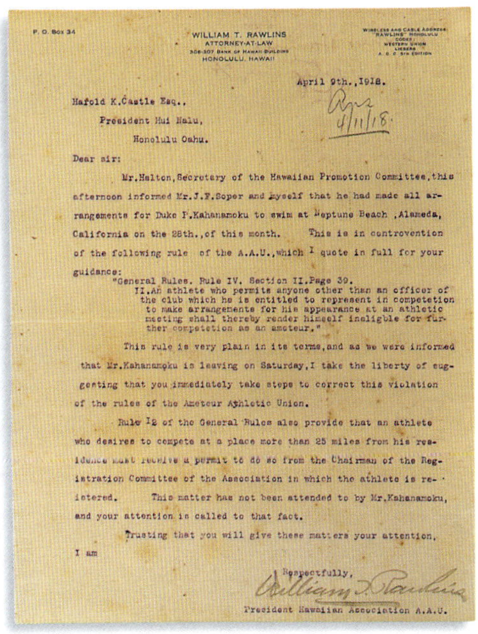

P. O. Box 34

WILLIAM T. RAWLINS
ATTORNEY-AT-LAW
306-307 BANK OF HAWAII BUILDING
HONOLULU, HAWAII

WIRELESS AND CABLE ADDRESS "RAWLINS" HONOLULU
CODES: WESTERN UNION LIEBERS A. B. C. 5TH EDITION

April 9th., 1918.

Apr 4/11/18.

Hafold K. Castle Esq.,
President Hui Nalu,
Honolulu Oahu.

Dear sir:

Mr. Halton, Secretary of the Hawaiian Promotion Committee, this afternoon informed Mr. J. F. Soper and myself that he had made all arrangements for Duke P. Kahanamoku to swim at Neptune Beach, Alameda, California on the 28th., of this month. This is in controvention of the following rule of the A.A.U., which I quote in full for your guidance:

"General Rules. Rule IV. Section II. Page 39.
II. An athlete who permits anyone other than an officer of the club which he is entitled to represent in competetion to make arrangements for his appearance at an athletic meeting shall thereby render himself ineligble for further competetion as an amateur."

This rule is very plain in its terms, and as we were informed that Mr. Kahanamoku is leaving on Saturday, I take the liberty of suggesting that you immediately take steps to correct this violation of the rules of the Ameteur Athletic Union.

Rule 12 of the General Rules also provide that an athlete who desires to compete at a place more than 25 miles from his residence must receive a permit to do so from the Chairman of the Registration Committee of the Association in which the athlete is reistered. This matter has not been attended to by Mr. Kahanamoku, and your attention is called to that fact.

Trusting that you will give these matters your attention,

I am

Respectfully,
William T. Rawlins
President Hawaiian Association A.A.U.

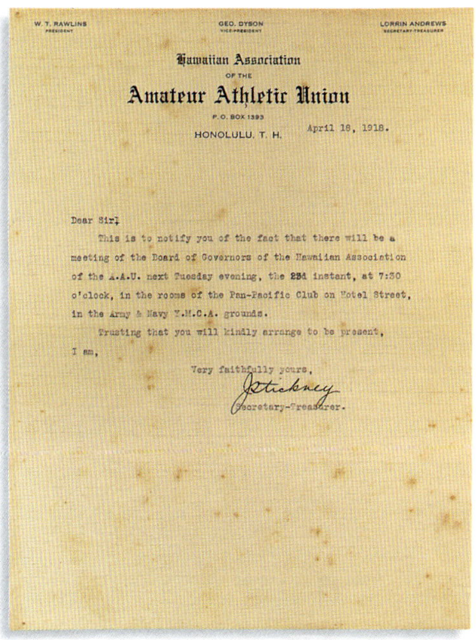

W. T. RAWLINS, PRESIDENT — GEO. DYSON, VICE-PRESIDENT — LORRIN ANDREWS, SECRETARY-TREASURER

Hawaiian Association
OF THE
Amateur Athletic Union
P. O. BOX 1393
HONOLULU, T. H.

April 18, 1918.

Dear Sir:

This is to notify you of the fact that there will be a meeting of the Board of Governors of the Hawaiian Association of the A.A.U. next Tuesday evening, the 23d instant, at 7:30 o'clock, in the rooms of the Pan-Pacific Club on Hotel Street, in the Army & Navy Y.M.C.A. grounds.

Trusting that you will kindly arrange to be present,

I am,

Very faithfully yours,
J Stickney
Secretary-Treasurer.

Surf-Board-Riding Waikiki, Honolulu.
Aloha Nui
FROM
HAWAIIAN ISLANDS

Diamond Head and Surf Board Riding, Honolulu, T. H.

Opposite page
Top left: **Aloha Nui Postcard.** Circa 1910. Entitled "Surf-Board-Riding, Waikiki, Honolulu." Mauna Kea Galleries, Kamuela, Hawaii. $40-60

Center left: **Real Photo Postcard.** Circa 1915. An interesting card showing a group of surfers at Queen's Surf, Waikiki. Mauna Kea Galleries, Kamuela, Hawaii. $60-90

Bottom left: **Postcard.** Circa 1915. Entitled "Diamond Head and Surf Board Riding, Honolulu, T.H." A cute card showing children frolicking on bellyboards in the surf at Waikiki. Mauna Kea Galleries, Kamuela, Hawaii. $40-60

Right: **Redwood, 8'1".** An unusually thin solid redwood board in the *alaia* style, circa 1915. A beautiful board in shape and style reflecting all the greatest elements of ancient Polynesian design and influence. Spencer and Annette Croul Collection. $6,000-9,000

Real Photo Postcard. Waikiki Beach, circa 1915. Mauna Kea Galleries, Kamuela, Hawaii. $100-150

Bellyboard Sometimes referred to as a "Paipo board," this type of small surfboard is usually used to ride waves in a prone position lying on the stomach.

Real Photo Postcard. Waikiki Beach, circa 1918. Mauna Kea Galleries, Kamuela, Hawaii. $60-90

Original Photograph of a Surfer. Circa 1920s. Mauna Kea Galleries, Kamuela, Hawaii. $80-120

Marshall's, Long Beach, Calif., For Rent Only, Bellyboard, 4'0". Redwood, circa 1920s. Allan Seymour, Pacific Coast Vintage Surf Auctions. $600-900

Take Off The act of catching a wave.

Souvenir Baggage Label from the Seaside Hotel and Cottages. Circa 1920s. Mauna Kea Galleries, Kamuela, Hawaii. $200-300

Real Photo Postcard of Unidentified Woman on Duke Kahanamoku's Surfboard. Circa 1915-1920. Quite the bathing beauty with stockings rolled to mid-calf. Mauna Kea Galleries, Kamuela, Hawaii. $300-500

Real Photo Postcard of a Bathing Beauty and her Board. Circa 1920. Entitled "The Surf-Rider Hawaii," this photograph was probably taken by Ray Jerome Baker some years earlier in his studio with a painted backdrop of Diamond Head. Here is shown a classic solid redwood board of the time period, measuring 10 feet or more. Mauna Kea Galleries, Kamuela, Hawaii. $200-300

Souvenir Pennant – *Surf Riding-Hilo, Hawaii*. A multitude of these pennants were made as souvenirs for various areas of Hawaii. This one is circa 1920. Mauna Kea Galleries, Kamuela, Hawaii. $100-150

Vintage Advertisement. Mauna Kea Galleries, Kamuela, Hawaii.

Redwood, 9'1". Solid redwood made in Hawaii in 1922. Board has a total weight of 62 pounds. Dick Metz, Dana Point, California. $4,000-6,000

Postcard. Circa 1920. Entitled "Surf-Board Riding, Honolulu." A classic image showing a takeoff at Canoes, Waikiki. Mauna Kea Galleries, Kamuela, Hawaii. $40-60

Clean When the surface of the sea and surf is glassy. The perfect surf conditions.

Greeting Card. Handtinted, circa 1920s. A great period image. Mauna Kea Galleries, Kamuela, Hawaii. $120-180

Redwood, 9'8". Lorrin Harrison's solid redwood board, circa 1922. Hoffman Collection. $8,000-12,000

Greeting Card. Circa 1920s. Mauna Kea Galleries, Kamuela, Hawaii. $60-90

Tandem Surf Photograph by Ray Jerome Baker. A silver print taken in the early 1920s, presumably at Waikiki. Mauna Kea Galleries, Kamuela, Hawaii. $400-600

Vintage Advertisement. Mauna Kea Galleries, Kamuela, Hawaii.

Print of a Watercolor by H. D. Christian - *Expert surf rider shooting ashore on a Waikiki wave.* Paradise of Pacific Magazine, Christmas Issue 1926. Mauna Kea Galleries, Kamuela, Hawaii. $40-60

Sportalbum f. dieſe Bilder
geg. Einſendung von 60 Pf.

Serie Schwimmſport
(Dieſe Serie = 100 Bilder)
Bild 17

D. Kahanamoku,
Hawai
einer der beſten Schwim-
mer der Welt

Greiling-Zigaretten
ſind wirklich gut!

Zigarettenfabrik
Richard Greiling A.G.
Dresden-A. 24

German Cigarette Premium. Richard Greiling, Dresden, Circa 1920. Mauna Kea Galleries, Kamuela, Hawaii. $300-500

Original Photograph of Duke Kahanamoku and Other Dignitaries, including the noted Polynesian Scholar Dr. Peter Buck. All are dressed in Hawaiian regalia, circa 1920. Mauna Kea Galleries, Kamuela, Hawaii. $200-300

Souvenir Koa Model Surfboard. Sold by Island Curio Company in the 1920s as a momento for tourist trade. Mauna Kea Galleries, Kamuela, Hawaii. $120-180

Original Photograph of Duke Kahanamoku and Friends. Circa 1920s. Hand-colored. Mauna Kea Galleries, Kamuela, Hawaii. $300-500

Real Photo Postcard of Duke Kahanamoku and Friends. Inscribed on reverse: *A youthful Duke Kahanamoku, fourth from left, and "beachboy" companions who, much as anything, contributed to making Waikiki a tourist mecca. This photo dates from approximately 1925.*
This photograph has some very interesting symbolism. Note that Kahanamoku, unlike his companions is attired with a feather cape, lei niho palaoa, and lance. While the others are portrayed as "commoners," Kahanamoku's portrayal is clearly that of ali'i. Most unusual photo of Kahanamoku not found in any of the several books about the "Duke" and his many exploits. Mauna Kea Galleries, Kamuela, Hawaii. $300-500

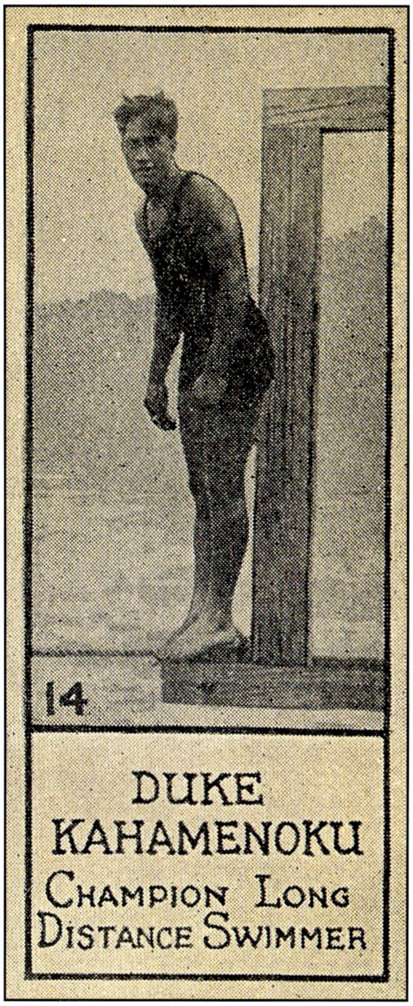

Duke Kahanamoku Champion Long Distance Swimmer Premium Card, 1925. Number 14 in the series produced by Wilbur Chocolate Company. Mauna Kea Galleries, Kamuela, Hawaii. $600-800

Original Photograph of Duke and Fred Cady. Circa 1923. This press photo by Pacific and Atlantic Photo Co. Inc., Los Angeles, shows Duke with the Los Angeles Athletic Club Swimming Coach. This particular image is signed and dated on reverse by the Duke and is very rare as such. Mauna Kea Galleries, Kamuela, Hawaii. As shown: $1,800-2,400

Original Photograph of Duke Kahanamoku and Babe Ruth. Taken on Waikiki Beach in the 1930s. Mauna Kea Galleries, Kamuela, Hawaii. $500-700

Hawaii Tourist Booklet. Cover art by the famous Hawaiian artist John Kelly, circa 1920s. Mauna Kea Galleries, Kamuela, Hawaii. $200-300

Redwood Plank Board, 11'0". Circa 1920s. Old repair near tail. This board was purchased in Waikiki in 1941 for $15 by two officers and was last ridden in the same year by Admiral Bull Halsey. Peter and Cathy Noble, Monterey, California. As shown: $6,000-8,000. Average: $4,000-6,000

John Mellville Kelly 1879-1962

This legendary island artist, born in Oakland, California, had his first drawing published at the age of seventeen. At twenty, he attended the prestigious Partington Art School in San Francisco. In 1908 he married Katherine Howland, an artist in her own right, who later won recognition as a sculptor. Moving to Honolulu, he worked for Charles Frazier in 1923 and was Art Director of the Star Bulletin Newspaper from 1927-1935. An avid surfer, he often reflected his love for the sport and the Hawaiian people in his artwork, his primary mediums being etchings and aquatints. His work was made popular not only in his early illustration work of the 1920s but especially so in the menus he designed for the Royal Hawaiian Hotel in the 1940s.

Surfing Souvenir. Inscribed *Hawaiian Surfrider, Souvenir of Honolulu*. These pieces were made in the 1920s for sale in the various curio stores in the Islands. Made of cheap pot metal and later plated with copper or bronze, they were often cast with little concern to the final finish, frequently resulting in inclusions, fractures and seam marks. Made in a multitude of sizes and styles, these curios really capture the golden age of surfing in Waikiki in the first quarter of the 20th century. Mauna Kea Galleries, Kamuela, Hawaii. As shown: $1,000-1,500 (7 inches in height)

Real Photo Postcard of George David "Dad" Center by Ray Jerome Baker. Circa 1920. Internationally renowned swimmer and surfer. Dad Center developed many of the swimming greats, including men and women such as Clarence "Buster" Crabbe, Stubby Kreuger, Ludy Langer, And Warren, and Pua Kealoha, among others. Mauna Kea Galleries, Kamuela, Hawaii. $300-500

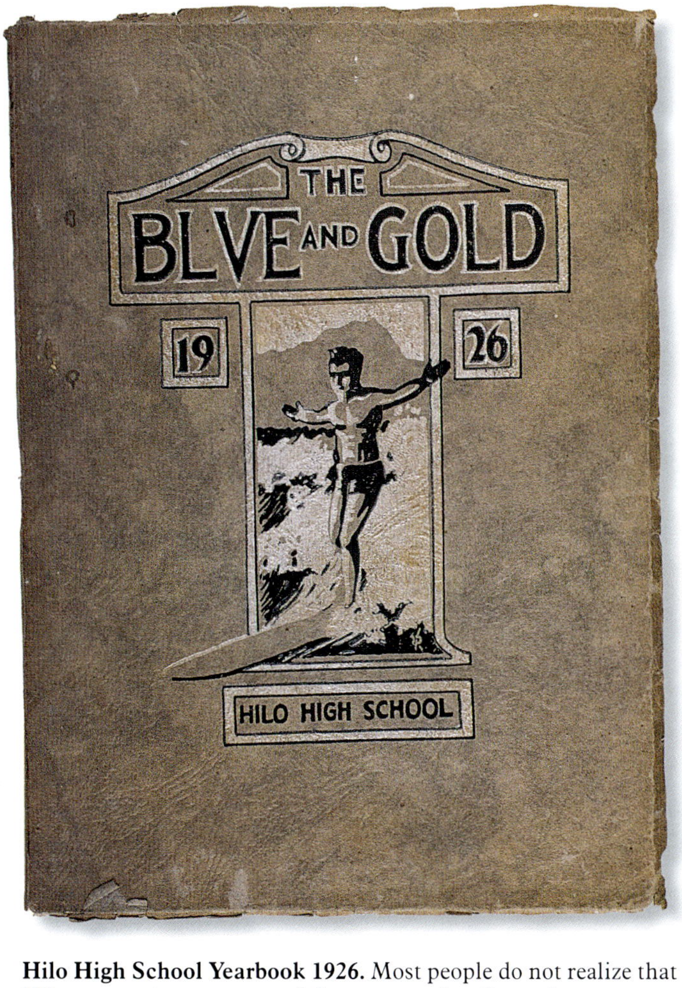

Hilo High School Yearbook 1926. Most people do not realize that Hilo, at one time, was one of the centers of surfing prior to construction of the breakwater and had seven various surf breaks. Even today, the author's favorite spot to surf, when the conditions are right, is at Bay Front, Hilo, where the longest ride in the state can be had. Mauna Kea Galleries, Kamuela, Hawaii. $60-90

Ray Jerome Baker 1880-1972

Born in Rockford, Illinois, and educated in St. Paul, Minnesota, he was Hawaii's premier photographer. Learning the photographic trade in Montana, he ran his first photo studio in Eureka, California, where he met and married Edith Frost. On a delayed honeymoon in 1908, he fell in love with Hawaii, returning two years later to open a studio in Honolulu. Baker photographed all aspects of Hawaiian life, especially the more romantic, truly capturing the "Aloha Spirit" with his photographic talents. He also produced the first two-reel feature film for the Hawaiian Tourist Bureau. Well traveled, he took pictures in over sixty countries, many of which were published in his book *Odyssey of a Cameraman* in 1956. In 1976, the Ray Jerome Baker Room was opened at Bishop Museum with an inventory of over 350,000 images of Hawaii dating back to 1845.

Johnny Noble's Royal Collection of Hawaiian Songs. Published by the Miller Music Corporation, 1929. Mauna Kea Galleries, Kamuela, Hawaii. $100-150

Wood Surfboards

Wood surfboards are the blue chip of surfing collectibles. Although many were made during the years of their production, very few remain today. The prices listed below are for good, clean examples with some minor imperfection acceptable. Early boards showing extensive repairs using the lost art of butterfly patching (in a manner like traditional Hawaiian calabashes) are worth 20% to 30% more than the prices listed. An unusual example of one with an important provenance also can be worth more than the listed prices.

Redwood, 10'1". A beautiful solid redwood board made in the late teens in Waikiki, with Hawaiian crest motif. Spencer and Annette Croul Collection. $8,000-12,000

Unusual Early Surf-Related Letter on Royal Hawaiian Hotel Stationery.

Honolulu Hawaii
Wednesday, Sept. 26, 1928
Dear John B,
Hello John. How are you. I don't forget you John. I hope you come back to Honolulu. The waves are so big now, John B. Mow. I got for surf board I will come over very soon. How is your Mother and Billy Frank, John B. Tell your mother write to me John B. I still got your picture John B. I always dream about you John. I hope you still got your ukulele. Can you play the ukulele John B. From now John B I feel so lonesome. Mow. Send your picture to Hank Shaw. John B. I want a good one. When are you coming to Honolulu John B. When you come over send some friend over to Hank Shaw. Mow. I am surf rider John B. Never forget your friend Hank Shaw is your best friend John B. I sure miss you John B. and much, but I will see you again John B. When. I hope you still got my picture John B. Keep and tell all about your friend you had a wonderful time in Waikiki Beach. I don't forget what you give me John B. You give a wonderful thing so that is nice, but I still got it John B. The picture you give me I took all over with me John B. because I don't miss your picture and also I miss the wonderful friend that is John B. Waikiki is good for you to come back to Honolulu Hawaii so I can teach you some more how to surf rider John B. You and I the best surf rider on the beach at Waikiki. You and I the best one on the beach to John B.
Yours truly,
From John Hank Shaw
Aloha oe to John B. love
This is my surf board now got my name on. This is the picture.
Aloha oe John B.
Mauna Kea Galleries, Kamuela, Hawaii. $800-1,200

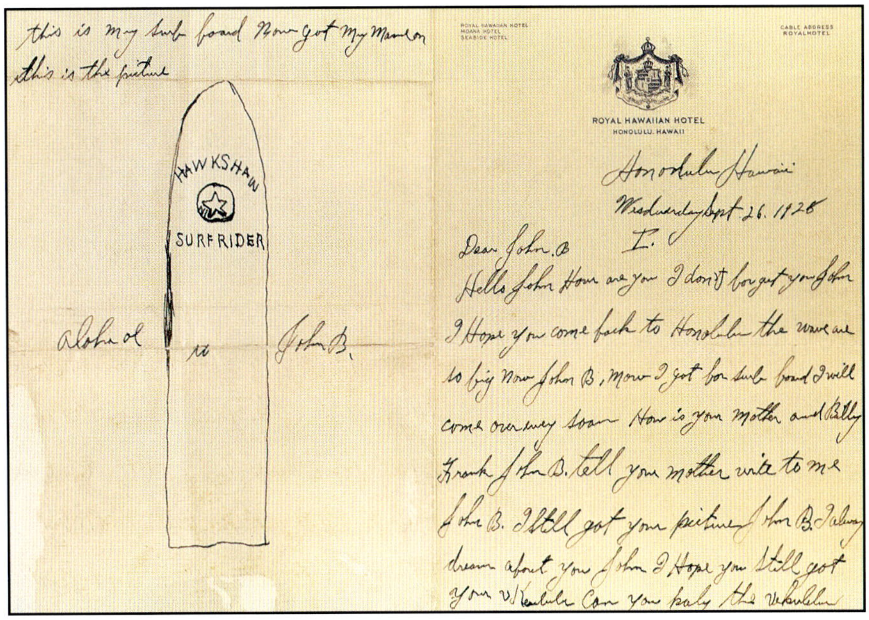
this is my surf board Now got My Name on
this is the picture
HAWKSHAW
SURFRIDER
Aloha oe to John B.

ROYAL HAWAIIAN HOTEL
HONOLULU, HAWAII

Honolulu Hawaii
Wednesday Sept 26. 1928
I.
Dear John. B
Hello John How are you I don't forget you John
I Hope you come back to Honolulu the waves are
so big Now John B, Mow I got for surf board I will
come over very soon How is your Mother and Billy
Frank John B. tell you mother write to me
John B. I still got your picture John B. I always
dream about you John I Hope you still got
your ukulele Can you play the ukulele

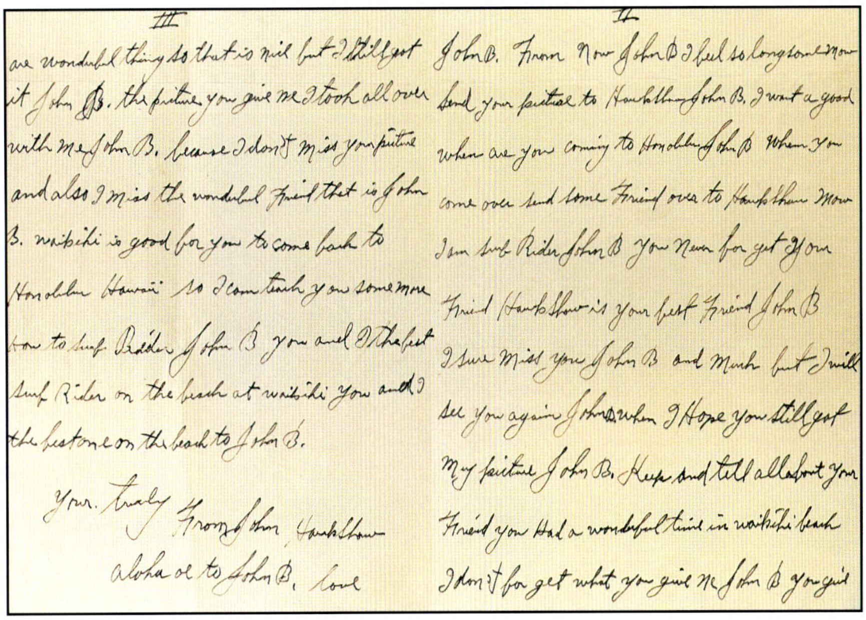
II
John B. From Now John B I feel so lonesome Mow
Send your picture to Hank Shaw John B. I want a good
When are you coming to Honolulu John B When you
come over send some Friend over to Hank Shaw Mow
I am surf Rider John B You Never for get your
Friend Hank Shaw is your best Friend John B
I sure miss you John B and Much but I will
see you again John B when I Hope you still got
My picture John B. Keep and tell all about your
Friend you Had a wonderful time in waikiki beach
I don't for get what you give me John B you give

III
a wonderful thing so that is nice but I still got
it John B. the picture you give me I took all over
with me John B. because I don't miss your picture
and also I miss the wonderful Friend that is John
B. waikiki is good for you to come back to
Honolulu Hawaii so I can teach you some more
how to surf Rider John B you and I the best
surf Rider on the beach at waikiki you and I
the best one on the beach to John B.
Your truly
From John Hank Shaw
aloha oe to John B. love

Real Photo Postcard – *Surf-riding at Waikiki Beach, Honolulu, T.H.* Circa 1920. Mauna Kea Galleries, Kamuela, Hawaii. $80-120

Redwood, 9'11". A solid redwood board made in Waikiki in the 1920s. Hoffman Collection. $5,000-7,000

Left Describes any wave breaking in a manner that causes a surfer taking off to turn to the left to stay ahead of the curl.

Vintage Advertisement. Mauna Kea Galleries, Kamuela, Hawaii.

Original Photograph of the Ala Wai Surfing Championships, January 1, 1927. Rare. Mauna Kea Galleries, Kamuela, Hawaii. $400-600

Right Describes any wave breaking in a manner that causes a surfer taking off to turn to the right to stay ahead of the curl.

Koa Cribbage Board. Beautifully carved in the shape of a surfboard with sea life motif. This item was carved on commission for Randolph Crossley in the 1930s. Mauna Kea Galleries, Kamuela, Hawaii. $300-500

Real Photo Postcard of Surfer and his Dog. Circa 1920. Mauna Kea Galleries, Kamuela, Hawaii. $80-120

Spruce and Redwood, 6'0". A classic late 1920s bellyboard used in Hermosa Beach as a rental. Hoffman Collection. $800-1,200.

Paddle Out To stroke out through the incoming surf to the lineup.

Real Photo Postcard of Waikiki Beach. Circa 1920s. Mauna Kea Galleries, Kamuela, Hawaii. $40-60

Stories of Hawaii. By Ann Shilt French, Cambridge, 1933, 1st edition. Great cover art. Mauna Kea Galleries, Kamuela, Hawaii. $60-90

Postcard – *Surf Rider*. Hawaii Masterseries Paintings by Sam MacLoed, published and copyrighted by Laszlo's Honolulu Arts. Circa 1930s. Mauna Kea Galleries, Kamuela, Hawaii. $40-60

C. H. L. Gartmann, Altona, Kakao- und Schokolade-Fabrik

Hawai,
ein Paradies im Ozean

Serie 646, Bild 2

Brandungsreiter

Kokospalmen, Kaffee- und Orangenbäume beschatten den Weg von den Villenanlagen der Amerikaner nach dem Strande. In unendlicher Weite liegt blau und schimmernd der Stille Ozean; die weißen Schaumkämme der Brandung rollen in ewiger Wiederkehr über den flachen Sand. Am Horizont Ozeandampfer, einsame Segler. Aber hier am Strande lustiges Leben. Die braunen, sehnigen Gestalten junger Amerikaner treiben den beliebten Sport des Brandungsreitens. Sie schwimmen mit einem schmalen Brett, das vorn und hinten bootähnlich zugespitzt ist, weit hinaus ins Meer, besteigen das Brett und lassen sich, indem sie sich, darauf stehend, im Gleichgewicht zu halten suchen, von den Wogen der Brandung auf den Strand treiben. Jubelndes Lachen ertönt, wenn ein Ungeschickter dabei kopfüber ins Wasser stürzt.

Nachdruck verboten!

Gr. A 44, (Ser. 646/60) Alb. 22

Stets wechselnde Serienbilder

German Chocolate Premium Card, *Gartmann Schokolade–Brandungsreiter–Serie 646, Bild 2*. Circa 1926. A very rare card and the first premium card ever produced showing multiple surfriders. Mauna Kea Galleries, Kamuela, Hawaii. $500-700

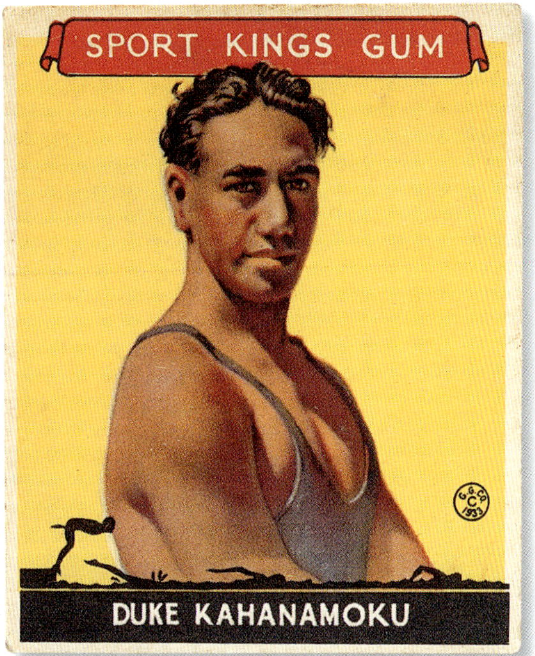

Duke Kahanamoku Premium Card, 1933.

— No. 20. –

DUKE KAHANAMOKU

(SWIMMING)

The world's record books of a few years ago, are filled with new marks established by Duke Kahanamoku. Greatest and most famous of all swimmers developed in the Hawaiian Islands, Duke safely holds his title as Sports King with his remarkable performances which mark him as the greatest all-round swimmer of all time. A great racer, an expert diver, a star performer on the surf-board and a marvelous water polo player, Duke leads them all. Traveled in many countries and established world's records in the 50 and 100 yard, 100 metres, 150 yards, and longer distances, both in open water and in tanks. In 1912, he thrilled spectators at Olympic Meet in Stockholm with a new record for the 100 metres, fee style, in 1 minute 2-2/5ths seconds. That year was crowned World's and Olympic Sprint Champion. Turned professional in 1917.

This is one of a series of noted athletes and sportsmen. The complete series includes all the leaders in every branch of sports. START YOUR COLLECTION NOW.

SPORT KINGS Chewing Gum Boston

The Goudey Gum Co.

Made by the originators of INDIAN and BIG LEAGUE GUM

Mauna Kea Galleries, Kamuela, Hawaii. $600-900

Original Photograph of David Kahanamoku. Circa 1920s. Mauna Kea Galleries, Kamuela, Hawaii. $150-250

Original Photograph of Duke Kahanamoku. Photo by Acme Newspictures, Inc., dated Jan. 23, 1932. Mauna Kea Galleries, Kamuela, Hawaii. $300-500

Original Photograph of the Honolulu Glee Club. Taken in 1932, this photograph shows many of the members of the club, including Duke Kahanamoku. Mauna Kea Galleries, Kamuela, Hawaii. $150-250

Duke Kahanamoku Los Angeles Olympiad Card, 1932. Card No. 9 of a series of 200 Olympic stars, these cards were published in Germany in the mid-1930s. Here Duke is seen with Amelia Earhart, Douglas Fairbanks and others. Mauna Kea Galleries, Kamuela, Hawaii. $250-350

Duke Kahanamoku Los Angeles Olympiad Card, 1932. Card No. 123 of a series of 200 Olympic stars, these cards were published in Germany in the mid-1930s. Duke is seen in front of his luggage. Mauna Kea Galleries, Kamuela, Hawaii. $200-300

Greeting Card. Circa 1930s. A large format card with a classic image of Duke Kahanamoku riding his board at Waikiki. Mauna Kea Galleries, Kamuela, Hawaii. $150-250

Lantern Slide, *Woman Wise*. Circa 1929. Another example of one of the many movies Duke Kahanamoku starred in. Mauna Kea Galleries, Kamuela, Hawaii. $200-300

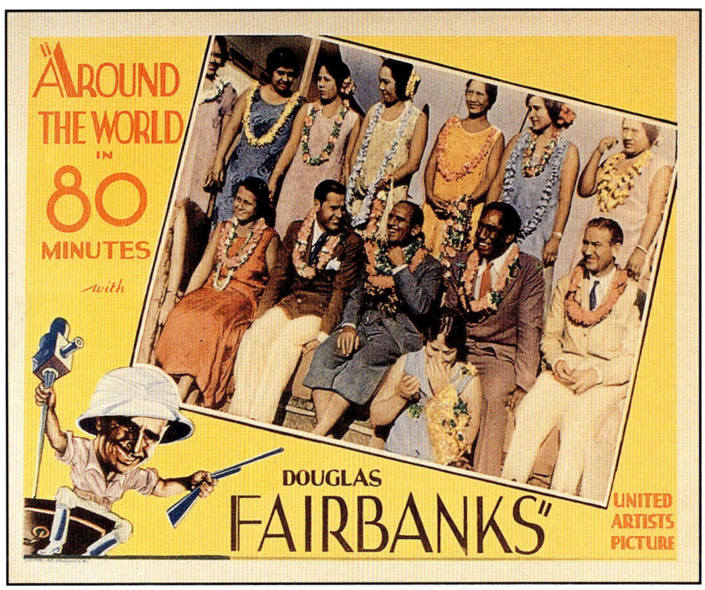

Lobby Card – *Around the World in 80 Minutes with Douglas Fairbanks – United Artists Picture.* A rare and unusual lobby card for one of the many movies Duke Kahanamoku appeared in. He is seated in the lower row, second from right. Circa early 1930s. Mauna Kea Galleries, Kamuela, Hawaii. $600-900

1932 Los Angeles Olympics Pass and Ticket. Issued to Duke Kahanamoku, who competed in both swimming and water polo. Having failed to place in the swimming trials, he earned a spot on the water polo team and was awarded a bronze medal. Rare. Ed and Randi Economy Collection. $2,000-3,000

Charles W. Bartlett Woodblock - *Surfriders*. Circa 1925. This print featured is considered his masterwork. His source of inspiration is Duke Kahanamoku and his friends surfing at Waikiki. Mauna Kea Galleries, Kamuela, Hawaii. $5,000-7,000

Charles W. Barlett 1860-1940

He was born in Bridport, England, and was first trained as a chemist. After studying at the Royal Academy in London, in 1883, and the Julian Academy in Paris, he became an artist in his own right with a residence in Japan, where he became fascinated with the art of woodblock printing. Arriving in Hawaii in 1917, he was met with an enthusiastic welcome by the Cooke family. He postponed his departure several times before finally deciding to remain in Hawaii. He was a frequent exhibitor at the Academy of Arts in Honolulu as well as the Royal Academy in London and the Salon des Beaux Arts in Paris. He is considered the most gifted woodblock artist ever to have worked in Hawaii.

***Hawaiian Surfriding* by Thomas Blake.** An unusual and rare booklet. Peter and Cathy Noble, Monterey, California. $400-600

Voyage 118 En route: Honolulu to Los Angeles
Wednesday, July 6, 1932
S. S. "City of Los Angeles"
Captain F. I. Hamma, Commander U.S.N.R.

BREAKFAST
Good Morning!

Juices: Tomato Sauerkraut Grapefruit Orange Pineapple

Hawaiian Pineapple California Prunes Grapefruit
Stewed Fresh Rhubarb Sliced Oranges Papaia
Bananas in Cream Chilled Cantaloupe
Preserved Apricots

Cream of Wheat Steamed Rice Rolled Oats
Puffed Wheat Rice Krispies Post Toasties
Shredded Wheat Wheaties Corn Flakes
All Bran Grape Nuts

Codfish Tongues and Sounds
Broiled Fresh Mackerel, Parsley Butter
Brookfield Farm Sausages

Creamed Chicken with Peppers on Toast
Fried Cornmeal Mush
Sugar Cured Ham Breakfast Bacon

TO ORDER
Sirloin Steak Pork Tenderloin

OMELETTES
Plain, Spanish, Parsley, Ham, Jelly, Cheese

EGGS
Scrambled, Poached, Fried, Shirred or Boiled

French Fried Potatoes Hashed Brown Potatoes

Butter Horns Napkin Rolls
Bran Muffins
Toast: White or Wholewheat
Buckwheat Cakes with Maple Syrup or Honey

Assorted California Preserves and Marmalades
Individual Hawaiian Preserves

English Breakfast, Ceylon, Banquet
and Green Teas
Postum Chocolate
Coffee

LOS ANGELES LASSCO STEAMSHIP CO.

MENU NO. 6

Ship's Menu Insert from the *City of Los Angeles, July 6, 1932*. Lassco Steam Ship Company, Los Angeles, California. Great surf image that fully captures the romance of the time period. Mauna Kea Galleries, Kamuela, Hawaii. $100-150

Thomas Edward Blake 1902-1994

Surfing's greatest innovator, he is one of the most influential names to be connected with surfing in the 20th century. Tom Blake was born in the small rural town of Washburn, Wisconsin. In 1912, at a local theater, there was a short newsreel clip showing, among other things, several Hawaiians surfing at Waikiki. His interest piqued, the wheels were set in motion. The following is a partial timeline of some of his many accomplishments and contributions to the sport of Surfing:

1920 In Detroit, meets the already famous Duke Kahanamoku and his teammates returning from Antwerp and accepts an invitation to visit Hawaii.

1921 Travels to Los Angeles to escape the misery of the aftermath of the worldwide flu epidemic that was now hitting Wisconsin. Once in Southern California, he is introduced to the personal health movement and becomes a vegetarian. First attempt at surfboard riding in Santa Monica. Becomes interested in swimming and trains at the Los Angeles Athletic Club after persuading the night watchman to let him use the pool facilities. After several months of practice asks the head coach, Fred Cady, for a spot on the swim team. After watching him swim, he takes a chance and places him on the team. A natural talent, Cady immediately begins working with Blake and within a year is sent to compete in the A.A.U. Ten Mile Open in Philadelphia. Against overwhelming odds and extremely frigid temperatures in the Delaware River, he wins his first of many swimming titles, including Long Distance Swimming Champion. Continues competing over the next seven years.

1922 Travels to Florida after the end of the swimming season and acts as a double for Ramon Navaro in the film *Where the Pavement Ends*. Becomes one of the first champion swimmers to perform water stunts in feature films. Over the next twenty years, he works in dozens of films, primarily standing in for leading stars of the day.

1924 Works as a lifeguard at the Santa Monica Swim Club and forms a close personal relationship with Duke Kanahamoku, who is a lifeguard at the Santa Monica Beach Club. With Duke's help, he masters basic surfing skills. Now stoked forever, he later travels to Hawaii.

1926 First recorded person to surf Malibu, along with Sam Reid. First attempt at surfboard design when he accidentally invented the hollow surfboard. While trying to replicate an ancient Hawaiian Olo board, he decides to drill the wood full of holes. After sealing the holes, he found that he had created a lighter surfboard that was well suited for paddleboard racing. This was a revolutionary moment in surfboard design and development.

Original Photograph of Tom Blake. Circa 1935. This is a unique piece of surfing history as Tom signed this in 1987 for his friend and surfing historian Gary Lynch. Tom Blake stands in front of a redwood board measuring 11 feet long, 23 inches wide and 3-1/4 inches thick. Next to it stands a red cedar board 12 feet long, good for fast paddling. The third board is hollow and used for big waves; it measures 14 feet 6 inches by 20 inches wide and weighs 120 pounds. The fourth is a reproduction of the ancient Hawaiian rider. The fifth board is a light, hollow board measuring 16 feet. The last one is a training board, which is solid and heavy. Mauna Kea Galleries, Kamuela, Hawaii. $1,200-1,800

Hawaiian Surfboard **by Thomas Blake.** Paradise of the Pacific Press, 1935, 95 pages. Issued bound in Samoan tapa cloth. Rarely seen with original dust jacket as shown. Mauna Kea Galleries, Kamuela, Hawaii. As shown with dust jacket $3,000-5000. Without dust jacket $1,500-2,500

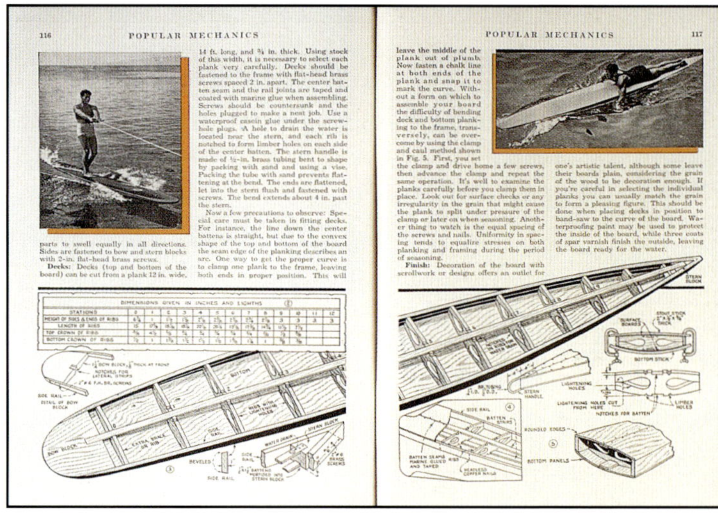

Popular Mechanics **Magazine, July 1937.** Issue with article entitled "Riding Breakers" by Tom Blake. This is the pioneering issue showing how to build a Hollow Hawaiian Surfboard. This particular copy is extremely rare as it was autographed by Tom Blake in 1989. Mauna Kea Galleries, Kamuela, Hawaii. As shown: $400-600, Average: $60-90

Vintage Advertisement. Mauna Kea Galleries, Kamuela, Hawaii.

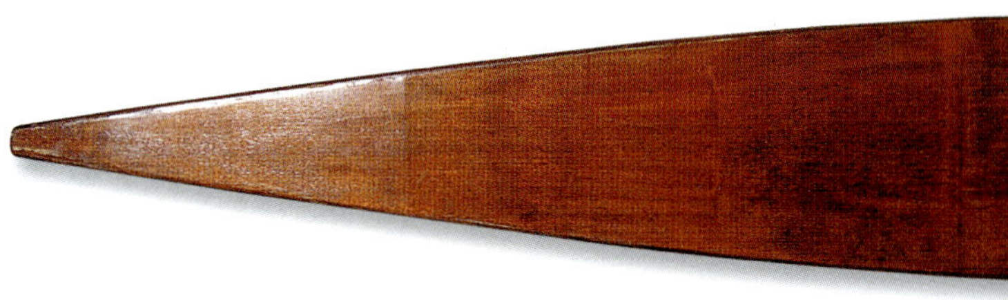

Paddleboard Invented by Tom Blake in 1926, it is a square-sided hollow board originally constructed of plywood. Today it is constructed of fiberglass and is much sleeker in design. These boards were used in long-distance racing competitions as well as a lifesaving tool.

1928 Wins the Pacific Coast Surfriding Championships using his own board design.
1929 Begins hollowing out chambers in solid wood planks. Builds the first waterproof camera using it extensively for surf photography.
1930 Competes and wins the Hawaiian Surfboard Championships on the Ala Wai canal, easily sweeping both events: the 100-yard Dash and the Half-Mile Open.
1931 After viewing an aircraft factory sometime earlier, he experiments with a design that uses bracing covered by either thin aircraft-grade hardwood veneer or thin solid wood, reducing board weight by 50 percent. Patents and manufactures the first production surfboard.
1932 Paddles his newly designed paddleboard from Point Vincente to Catalina, a distance of over 26 miles. Promotes his new paddleboard as the fastest, safest way to make open-water rescues.
1933 Thomas Rogers begins producing a variety of Blake's designed boards. The American Red Cross endorses and adopts them as rescue equipment. Gaining popularity, the Blake paddleboard craze sweeps across the country, being primarily used on lakes and rivers
1935 Adds the first fin (skeg) onto a surfboard. Authors the first definitive book on surfing, *Hawaiian Surfboard*, drawing upon the true source and soul of surfing – the ancient Hawaiians. Has first surfing photo spread in a national magazine.
1940 Designs the first sailing surfboard and aluminum torpedo rescue buoy.
1942 Enters Coast Guard.
1957 Quits surfing full-time.

For the rest of his life, Blake was the ultimate waterman, receiving numerous accolades. Duke Kahanamoku and Tom Blake were the only two watermen to be inducted into both Florida's Swimming Hall of Fame and California's International Surfing Hall of Fame. A true Renaissance and ladies man, it is said he had numerous affairs throughout his life with Hollywood starlets, including, among others, Marilyn Monroe. After many years spent in Hawaii and California, he retreats, at the end of his life, to Ashland, Wisconsin, where he spends time reflecting on his truly remarkable life.

Hawaiian Paddleboard, 14'0". A Tom Blake hollow mahogany veneer construction, circa 1930s. Spencer and Annette Croul Collection. $8,000-12,000

Postcard of Surfers at Canoes, Waikiki. This postcard from the 1930s was sent to Tom Blake in 1988 by the surf historian Gary Lynch, with the note:
Can you identify these riders? *Some.*
Are they the Kahanamoku brothers? *No.*
Standing Riders – R to L.
1. Waldo Bowman
2. Looks like Chuck Daniels
3. Wilbur Crow
A rare and unique piece of surfing history. Mauna Kea Galleries, Kamuela, Hawaii. $500-700

Original Photograph of David Kahanamoku. Circa 1915. Mauna Kea Galleries, Kamuela, Hawaii. $100-150

Redwood, 8'9". An historic solid redwood board made in Makaha in 1935 and previously owned by David Kahanamoku. Old butterfly repairs of koa wood. Dick Metz, Dana Point, California. As shown: $8,000-12,000. Average: $6,000-9,000

Duke Kahanamoku's Service Station Ledger Book. Original ledger book kept by Duke for his Union gasoline service station in Waikiki in the 1930s. Originally sold by Tusitalia Book Shop in Kailua, Oahu, to surf historian Mark Fragale who, in turn, gave it to Ed Economy. Ed and Randi Economy Collection. $3,000-5,000

Vintage Advertisement. Mauna Kea Galleries, Kamuela, Hawaii.

Face The unbroken front surface of a wave between the crest and the trough.

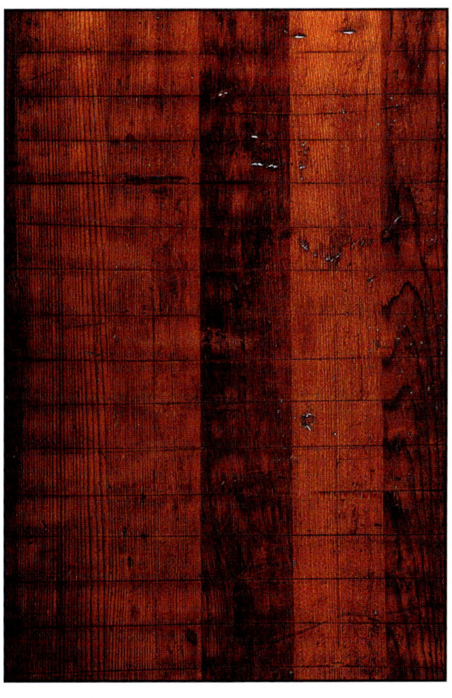

Redwood, 7'11". A hollow plank board with unusual grooves for traction, circa 1930s. Spencer and Annette Croul Collection. $4,000-6,000

Redwood, 8'1". A planked board inspired by the ancient Hawaiian *alaia* shape. This board was made and used in Huntington Beach in the 1930s. Unusual painted decoration on both sides. Hoffman Collection. $6,000-9,000

Hot Curl A term used in the 1930s to describe a fast, challenging wave.

Vintage Advertisement. Mauna Kea Galleries, Kamuela, Hawaii.

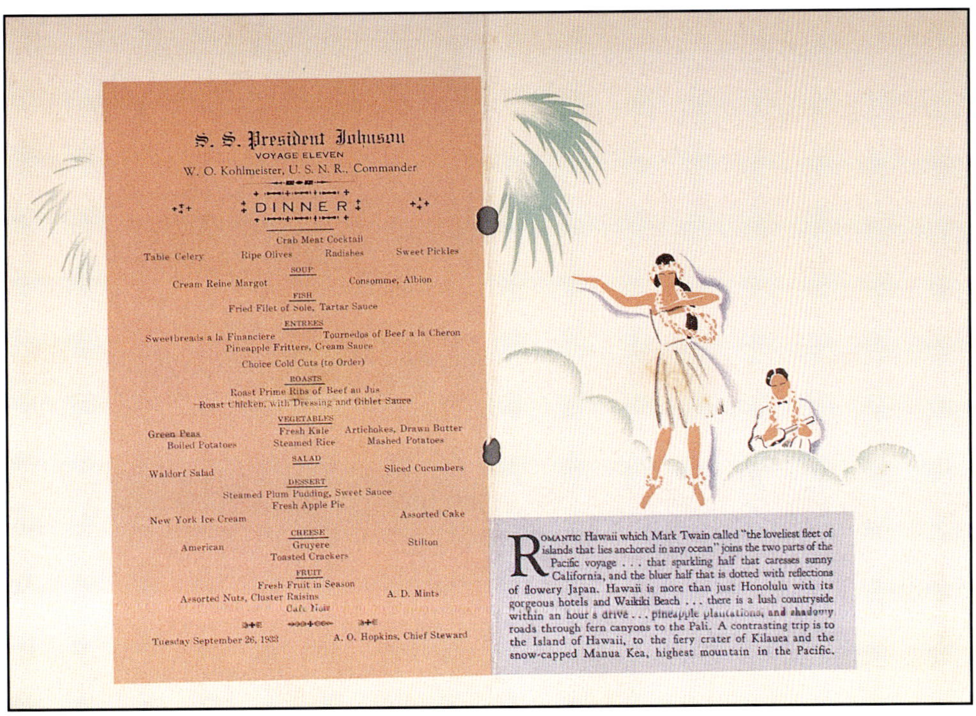

Ship's Menu from the *S.S. President Johnson*, September 1933. Mauna Kea Galleries, Kamuela, Hawaii. $120-180

Original Gelatin Silv Print. Entitled "Sea Gods," by Warren Photographers, Honolulu, circa 1930s. This print is signed and titled on lower mat. Th image was later used by Don Blanding as an actual illustration and inspiration in two of h books. This photo real captures the feel of surfing at Canoes, Waikiki, at the time period and shows that was a popular and crowded surf spot even 75 years ago. Mauna Ke Galleries, Kamuela, Hawaii. $800-1,200

Redwood, 11'0". Circa late 1920s early 1930s. An interesting example of a hollowed-out board with slots for support spars, so classic in early paddleboard construction. This board is possibly an altered solid redwood board dating from the 1920s. Dick Metz, Dana Point, California. $2,000-3,000

Redwood, 9'10". A solid redwood hot curl board made in Black Point, Oahu, in the 1930s. A good example of the ancient Hawaiian technique of butterfly repair, which was often used on the treasured heirloom calabashes. Hoffman Collection. $8,000-12,000

Original Dry Point Etching. A very rare print done in the 1930s by Ronald Riggs, who was an illustrator and did a number of Hawaiian prints for Dole Pineapple and Matson Navigation. This particular print came from a purser for the Matson ship *Mariposa*. Mauna Kea Galleries, Kamuela, Hawaii. $5,000-7,000.
A word of caution: The author has seen numerous fraudulent copies of Riggs prints appearing on the Internet being sold as genuine. Know your source!

Fin A projection sometimes referred to as a skeg affixed to a surfboard's bottom adding to the board's stability and drive. Invented by Tom Blake in 1935.

Redwood and Balsa, 10'6". This beautiful board is composed of a redwood deck and a redwood and balsa bottom. Built by Gary Larson in the 1930s. Hoffman Collection. $8,000-12,000

Vintage Advertisement. Mauna Kea Galleries, Kamuela, Hawaii.

Vintage Advertisement. Mauna Kea Galleries, Kamuela, Hawaii.

Redwood, 6'0". A short planked redwood design, circa 1930s. Dick Metz, Dana Point, California. $2,000-3,000

Vintage Advertisement. Mauna Kea Galleries, Kamuela, Hawaii.

Belly The convex bottom of a surfboard.

Waikiki Surf Board, Mfd. by Pacific System Homes Inc., Los Angeles, Calif., 10'3". Redwood and balsa, this board was purchased new in 1942 and still retains its original receipt for $31.50, a huge sum in those days. Spencer and Annette Croul Collection. As shown: $15,000-20,000. Average: $8,000-12,000

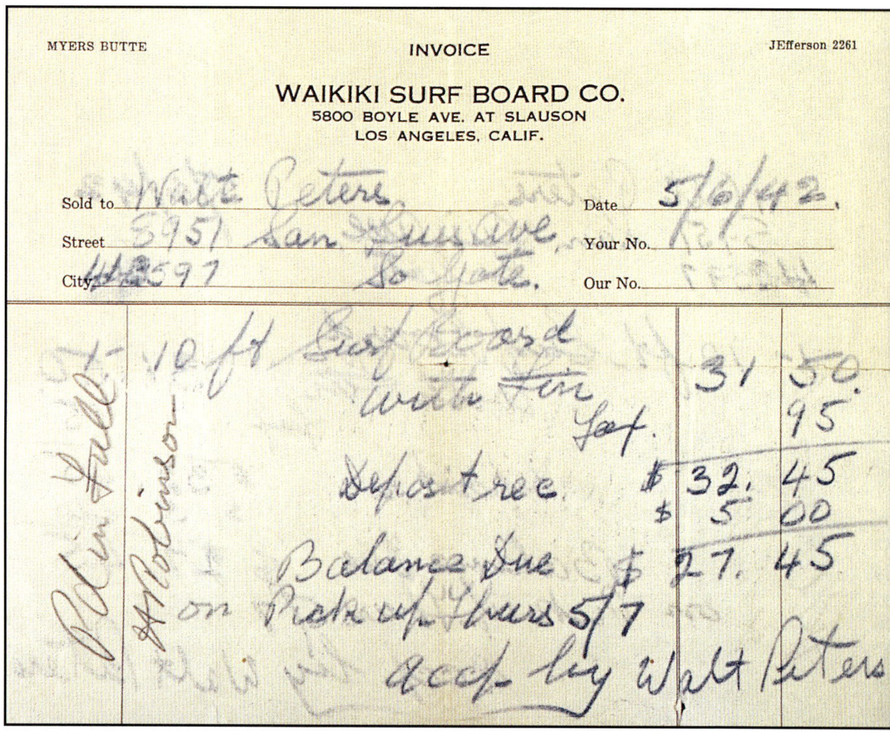

MYERS BUTTE — INVOICE — JEfferson 2261

WAIKIKI SURF BOARD CO.
5800 BOYLE AVE. AT SLAUSON
LOS ANGELES, CALIF.

Sold to Walt Peters — Date 5/6/42
Street 5951 San Juan Ave. — Your No.
City 597 So Gate. — Our No.

Pd in Full / H Robinson	10 ft Surf Board with Fin	31	50
	Tax		95
		$ 32	45
	Deposit rec.	$ 5	00
	Balance Due on Pick up Thurs 5/7	$ 27	45
	acc. by Walt Peters		

Waikiki Surf-Board Co., A Subsidiary of Pacific System Homes Inc., Los Angeles, California. A rare promotional pamphlet/pricelist, circa early 1930s. Spencer and Annette Croul Collection. $300-500

Waikiki Surf Boards Mfd. by Pacific System Homes Inc., Los Angeles, California, Bellyboard, 5'0". Redwood and pine with nose rocker, circa 1930s. This one is unusual because the logo is still strong and distinct. Mauna Kea Galleries, Kamuela, Hawaii. As shown: $4,000-6,000. Average: $2,000-3,000

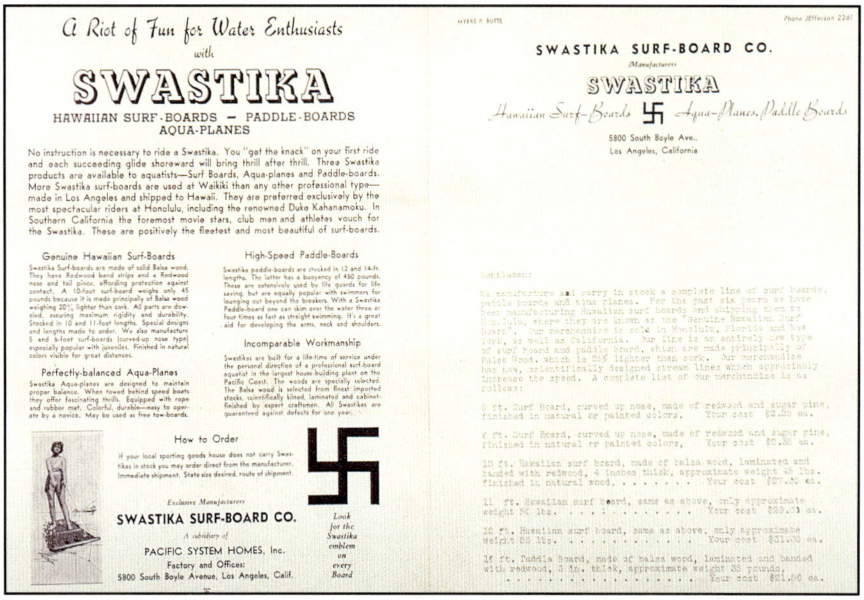

A Riot of Fun for Water Enthusiasts
with

SWASTIKA

HAWAIIAN SURF-BOARDS – PADDLE-BOARDS
AQUA-PLANES

No instruction is necessary to ride a Swastika. You "get the knack" on your first ride and each succeeding glide shoreward will bring thrill after thrill. Three Swastika products are available to aquatists—Surf Boards, Aqua-planes and Paddle-boards. More Swastika surf-boards are used at Waikiki than any other professional type—made in Los Angeles and shipped to Hawaii. They are preferred exclusively by the most spectacular riders at Honolulu, including the renowned Duke Kahanamoku. In Southern California the foremost movie stars, club men and athletes vouch for the Swastika. These are positively the fleetest and most beautiful of surf-boards.

Genuine Hawaiian Surf-Boards

Swastika Surf-boards are made of solid Balsa wood. They have Redwood band strips and a Redwood nose and tail piece, affording protection against contact. A 10-foot surf-board weighs only 45 pounds because it is made principally of Balsa wood weighing 20% lighter than cork. All parts are doweled, assuring maximum rigidity and durability. Stocked in 10 and 11-foot lengths. Special designs and lengths made to order. We also manufacture 5 and 6-foot surf-boards (curved-up nose type) especially popular with juveniles. Finished in natural colors visible for great distances.

Perfectly-balanced Aqua-Planes

Swastika Aqua-planes are designed to maintain proper balance. When towed behind speed boats they offer fascinating thrills. Equipped with rope and rubber mat. Colorful, durable—easy to operate by a novice. May be used as free tow-boards.

High-Speed Paddle-Boards

Swastika paddle-boards are stocked in 12 and 14-ft. lengths. The latter has a buoyancy of 450 pounds. These are extensively used by life guards for life saving, but are equally popular with swimmers for lounging out beyond the breakers. With a Swastika Paddle-board one can skim over the water three or four times as fast as straight swimming. It's a great aid for developing the arms, neck and shoulders.

Incomparable Workmanship

Swastikas are built for a life-time of service under the personal direction of a professional surf-board aquatist in the largest house-building plant on the Pacific Coast. The woods are specially selected. The Balsa wood is selected from finest imported stocks, scientifically kilned, laminated and cabinet-finished by expert craftsmen. All Swastikas are guaranteed against defects for one year.

How to Order

If your local sporting goods house does not carry Swastikas in stock you may order direct from the manufacturer. Immediate shipment. State size desired, route of shipment.

Exclusive Manufacturers
SWASTIKA SURF-BOARD CO.
A subsidiary of
PACIFIC SYSTEM HOMES, Inc.
Factory and Offices:
5800 South Boyle Avenue, Los Angeles, Calif.

Look for the Swastika emblem on every Board

MYERS P. BUTTE

Phone JEfferson 2261

SWASTIKA SURF-BOARD CO.
Manufacturers
SWASTIKA
Hawaiian Surf-Boards *Aqua-Planes, Paddle Boards*
5800 South Boyle Ave.,
Los Angeles, California

Gentlemen:

We manufacture and carry in stock a complete line of surf boards, paddle boards and aqua planes. For the past six years we have been manufacturing Hawaiian surf boards and shipping them to Honolulu, where they are known as the "Genuine Hawaiian Surf Board". Our merchandise is sold in Honolulu, Florida and New York, as well as California. Our line is an entirely new type of surf board and paddle board, which are made principally of Balsa Wood, which is 25% lighter than cork. Our merchandise has new, scientifically designed stream lines which appreciably increase the speed. A complete list of our merchandise is as follows:

5 ft. Surf Board, curved up nose, made of redwood and sugar pine, finished in natural or painted colors. Your cost $2.25 ea.

6 ft. Surf Board, curved up nose, made of redwood and sugar pine, finished in natural or painted colors, Your cost $2.35 ea.

10 ft. Hawaiian surf board, made of balsa wood, laminated and banded with redwood, 4 inches thick, approximate weight 45 lbs. finished in natural wood, ... Your cost $27.50 ea.

11 ft. Hawaiian surf board, same as above, only approximate weight 50 lbs. . . . . Your cost $29.00 ea.

12 ft. Hawaiian surf board, same as above, only approximate weight 55 lbs. . . . . Your cost $31.00 ea.

16 ft. Paddle Board, made of balsa wood, laminated and banded with redwood, 3 in. thick, approximate weight 35 pounds, ... Your cost $21.50 ea.

Swastika Hawaiian Surf-Boards, Manufactured by Pacific System Homes Inc., Los Angeles, California. Circa early 1930s. Spencer and Annette Croul Collection. $300-500

Windansea The famous La Jolla, California, surf break popularized in the 1930s and 1940s and the site of the well-known surf club by the same name.

Pacific System Homes Inc., Los Angeles, California, 11'2". Redwood and balsa, circa early 1930s. Famous Swastika model. Spencer and Annette Croul Collection. $8,000-12,000

Pacific System Homes Inc., Los Angeles, California, 9'6". Redwood and balsa, circa 1936. Two unusual elements on this board are the addition of a running board tread off of a Ford Model T and the Swastika motif, which had been routed out to look like a window instead of the unpopular symbol it became during World War II. Original owner of board was Ed Thomas, whose fiancé posed in front of the board at Solona Beach, California (see photo). Spencer and Annette Croul Collection. $6,000-9,000

Swastika Surf Board Company, Manufactured by Pacific System Homes Inc., Los Angeles, California. Rare early promotional pamphlet, circa early 1930s. Spencer and Annette Croul Collection. $400-600

Lip. The edge at the top of a wall of breaking waves.

Vintage Advertisement. Mauna Kea Galleries, Kamuela, Hawaii.

Redwood, Balsa and Spruce, 10'3". An early 1930s planked board made, most likely, by Pacific Homes and cut down in Hawaii in the late 1940s to a big wave gun. Shaped by hand, this historic board may actually be one of the first gun shapes ever produced. Mauna Kea Galleries, Kamuela, Hawaii. $12,000-18,000

Original Photograph. A classic image with captions and notes by Tom Blake. Mauna Kea Galleries, Kamuela, Hawaii. $500-700

Vintage Advertisement. Mauna Kea Galleries, Kamuela, Hawaii.

Left: **Tom Blake, 10'0".** A hollow spruce paddleboard design with brass drain plug, circa 1930s. Spencer and Annette Croul Collection. $6,000-9,000

Right: **Pacific System Homes Inc., Los Angeles, 14'0".** Classic Swastika design hollow paddleboard constructed of spruce and redwood, circa 1933. Spencer and Annette Croul Collection. $6,000-9,000

Rail The outside edge of a surfboard.

Redwood and Plywood Planked Board, 10'10". Boat nose, circa 1930s. Unusual hollow core added at a later time for lightness. The plywood used was most likely steam bent. Spencer and Annette Croul Collection. $4,000-6,000

Rare *Honolulu Star Bulletin* Christmas Gift Print, December 1940 – *Huki*. To our knowledge, it is the first in a series of gift prints given out every year to the newspapers best customers. This beautiful lithographic print is reproduced in full color from the original painting by the noted Hawaiian artist Lionel Walden. This is the only gift print with a surfing subject matter, and under image is a lengthy story about surfing. Mauna Kea Galleries, Kamuela, Hawaii. $600-900

Valentine Greeting Card. Circa late 1930s. Great graphic art that was later used in the 1940s as a magazine cover. Large format. Mauna Kea Galleries, Kamuela, Hawaii. $100-150

Redwood, 11'8". A solid redwood Waikiki board in the classic *alaia* shape, circa 1930s. Hoffman Collection. $6,000-9,000

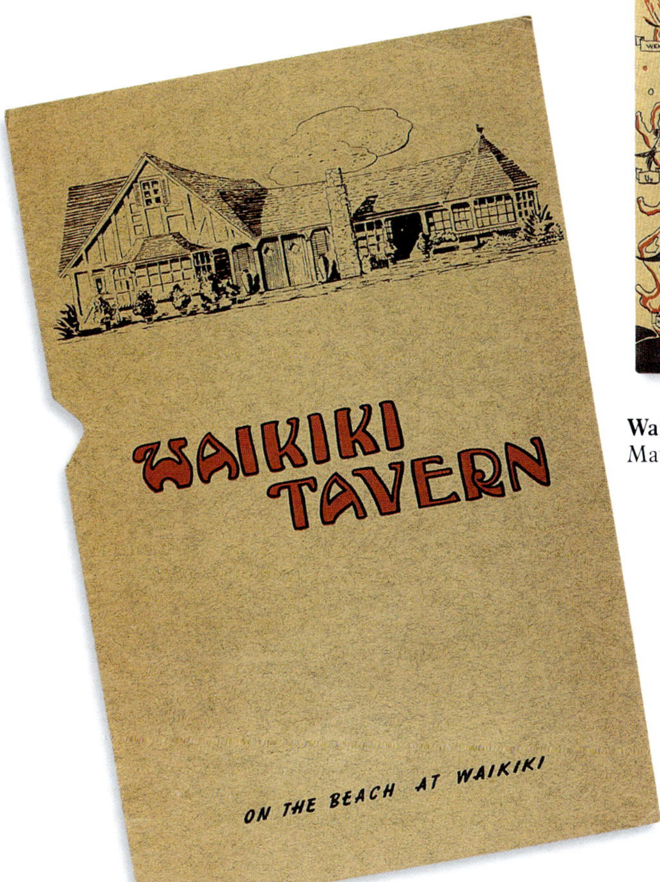

Waikiki Tavern Souvenir Menu. Circa 1930s. Mauna Kea Galleries, Kamuela, Hawaii. $100-150

Menu Cover Queen's Surf, Waikiki. Circa 1940s. Mauna Kea Galleries, Kamuela, Hawaii. $80-120

Original Photograph of Shirley Temple and Duke Kahanamoku. Circa 1940. Inscribed on reverse in pencil, *Sherlie and Duke Kahanamoku the Sheriff discussing her doll.* Mauna Kea Galleries, Kamuela, Hawaii. $200-300

Redwood and Spruce, 10'6". This planked board was made by Lorrin Harrison in the 1940s. Original metal nose guard. Hoffman Collection. $6,000-9,000

Vintage Advertisement. Mauna Kea Galleries, Kamuela, Hawaii.

Curl The curved breaking portion of any wave.

Original Photograph of Amelia Earhart and Duke Kahanamoku, Honolulu. Circa 1940. Inscribed on reverse in pencil, *Amelia and Duke Kahanamoku eating pineapple. The man is the sheriff down here. Also a great swimmer.* Mauna Kea Galleries, Kamuela, Hawaii. $200-300

Redwood Hot Curl, 10'5". Hollow core with laminated doweled plank, circa 1940. Spencer and Annette Croul Collection. $6,000-8,000

Original Photograph of Louis Kahanamoku. Circa early 1940s. Mauna Kea Galleries, Kamuela, Hawaii. $60-90

Buy U. S. War Savings Bonds and Stamps

VOLUME LXXXVI — NUMBER THREE

THE NATIONAL GEOGRAPHIC MAGAZINE

SEPTEMBER, 1944

How We Fight with Photographs — With 22 Illustrations — F. BARROWS COLTON

Rhodesia, Hobby and Hope of Cecil Rhodes — With 13 Illustrations and Map, 10 Natural Color Photographs — W. ROBERT MOORE

Bare Feet and Burros of Haiti — With 10 Illustrations and Map — OLIVER P. NEWMAN

Haiti Goes to Market — 10 Natural Color Photographs — B. ANTHONY STEWART

Salt for China's Daily Rice — 11 Illustrations

When GI Joes Took London — With 18 Illustrations — FREDERICK SIMPICH, JR.

Surf-Boarders Capture California — 8 Illustrations — J. H. BALL

Other Working Dogs and the Wild Species — With 12 Illustrations from Photographs, 9 Original Paintings — STANLEY P. YOUNG, WALTER A. WEBER

Twenty-four Pages of Illustrations in Color

PUBLISHED BY THE NATIONAL GEOGRAPHIC SOCIETY
WASHINGTON, D.C.

$4.00 A YEAR — 50¢ THE COPY

362 — The National Geographic Magazine

J. H. Ball

Tom Blake Rides with His World-champion Dog Surfer, Rusty

Though the spaniel prefers to go out with his master, a famous rider, he is so fond of the sport that he will beg anyone launching a board to take him along. Surfers steer their boards by shifting the balance from side to side. Sometimes they "slide" down a wave, cut over, and skim at an angle to make the ride longer. (See "Waves and Thrills at Waikiki," by Thomas Edward Blake, NATIONAL GEOGRAPHIC MAGAZINE, May, 1935.)

***National Geographic*, September 1944.** A scarce issue with the article by Doc Ball, entitled "Surf-boarders Capture California." This particular issue was autographed by Doc Ball in 1988. Mauna Kea Galleries, Kamuela, Hawaii. As shown: $150-250. Average: $50-70

Receipt Signed and Annotated by Doc Ball. An unusual item of surfing ephemera given with the purchase of Doc Ball's book, *California Surfriders*, circa 1940s. This receipt is annotated with names of the surfriders pictured on the receipt. Left to right: Trux Oehrlin, Hal Pearson and Donnie Grannis. Mauna Kea Galleries, Kamuela, Hawaii. $300-500

Paddleboard, 12'0". Mahogany, circa late 1930s/early 1940s. Allan Seymour, Pacific Coast Vintage Surf Auctions. $800-1,200

Paddleboard, 12'5". Red mahogany, circa 1930s-40s. An unusual piece of Americana. Allan Seymour, Pacific Coast Vintage Surf Auctions. $1,200-1,800

Los Angeles Ladder Co., 14'0". A Tom Blake hollow paddleboard design, spruce plank, with brass screws and drain plug, circa early 1940s. Spencer and Annette Croul Collection. $6,000-9,000

Flat Refers to a waveless ocean.

Vintage Advertisement. Mauna Kea Galleries, Kamuela, Hawaii.

Plywood and Balsa, 10'5". A very rare Bob Simmons sandwich board, circa 1946-1947. This important board was the first board ever produced utilizing foam. A rare and historic item in the history of surfboard production. Hoffman Collection. $12,000-18,000

Bob Simmons

A surfer from Southern California with an engineering background, he made numerous contributions to the sport and surfboard design by experimenting with different materials, such as sandwiching together balsa, plywood and foam. He also was the first person credited with using fiberglass on lightweight materials and the first person to experiment with foam in a surfboard. Tragically, he was killed in 1954 when he was hit by his own surfboard while surfing at Windansea, La Jolla, California.

Bob Simmons, 10'2". A rare and historic early transitional board with styrofoam core, veneer laminated with balsa wood rails utilizing aircraft fiberglass. This twin-fin board has a concave deck, which is often referred to as a spoon. Dick Metz, Dana Point, California. $12,000-18,000

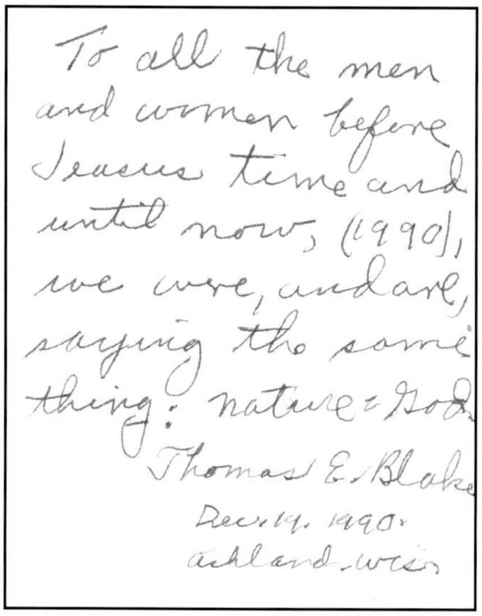
To all the men
and women before
Jesus time and
until now, (1990),
we were, and are,
saying the same
thing: nature = God
Thomas E. Blake
Dec. 19. 1990.
ashland. wis.

Tom Blake Photograph and Note. Both items are in Tom's own hand and reflect his whole essence and outlook on life. Rare. Mauna Kea Galleries, Karnuela, Hawaii. $1200-1800.

Hot Curl Board A term used in the early 1950s for a big wave riding board. The term was later changed to "gun."

Left & below: **Matt Kivlin Hot Curl, 9'9".** Redwood with oak butterfly repairs, shaped in 1948. This board was once a community plank at Waikiki when Dave Rochlein decided to bring the board back to Malibu. Dave owed Matt some money for fiberglass supplies, and in lieu of the bill Dave traded the board to Matt. Matt then re-shaped the board into a hot curl board for his personal use. Matt later traded the board to Con Colburn for a wetsuit. Peter and Cathy Noble, Monterey, California. As shown: $6,000-8,000

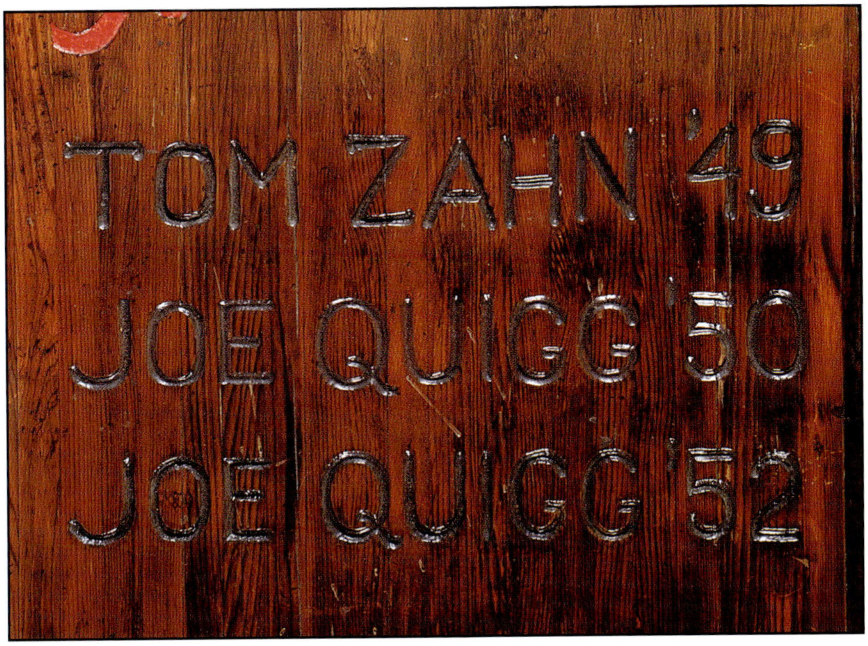

Rare Malibu Perpetual Board Trophy, 9'6". Hot curl board shaped by Joe Quigg and Matt Kivlin. Board was a sinker and unrideable, subsequently donated as a trophy board. Board was found bolted to a fence in Las Vegas and rescued by the present owner. Peter and Cathy Noble, Monterey, California. $4,000-6,000

Joe Quigg – Joe began surfing in the 1930s and was an avid paddler, winning many contests in the 1940s and 1950s. A native of Santa Monica, California, he was a master craftsman, shaping his own line of balsa boards in Newport Beach, California, in the 1950s.

Comic Postcard. Circa 1940s. Entitled "In Hawaii – and How!" Lower caption reads "Perfect form on the water hazard at Waikiki." Mauna Kea Galleries, Kamuela, Hawaii. $40-60

Advertising Label, American Sanitary Laundry Ltd. Circa 1940s. Mauna Kea Galleries, Kamuela, Hawaii. $60-90

Close Out Waves that become too large to form properly for surfing - the entire length of the wave breaks at the same time.

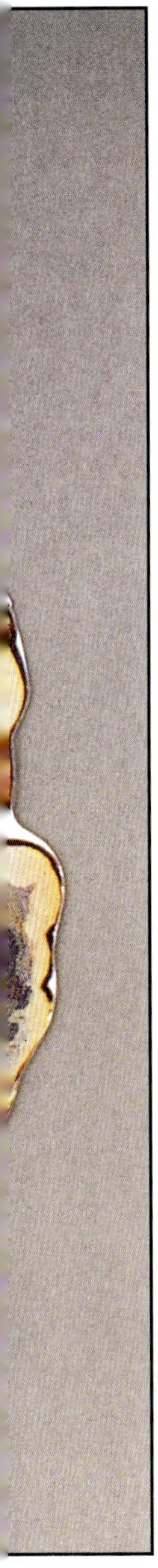

Comic Souvenir Postcard by Mundorff. This unusual and amusing postcard is from the 1940s. Mauna Kea Galleries, Kamuela, Hawaii. $80-120

Balsa, 10'5". An early use of concave shape adding to its aerodynamic design, this twin-fin channel bottom board was made in the late 1940s and recently restored by Dale Velzy. Hoffman Collection. $6,000-9,000

Balsa Boards

Balsa wood was first used by Lorrin Thurston in surfboard construction in Honolulu in 1926. Balsa was later used laminated with other materials such as spruce and redwood in the 1930s, and by the 1940s the all-balsa board was developed, which was popular until the advent of the foam era in or around 1957. It has been said that the all-balsa board helped popularize the sport of surfing due to their light weight, which encouraged more people to get into surfing.

Velzy Surfboards – Dale Velzy started shaping boards in the late 1940s, and by the early and mid-1950s his very popular Hawk model was being ridden at all the popular surf spots of Southern California. In 1960, he had one of his most famous models, the 7-11, selling nearly 2,000 units. He is credited with being the first person to really put surfboards within reach of the average person through mass production using lighter, less costly materials.

Dale Velzy's Working Tools. Circa early 1950s. An interesting group representing surfboard production in its infancy. Spencer and Annette Croul Collection.

Dale Velzy's Hot Curl and Semi-Pig Templates. Circa 1950s. Spencer and Annette Croul Collection.

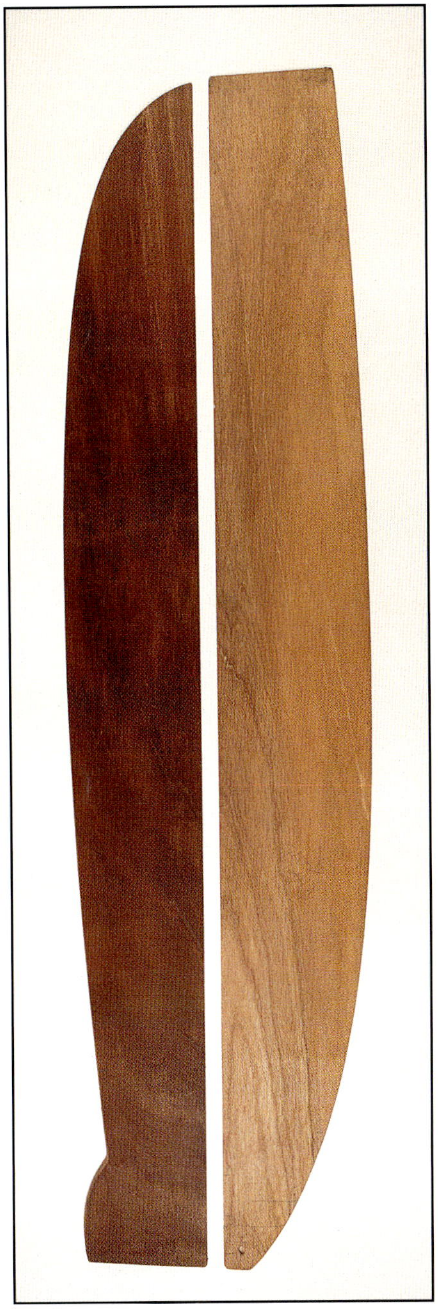

Dale Velzy's Pigtail and Banjo Templates. Circa 1950s. Spencer and Annette Croul Collection.

Balsa and Redwood Board, 9'3". A very rare and important board, being the first board made by Greg Noll. This board is a transitional piece of surf history, as, in 1951, with the appearance of streamlined, lighter-weight boards made entirely of balsa and fiberglass, the heavily varnished redwood and balsa boards were rendered obsolete. Because of the high cost of these new boards, many resourceful surfers overhauled their existing redwood and balsa boards to replicate the new models. Lifeguard Jerry Cunningham brought the Pacific Systems Homes board featured here to Dale Velzy's shop in Manhattan Beach, where a 14-year-old Greg Noll cut off the redwood rails, replaced them with balsa, and coated the board with fiberglass. Spencer and Annette Croul Collection. $25,000-35,000

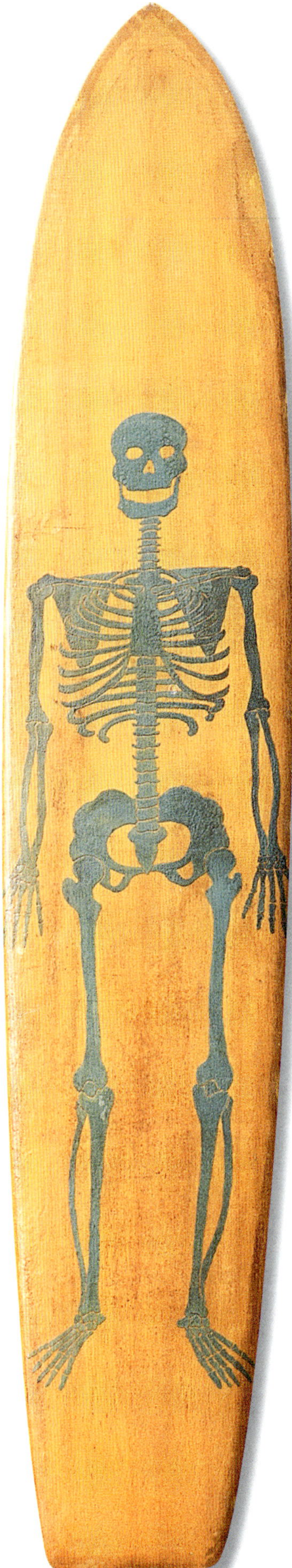

Vintage Advertisement. Mauna Kea Galleries, Kamuela, Hawaii.

Left: **Joe Quigg, 10'.** A beautiful and unusual all balsa board shaped by Quigg in the 1950s. The board was used by a female surfer who had the skeleton design put on by her mother, an art teacher at Punahou School, Honolulu. Mauna Kea Galleries, Kamuela, Hawaii. $5,000-7,000

Far left: **Joe Quigg, 10'2".** An unusual balsa board, laminated by Dale Velzy, and one of only two made. The thick nose of this board made it very difficult to handle. Peter and Cathy Noble, Monterey, California. As shown: $4,000-6,000

John Rochelan, 10'6". Balsa board shaped in 1953 at Point Dume, California, for Rene Calliet. Peter and Cathy Noble, Monterey, California. $2,500-3,500

Balsa, 10'2". An early Makaha big wave gun, shaped by George Downing. Early use of slot box receptacle for fin. Woody Brown was the original designer of this style. Hoffman Collection. $10,000-15,000

Balsa and Redwood, 11'0". A beautifully fabricated inlaid big wave gun produced in the early 1950s. This board was built for a Waianae fire chief and then was passed to Donald DuPont in 1955. This board carries the nameplate of Jerry Pregill. Hoffman Collection. $8,000-12,000.

Big Wave Guns – The most machismo of the surfboards, these highly specialized boards were designed to pit man against nature, resulting in an intense bond between the shaper and the rider.

The first big wave breaks recorded in modern surfing history were located in Hawaii on the island of Oahu in the 1930s and 1940s, mainly on the South Shore, Zero Break being the most famous. Around the same time, the West Shore of Oahu at Makaha was being explored, and by the late 1950s and early 1960s, the infamous Waimea, Sunset and Pipeline were all being ridden on the North Shore of Oahu.

The name 'Big Gun' was given to these boards, according to Joe Quigg, by Buzzy Trent in the late 1950s. According to Quigg, Buzzy had an intense infatuation with his stepfather's collection of firearms and was constantly referring to it. While Joe was shaping a big wave board for Buzzy, Buzzy blurted out the following: "You don't go out hunting elephants with a BB gun – you hunt elephants with an elephant gun. Make me an elephant gun to shoot big waves with." Thus, the legend was born.

Today, these big wave guns are the hottest area of the surfboard collectible market – and provenanced guns ridden by famous big wave riders present an area of tremendous investment growth potential.

ADVENTURE

SUNBURNS AND FLOOR BURNS - - - -

Go hand in hand for surfboard enthusiasts. Introduced in Hawaii, pastime now a favorite among the summer set in the north, and an all-year-round exerciser in southern Florida and California. With spray flying from polished boards from the Pacific to the Atlantic, followers paddle like geese getting up flying speed, stand erect as wave speeds them to shore.

CARD NO. 26

PRINTED IN U. S. A.
© GUM PRODUCTS, INC. 1956

Surfing Premium Card, 1956, Adventure Gum. Mauna Kea Galleries, Kamuela, Hawaii. $25-35

Presentation Miniature Surfboard. This miniature surfboard was presented to Jack Cheshire while preparing to move from Hawaii to California in 1955.

It was made by "Dukey" a part-time Beachboy at the Outrigger Canoe Club. The club was located on the beach at Waikiki between the Royal Hawaiian Hotel and the Moana Hotel. The board measures 6" by 24" and is made from a hardwood. The Outrigger was the location the Beachboys used as their headquarters to give surfing lessons and canoe rides. The Beachboys Captain was "Sally" Hale. "Sally" scheduled the lessons and took in the loot. The board is signed by most of the guys that worked the beach at that time, namely, "Steamboat" Mokuahi, "Rabbitt" Kekai, "Turkey" Love, "Curley" Cornwall, "Splash" Lyons, "Steamboat Jr.," "Sally," "Panama" Baptist – some well known, some not so well known, but all a part of the Hawaii that was the best of times. In addition, we must not forget the famous Hawaiian Olympian and Honolulu Sheriff "Duke" Kahanamoku, his brother David, and the one and only "Chick" Daniels, head Beachboy at the Royal. As you can see, there are more signatures than mentioned above, most of them gone, but not forgotten, and will be remembered as the Hawaii that was.

Mahalo,

Jack Cheshire

Courtesy of Jack and Mona Cheshire, Newport Beach, California.
$6,000-8,000

Makaha Surfing Champion Souvenir Programs. One of the most sought after of Hawaiian surf collectibles, these programs tell the story of surfing competition in Hawaii from its inception in 1954 to the present contests. Championships were originally sponsored by the Waikiki Surf Club and The Waianae Lions Club.

1954 $600-900
1955 $400-600
1956 $400-600
1957 $300-500
1958 $400-600
1959 $300-500
1960 $300-500
1961 $300-500
1962 $250-350
1963 $200-300
1964 $200-300
1965 $200-300
1966 $200-300
1967 $200-300
1968 $200-300
1969 $200-300

All programs shown, Mauna Kea Galleries, Kamuela, Hawaii.

Lineup Most often used to describe surfers sitting waiting to catch a wave.

Catalina Equipment Company, Los Angeles, 11'7". A Tom Blake hollow plywood paddleboard design, circa early 1950s. Spencer and Annette Croul Collection. $6,000-9,000

Candy Box from Kay's Candies, Honolulu. An unusual use of a surfing image in a confectionery box design, circa early 1950s. Mauna Kea Galleries, Kamuela, Hawaii. $100-150

Original Photograph of David Kahanamoku. Circa 1950s. Mauna Kea Galleries, Kamuela, Hawaii. $60-90

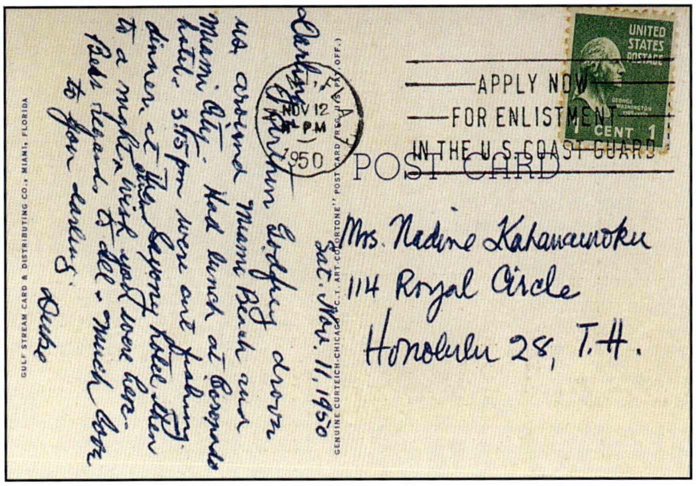

Postcard of Hotel Row, Miami Beach, Florida. Circa 1950. A poignant postcard addressed by Duke Kahanamoku to his wife, Nadine, while he was in Miami with Arthur Godrey opening a hotel in Miami Beach.

Saturday, November 11, 1950.

Darling, Aurthor Godfrey drove us around Miami Beach and Miami city. Had lunch at Coronado Hotel, 3:15 PM were out fishing. Dinner at the Saxony Hotel, then to a night out. Wish you were here. Best regards to all. Much to you darling. Duke

Rare. Mauna Kea Galleries, Kamuela, Hawaii. $800-1,200

Radiogram Sent by Duke Kahanamoku. Sent in 1952 to his wife Nadine, confirming his arrival and flight information. Ed and Randi Economy Collection. $80-120

Original Photograph of the Kahanamoku Brothers. Circa 1950s. An interesting photograph of unknown origin with the image of Duke Kahanamoku added. Mauna Kea Galleries, Kamuela, Hawaii. $100-150

Hobie Surfboards – Founded by all-around waterman Hobart "Hobie" Alter in the 1950s, his surfboards were the winningest of all in the major surfboard competitions of the 1960s. His first shop was opened in Dana Point, California, and, by the mid-1960s, he had dealerships in all the major surfing centers of the U.S. Today, the Hobie name is still synonymous with surfing.

Hobie Surfboards, Dana Point, California. Hobart L. Alter's personal card. Peter and Cathy Noble, Monterey, California. $100-150

Hobie, 10'0". Fiberglass-coated balsa, circa 1952. Rare early logo being one of the first boards produced in Hobie's garage, pre surf shop. A classic design representative of Velzy's Malibu chip fin, which Velzy based upon a shark's dorsal fin. Spencer and Annette Croul Collection. $3,000-5,000

Hobie Surfboards, Dana Point, California, Decal. Peter and Cathy Noble, Monterey, California. $60-90

Hobie, Dana Point, Calif., 11'1". Solid balsa, circa early 1950s. Re-glassed at Hobie factory. Allan Seymour, Pacific Coast Vintage Surf Auctions. As shown: $2,500-3,500

Hobie, Dana Point, Calif., 11'9". Balsa, circa 1954 or earlier. Serial No. 377. Illustration on nose by Warren Miller, 1958. Dick Metz, Dana Point, California. $3,000-5,000

Hobie, Dana Point, California, Decal. Peter and Cathy Noble, Monterey, California. $60-90

Hobie, Dana Point, California, 10'0". Balsa board, circa 1956. Made for Bob Williamson of Newport Beach, California. Spencer and Annette Croul Collection. $3,500-4,500

Vintage Advertisement. Mauna Kea Galleries, Kamuela, Hawaii.

Gremmie A late 1950s term for a preteen who inhabits surfing areas, idolizing surfers, is inexperienced himself but stoked about surfing. Also used to describe a young, rude beginner surfer.

Hobie Surfboards Patch. Peter and Cathy Noble, Monterey, California. $30-50

Hobie, Dana Point, Calif., 9'10". Solid balsa with scarfed nose, circa late 1950s. Allan Seymour, Pacific Coast Vintage Surf Auctions. $1,500-2,500

Hobie, Dana Point, California, 9'8". Single stringer, foam with balsa, foam fin, circa 1959. This type of board is known as an "Easter Board." Hobie Alter and Grubby Clark were pioneers in foam development. Some people give credit to Dave Sweet, but it was their contribution that was most commercially significant. Hobie and Grubby hid foam blanks on roofs all over Orange County, California, testing the UV and heat/cold reactions. Some of the formulas would swell to twice their original size, while others would disintegrate due to exposure to the elements. The foam didn't blow clean and wormholes (bubbles) developed. This would not be discovered until the blank was shaped, resulting in the usage of multi-stringer setups in completely pigmented boards in the 1960s. Boards were pigmented solid light blue, violet or yellow in order to hide the imperfections in the foam, hence the term "Easter Board." Early models, like this one, used an ink stamp logo, while later boards used a silver mylar sticker. Peter and Cathy Noble, Monterey, California. $1,200-1,800

Floaty A surfboard that is overly buoyant resulting in a board that floats high in the water.

Vintage Advertisement. Mauna Kea Galleries, Kamuela, Hawaii.

Vintage Advertisement. Mauna Kea Galleries, Kamuela, Hawaii.

Robert Shepherd, Honolulu, Hawaii, 8'10". Balsa, circa mid-1950s. Spencer and Annette Croul Collection. $3,000-5,000

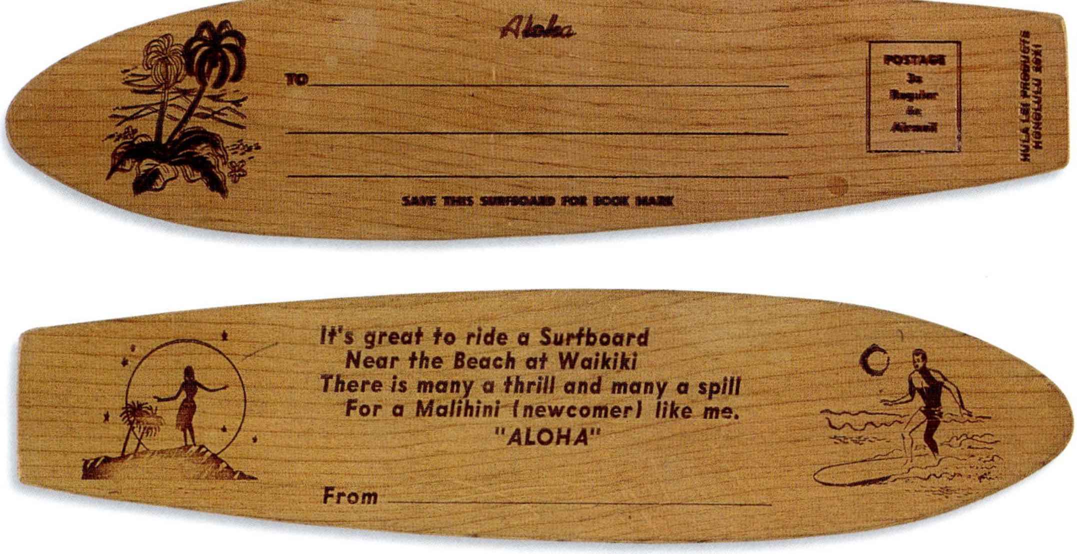

Surfboard-shaped Wood Postcard. An unusual and fun item made for the tourist market in Hawaii in the 1950s or earlier. Mauna Kea Galleries, Kamuela, Hawaii. $150-250

Balsa, 9'6". Joe Quigg shaped board, made for Buzzy Trent, mid-1950s. Hoffman Collection. $5,000-7,000

Slippery When Wet**.** A Bruce Brown film, circa 1958. Courtesy of Buck Labadie/ Artstuff. As shown: $400-600. Average: $250-350

Balsa and Redwood , 11'6". Six stringer, big wave gun, balsa with redwood, circa late 1950s/ early 1960s. Possibly shaped by Bob Shephard and Pat Curren. Hole in fin was used to secure board with a cable lock. Previous owner was Rob Lunquist, Santa Cruz lifeguard. Ed and Randi Economy Collection. $6,000-9,000

Bail Jumping or diving off the board.

Double Feature Program for *Slippery When Wet* and *Surf Crazy*. Bruce Brown films, circa late 1950s/early 1960s. Courtesy of Buck Labadie/Artstuff. As shown: $350-450. Average: $200-300

***Surf Crazy*.** A Bruce Brown film, circa 1959. Courtesy of Buck Labadie/Artstuff. As shown: $350-450. Average: $200-300

Surf Posters

This is the most under-priced area in the surf collectibles marketplace and offers tremendous growth potential. Surf posters, for the most part, were highly disposable – an inexpensive way of promoting a particular movie or event. Due to this, most posters were produced on shoestring budgets using very poor materials. These posters often were tacked up on telephone poles, sides of buildings, etc., with the result being that very few examples survive today. Prices listed below are for blemish-free copies, free from all punctures. Folded copies are acceptable in the case of some titles, as this is the way they were produced. Super clean, mint condition copies are worth more than the prices listed below. All posters with a Hawaiian venue carry a minimum of a 100% premium. Also, a word of warning: There has been a splurge of fake or reproduction posters being sold as genuine. Know your source!

Greg Noll Surfboards – One of the most legendary names in the industry, Greg Knoll shaped his first board at age 14 in the backyard of his parents' house in Manhattan Beach, California. An early apprentice to Dale Velzy, he started his first factory in Hermosa Beach, California, in the late 1950s. He is credited with being one of the first to produce and blow his own foam, which was quite an accomplishment considering the time period. Besides being a producer of surfboards, he was also an accomplished film producer. His real strength in the marketplace was his ability to capture the "big wave" market. Every year, he spent about six weeks in Hawaii promoting his boards as well as surfing where his big-wave-riding feats were of legendary proportions. Greg Noll had many dealers across the East Coast and Texas and, in the mid-1960s, licensed Charlie Galanto to produce boards in Hawaii. His boards were ridden by many legendary surfers, including Fred Van Dyke, Peter Cole, George Downing and Ricky Grigg.

Greg Noll Surf Boards and Film Productions, 8'5". An outstanding example of a balsa board with balsa and redwood fin, circa late 1950s. Spencer and Annette Croul Collection. $6,000-9,000

Decals

Decals are highly collectable and are extremely fragile, as is the case of the early water transfer examples. The prices listed are for decals in mint condition with no crazing, cracking or other imperfections.

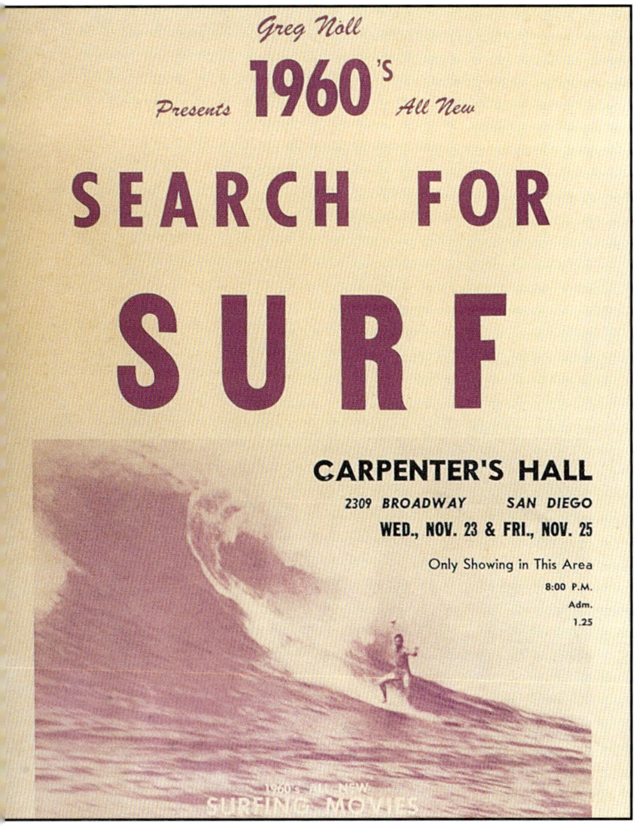

Search for Surf. Originally filmed in 1957, Greg Noll was constantly re-editing this masterpiece as shown by this edition of this poster. Mauna Kea Galleries, Kamuela, Hawaii. $200-300

Greg Noll Surf Boards Decal. Peter and Cathy Noble, Monterey, California. $100-150

Doggers A 1950s terms for multi-colored swimming trunks constructed of canvas or an equivalent tough fabric.

Greg Noll Surf Boards and Film Productions Decal. Courtesy of Buck Labadie/Artstuff. $150-250

Greg Noll Surfboards, Hermosa Beach Price List. Circa early 1960s. Mauna Kea Galleries, Kamuela, Hawaii. $300-500

Grading Surfboards

Foam surfboards are priced and collected on a 1 to 10 grading scale, with 10 being absolutely mint and out-of-the-box. It has been my experience that the majority of people involved in buying, selling, and collecting boards tend to over-grade them, sometimes to the point of absurdity. As someone who was involved (at a very early age) in another field where grading is all-important, I have come up with the following guidelines after considerable thought and numerous discussions with fellow enthusiasts. Remember, as with all collectable items, condition is the most important factor in considering price, with rarity and provenance also playing an integral part.

Grade 10 Absolutely mint and out-of-the-box. Foam should be absolutely as white as newly driven snow. No dings whatsoever.
Grade 9 Two minor dings or less plus one minor pressure ding allowed. All of the dings should not be serious enough to cause the fiberglass skin to fracture. Absolutely no areas of restoration or fading or yellowing from exposure to the sun.
Grade 8 Three minor dings or less plus two minor pressure dings allowed. All of the dings should not be serious enough to cause the fiberglass skin to fracture. Absolutely no areas of restoration or fading or yellowing from exposure to the sun.
Grade 7 Four minor dings or less plus three minor pressure dings allowed with two fracture dings of either type resulting in minor but not unsightly discoloration of the foam from contact with the water. No areas of restoration, but minor sun fading is allowed.
Grade 6 Five dings or less plus four pressure dings allowed with three dings of either type resulting in discoloration of foam from contact with the water. No areas of restoration, but sun fading is allowed.
Grade 5 Six dings or less plus five pressure dings allowed, with four dings of either type resulting in discoloration of foam from contact with the water. No areas of restoration, but sun fading is allowed.
Grade 4 Seven dings or less plus six pressure dings allowed, with five dings of either type resulting in discoloration of foam from contact with the water. Moderate to heavy sun fading. Moderate eye-appeal.
Grade 3 Eight dings or less plus seven pressure dings allowed, with six dings of either type resultling in discoloration of foam from contact with the water. Heavy sun fading. Moderate eye-appeal.
Grade 2 Nine dings or less plus eight pressure dings allowed with seven dings of either type resulting in discoloration of foam from contact with the water. Heavy sun fading. No eye-appeal.
Grade 1 Trashed. Includes boards that were broken and restored.

All prices for boards listed in this book are for Grade 7, unless otherwise noted in the caption.

"**Re-dos**" - There has been considerable talk by fellow collectors about reconditioned boards. I feel they are fine as long as they are described as such. Most of these boards have had their dings and other surface blemishes filled and re-glassed, with the surfaces repainted, resulting in the hiding of all visible defects, including sun fading, etc. I would consider them Grade 6, if fully restored and at first glance appearing in mint condition.

Grades 5 and below have no place in the collectors' market. Instead, they should be sold as wall hangers, props, etc., and should only be bought by a true collector as a board to restore or, in the case of a really rare and unusual item, as an example to fill a gap in the collection.

Ding refers to any damaged place on a surfboard such as a dent, hole, or deep scratch. All dings on a surfboard that is actively being used for surfing should be repaired immediately so that water does not enter the foam and discolor it or add excess weight to the board. Duct tape is often used as a quick fix until the area can be properly repaired.

Walker Foam Decal. Peter and Cathy Noble, Monterey, California. $60-90

Stringer The wooden runner or runners (1/16 to 1/4 inch thick) that most well-made surfboards have inside of them for the purpose of strengthening the foam and fiberglass. All wooden runners are included in our stringer counts. The stringer also sets the rocker, meaning that it determines how much curvature or nose scoop the board will have.

Harold Walker Blanks, San Clemente, California. Circa early 1960s. A two-sided advertising sheet. Mauna Kea Galleries, Kamuela, Hawaii. $100-150

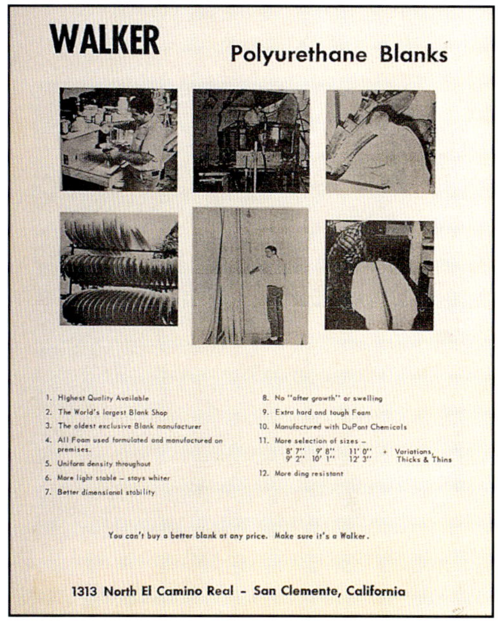

WALKER Polyurethane Blanks

1. Highest Quality Available
2. The World's largest Blank Shop
3. The oldest exclusive Blank manufacturer
4. All Foam used formulated and manufactured on premises.
5. Uniform density throughout
6. More light stable – stays whiter
7. Better dimensional stability
8. No "after growth" or swelling
9. Extra hard and tough Foam
10. Manufactured with DuPont Chemicals
11. More selection of sizes – 8' 7" 9' 8" 11' 0" 9' 2" 10' 1" 12' 3" + Variations, Thicks & Thins
12. More ding resistant

You can't buy a better blank at any price. Make sure it's a Walker.

1313 North El Camino Real - San Clemente, California

Greg Noll Surfboards, 11' 3". Three-stringer, big wave elephant gun, foam with redwood, circa early 1960s. A beautiful and historic board that Joyce Hoffman rode in a Makaha contest. Hoffman Collection. As shown: $8,000-12,000. Average: $4,000-6,000.

Longboard Surfboards usually nine to twelve feet long.

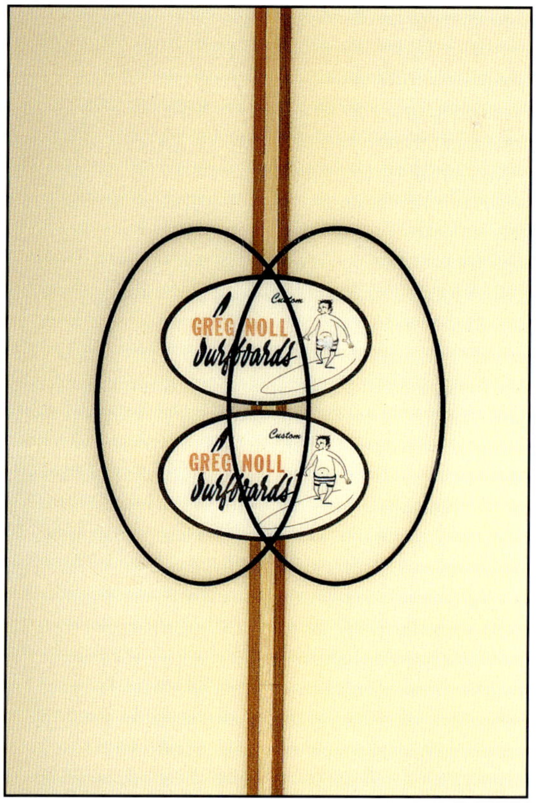

Greg Noll Custom Surfboards, 9'8". Three stringer, foam with redwood and balsa, Atomic logo, circa early 1960s. Allan Seymour, Pacific Coast Vintage Surf Auctions. $1,500-2,500

North Swell. A Grant Rohloff film, circa 1963. Mauna Kea Galleries, Kamuela, Hawaii. $200-300

Swell Unbroken waves often originating from storms far out at sea.

Greg Noll, 10'7". Wide single stringer, big wave gun, foam with balsa and redwood, circa 1963. Unusual Murphy big gun logo. This board was designed bigger and wider for the big surf at Makaha. An interesting combination of Royal Hawaiian colors of yellow and red used in design element. Ed and Randi Economy Collection. $5,000-7,000

Stop the Wave, I Want to Get Off. A Jim Wilhoite film, circa 1965. A film combining surfing, skim boards and skateboarding in Hawaii and California. Mauna Kea Galleries, Kamuela, Hawaii. $150-250

Vintage Advertisement. Mauna Kea Galleries, Kamuela, Hawaii.

Da Cat – Originally sold and produced by Greg Noll Surfboards in the mid-1960s for around $175. This Mickey Dora signature model was shorter and thicker than most of the boards of this era and had a scooped-out area on the nose – supposedly giving more edge control when on the lip. This model also was available in a pintail version with a removable fin.

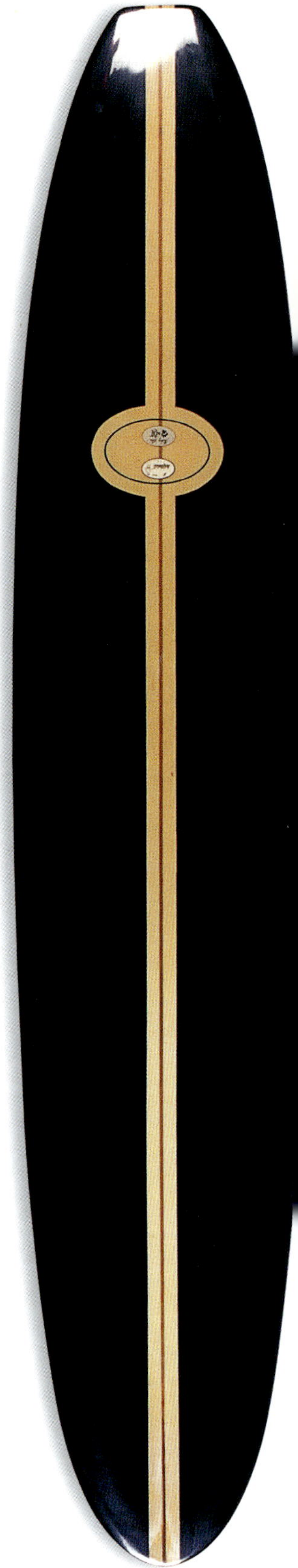

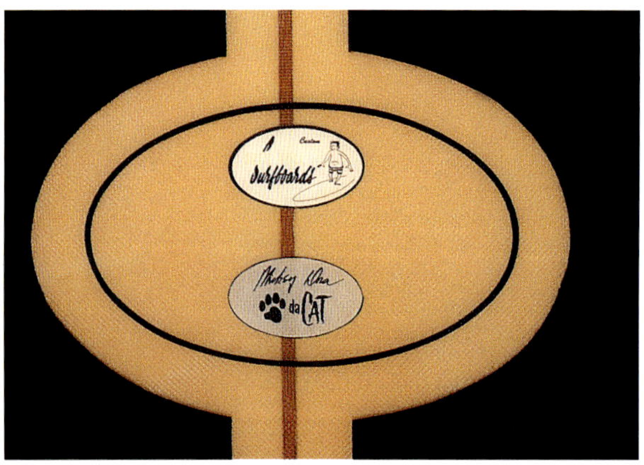

Greg Noll Surfboards – Mickey Dora "da Cat," 9'7". Single stringer, foam with redwood, circa 1966. Collectors should be wary of the very well-produced fakes that have shown up in the marketplace. Hoffman Collection. $3,000-5,000

Don Brown Presents the 3rd Annual Surf-O-Rama. Mauna Kea Galleries, Kamuela, Hawaii. $150-250

Greg Noll, 10'10". Single stringer, big wave gun, foam with redwood, circa 1967. Classic Royal color of Hawaii, reportedly influenced by Peter Cole. Ed and Randi Economy Collection. $4,000-6,000

Greg Noll Surf Boards and Film Productions Business Card. Peter and Cathy Noble, Monterey, California. $100-150

Greg Noll Surfboards, Fains Formula II, 7'6". Foam, circa late 1960s. Great psychedelic logo. Allan Seymour, Pacific Coast Vintage Surf Auctions. $500-700

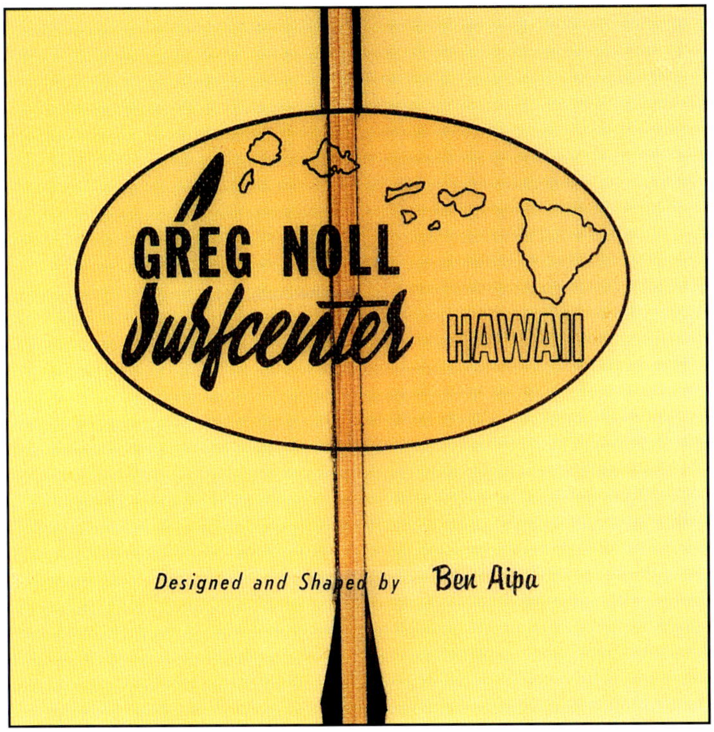

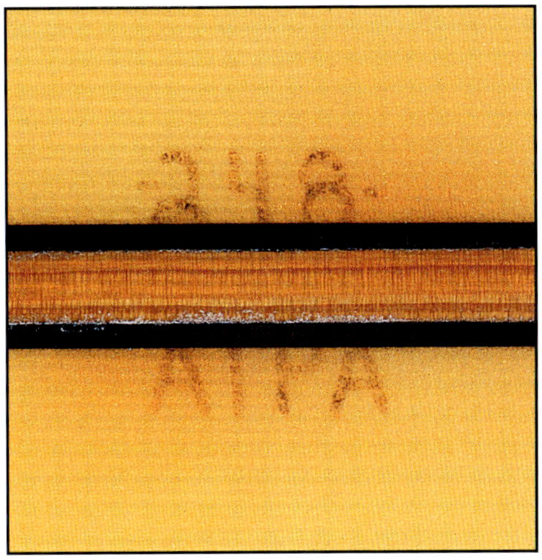

Greg Noll, 10'0". Single stringer, big wave gun, foam with redwood, with an unusual long and narrow based fin, circa 1969. A Ben Aipa shaped and designed transitional board for Greg Noll's Surfcenter Hawaii shop. Max Lim's personal North Shore big wave gun. Ed and Randi Economy Collection. $6,000-9,000

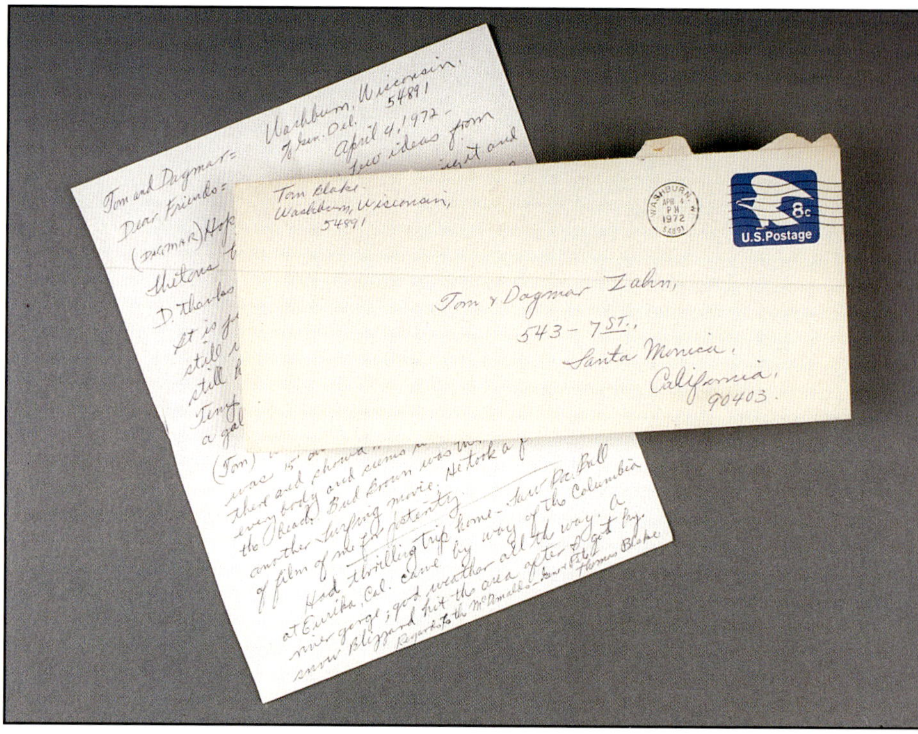

Tom Blake Letter. Sent in 1972 to the Zahn brothers. An interesting letter with great surf history content.
Washburn, Wisconsin
c/o Gen. Del. 54891
April 4, 1972
Tom and Dagmar =
Dear Friends=
(Dagmar) Hope you got a few ideas fom Shetons book. thanks for returning it and D. thanks for the beautiful winter scene. It is just like up here. The fields are still white with clean snow, the lake still has 3 feet of ice; snowmobiles abound. Temp last nite –20 today about 30° and a gale wind, which blows the snow along.
(Tom) Went by Santa Cruze on way here – Surf was 15' and a contest on. Sam Ried was there and showed me around. He knows everybody and seems to be important around the beach. Bud Brown was there, shooting another Surfing movie. He took a few frames of film of me for posterity.
Had thrilling trip home – Saw Doc Ball at Eurika, Cal. came by way of the Columbia River Gorge; good weather all the way. A snow blizzard hit the area after I got by.
Regards to the McDonalds – Gene & Pete –
Thomas Blake
Mauna Kea Galleries, Kamuela, Hawaii. $400-600

Joe Quigg Surfboards, 9'8". Wide t-bar stringer, foam with balsa, circa 1961. This was Tommy Zahn's personal board that he used to surf Makaha. Tommy's largest wave ridden with this board was 20 feet. Peter and Cathy Noble, Monterey, California. As shown: $4,000-6,000. Average: $1,500-2,500

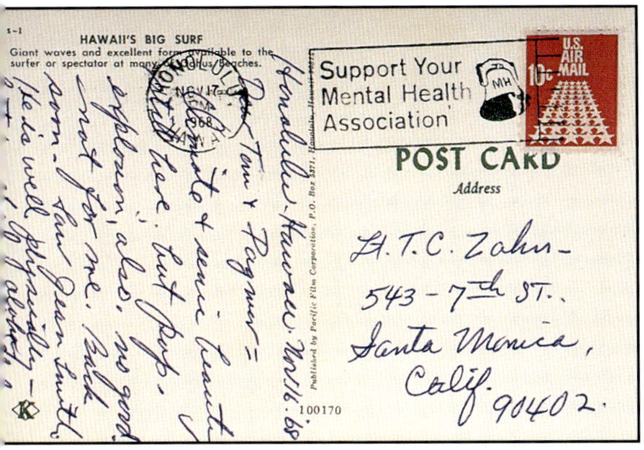

Postcard - *Hawaii's Big Surf*. An interesting piece of surf history as the card was sent by Tom Blake to Tommy Zahn in 1968. Mauna Kea Galleries, Kamuela, Hawaii. $300-500

***Have Board Will Travel*.** A Don Brown film, circa 1963. To the author, this is the most desirable and unique surf poster of the 1960s. It was issued in two sizes. All known copies of the large posters were folded once. Mauna Kea Galleries, Kamuela, Hawaii. Small: $400-600. Large: $600-900

Stoked An excited and thrilled feeling about surfing and life in general.

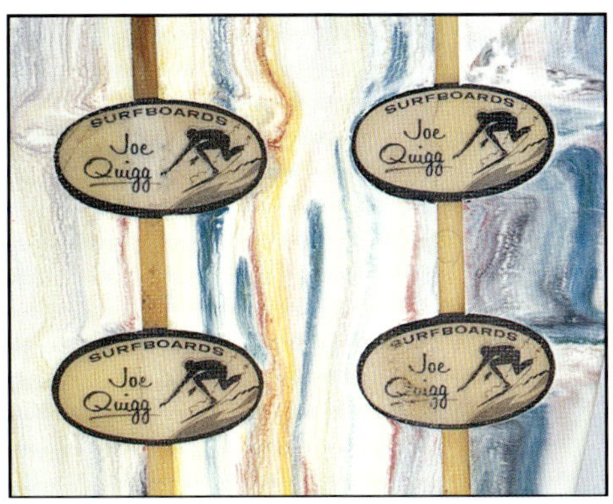

Joe Quigg Surfboards, 8'1". Two stringer, foam with balsa, circa mid-1960s. Don Browner, shaper. Hoffman Collection. $1,000-1,500

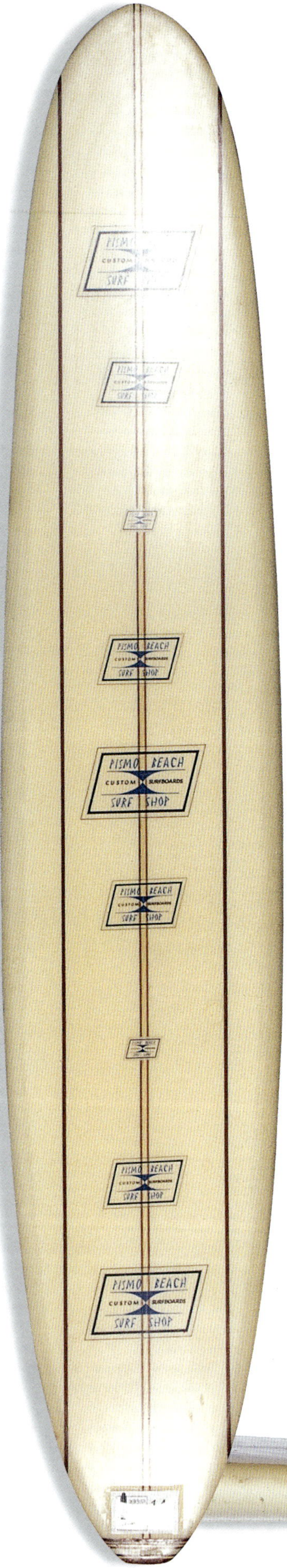

Los Angeles Surf Fair. A rare poster from 1963 featuring the original members of the Beach Boys holding a board. Mauna Kea Galleries, Kamuela, Hawaii. $400-600

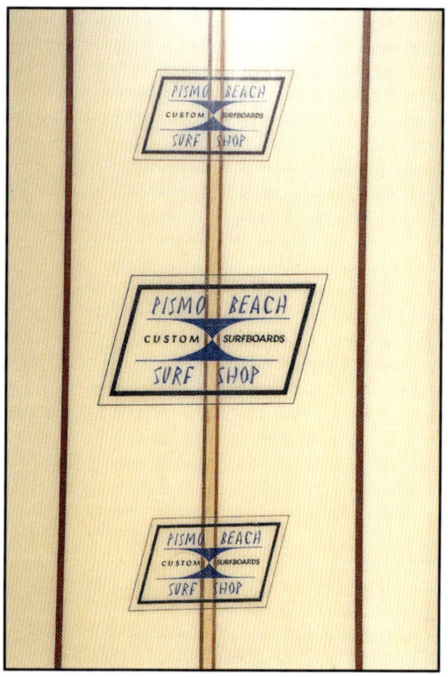

Pismo Beach Surf Shop, 9'5". Purchased in 1965 by the original owner to surf in Hawaii, which never happened. Five stringer, foam with redwood and balsa. Unusual multiple logo motif. Peter and Cathy Noble, Monterey, California. $800-1,200

Beach Party. Circa 1964. Mauna Kea Galleries, Kamuela, Hawaii. $300-500

Surf Party. Starring Bobby Vinton. Circa 1964. Mauna Kea Galleries, Kamuela, Hawaii. $250-350

Muscle Beach Party. Circa 1964. Mauna Kea Galleries, Kamuela, Hawaii. $300-500

Leedy of Costa Mesa, California, 9'8". Seven stringer, foam with redwood and balsa. This was the Cadillac of the Leedy surfboards and was produced in 1965 at a cost of $300. This particular board was used in the 1965 Leedy ad campaign in *Surfer Magazine*. Peter and Cathy Noble, Monterey, California. $1,200-1,800

Goofy Foot Riding a surfboard with the right foot forward and the left back – the opposite of a "natural" footed surfer.

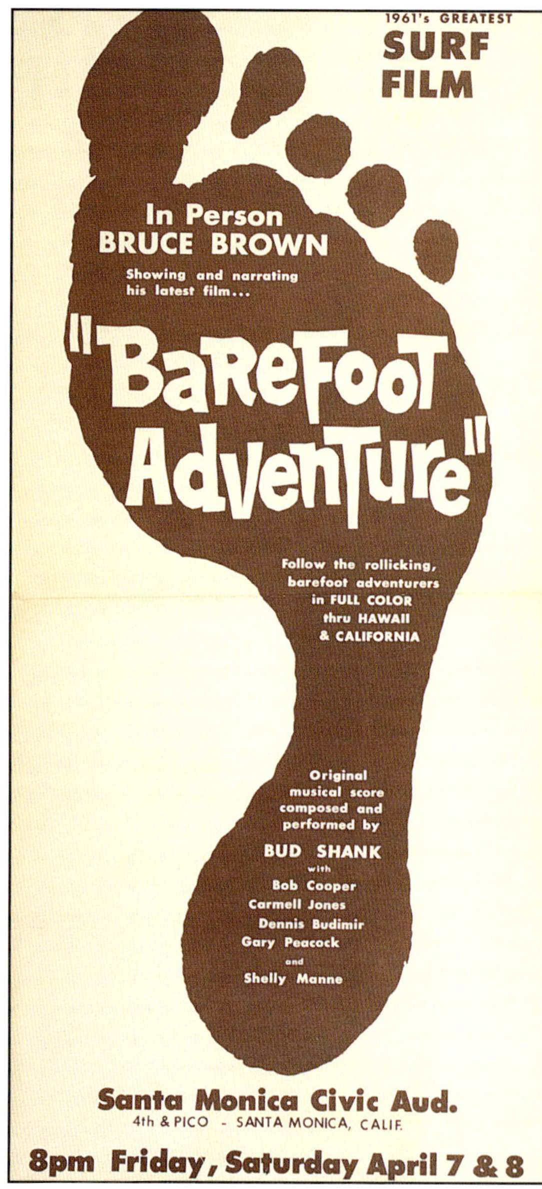

Barefoot Adventure. A Bruce Brown film, circa 1961. Courtesy of Buck Labadie/Artstuff. $150-250

Barefoot Adventure. A Bruce Brown film, circa 1961. Great graphics. Mauna Kea Galleries, Kamuela, Hawaii. As shown $300-500. Average $200-300

Barefoot Adventure. A Bruce Brown film, circa 1961. Courtesy of Buck Labadie/ Artstuff. $250-350

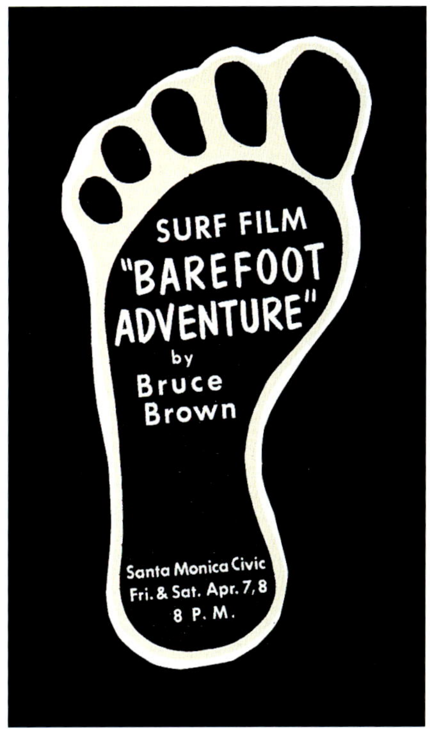

Surf Film *Barefoot Adventure* by Bruce Brown Decal. Santa Monica Civic, Fri. & Sat., Apr. 7, 8, 8 P.M. Peter and Cathy Noble, Monterey, California. $120-180

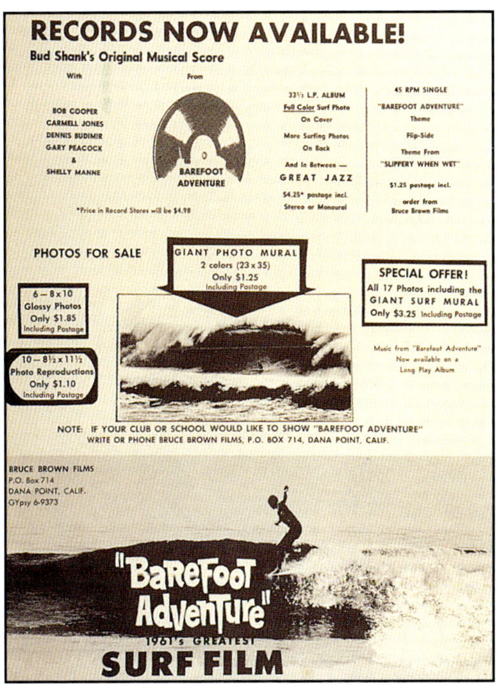

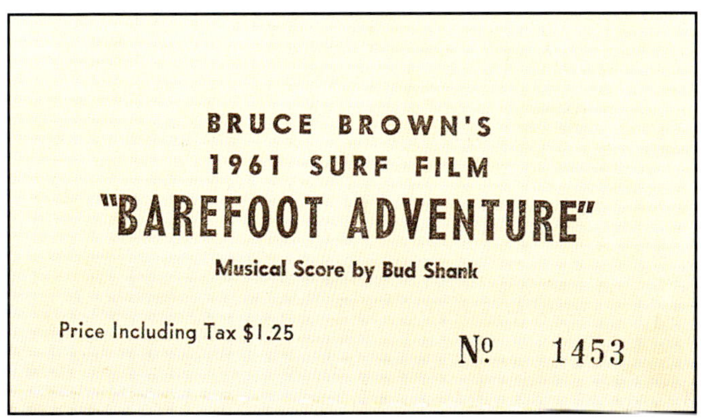

***Barefoot Adventure* Admission Ticket Stub.** A Bruce Brown film, circa 1961. Courtesy of Buck Labadie/Artstuff. $30-50

Foam Usually used to describe the hard plastic, cellular structure that is shaped into a surfboard. A chemically produced substance composed of polyurethane, it was developed and used for the first time in surfboard production by Dave Sweet of Santa Monica in 1956. Although it had been used previously by the likes of Bob Simmons and Lorrin Harrison, it was Sweet who really brought it to its rightful forefront. It was Hobie Alter, though, who came out with the first commercially successful board design in 1958, followed by Gordon "Grubby" Clark, who formed Clark Foam in 1961, perfecting the process. Today Clark Foam is the largest manufacturer of foam blanks in the world.

Custom by Leedy Productions, Costa Mesa, 9'8". Wide single stringer, foam with balsa, circa mid-1960s. Allan Seymour, Pacific Coast Vintage Surf Auctions. $600-900

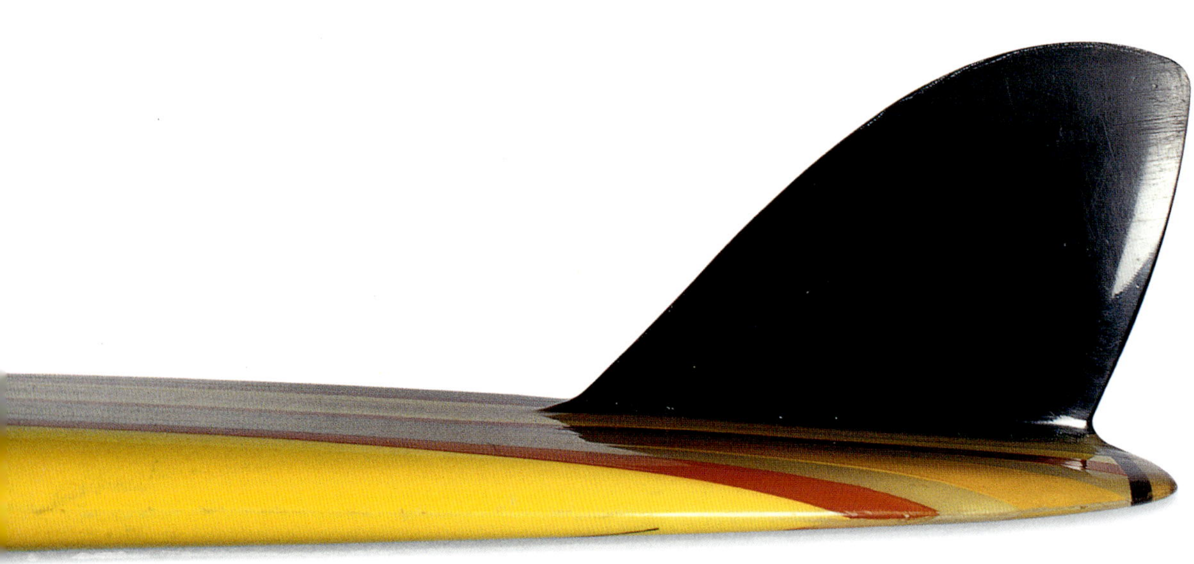

Hobie Surfboards, Dana Point, California Decal. Peter and Cathy Noble, Monterey, California. $40-60

Surf Classics**.** A John Severson film, circa 1964. Mauna Kea Galleries, Kamuela, Hawaii. $150-250

Hobie – Joyce Hoffman Model, 9'1". Single stringer, foam with redwood, circa 1962-63. Hoffman Collection. $1,000-1,500

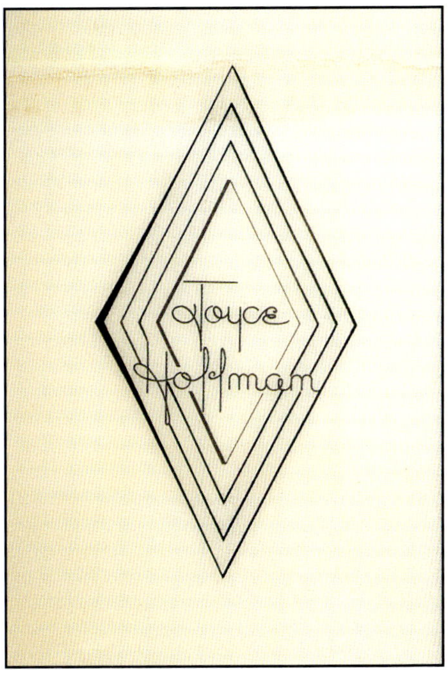

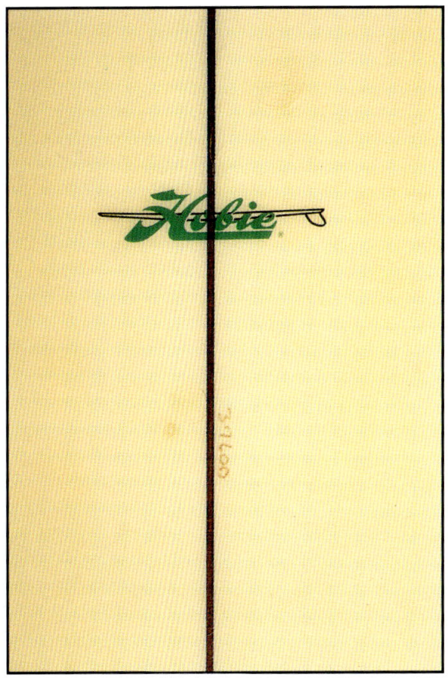

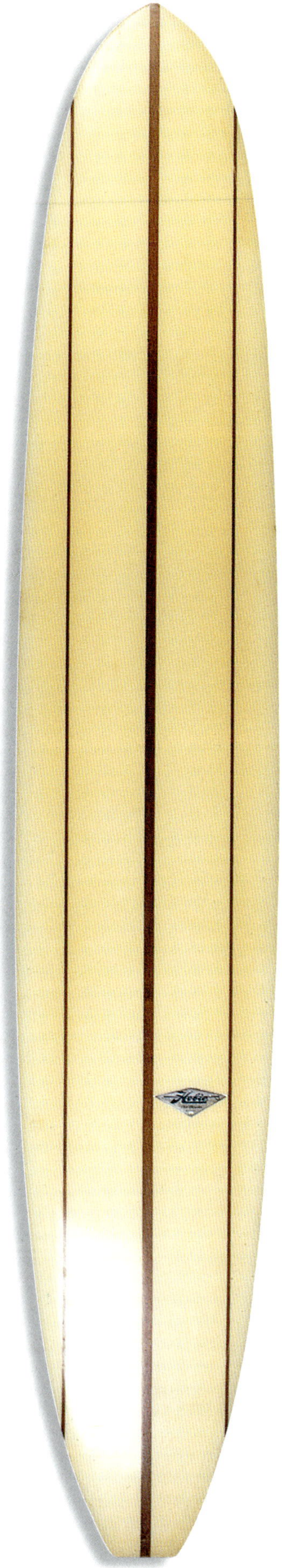

Hobie – Phil Edwards Model Decal. Peter and Cathy Noble, Monterey, California. $100-150

Clark Foam Decal. Peter and Cathy Noble, Monterey, California. $30-50

Hobie, Phil Edwards Model, 10'2". Classic three stringer, foam with redwood, circa 1964. This was the first signature model ever produced. An interesting note on this board is the foil license from Newport Beach, California, dated 1968, when local municipalities often required surfboard licenses at the peak of the surf craze in the 1960s. The fee was $3-5 depending on the location. Spencer and Annette Croul Collection. As shown: $3,000-5,000. Average: $1,200-1,800

Hobie Surfboards, Dana Point, Calif., 9'9". Three stringer, foam with redwood Multi Board, circa 1964. This board was built for the movie *Endless Summer* and was designed to travel around the world. It became known as the Suitcase Board. This board was never ridden and has a beautiful laminated wood and fiberglass fin. Dick Metz, Dana Point, California. $5,000-$7,000

The Endless Summer

This timeless Bruce Brown-produced masterpiece of 1964 brought movie-goers the surfing adventures of Robert August and Mike Hynson, who traveled worldwide in search of the perfect wave. This was the first surf film to reach a national audience and is probably the most sought-after classic surf memorabilia from the 1960s.

Vintage Advertisement. Mauna Kea Galleries, Kamuela, Hawaii.

Robert August today in the white shirt

***True* Magazine, August 1967.** With the famous article *How Bruce Brown's Endless Summer of Surfing made him $1,000,000*. Courtesy of Buck Labadie/Artstuff. $40-60

***The Endless Summer* Poster.** A Bruce Brown film, circa 1964. Mauna Kea Galleries, Kamuela, Hawaii. $400-600

***The Endless Summer* Movie Program.** A Bruce Brown film, circa 1964. Multi-paged with great advertisements and stories about the two surfers featured in the film. Mauna Kea Galleries, Kamuela, Hawaii. As shown $400-600

***The Endless Summer* Broadsheets.** A Bruce Brown film, circa 1964. Mauna Kea Galleries, Kamuela, Hawaii. $500-700

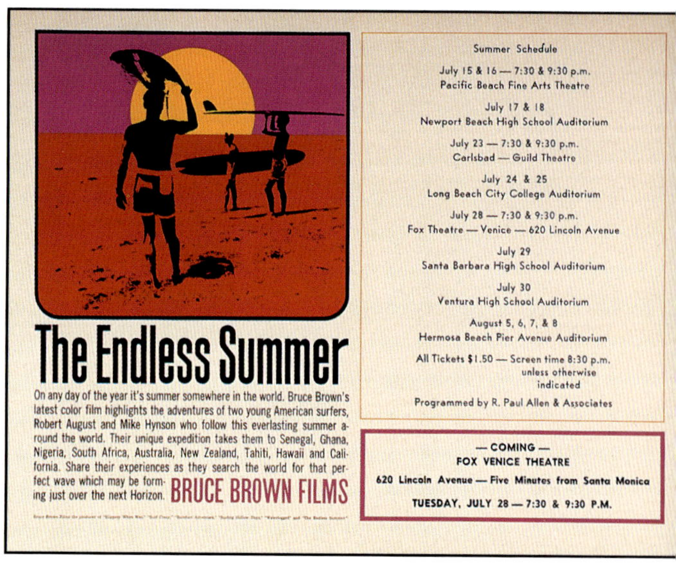

Hobie, Dana Point, California, 10'0". Balsa with redwood stringer with original protective bumblebee stripes on the nose. Circa 1964. Peter and Cathy Noble, Monterey, California. $2,000-3,000

Hobie

SURFBOARD PRICES

Up to 8' 3"	$ 85.00	9' 9" to 10'	100.00
8' 3" to 9'	90.00	Up to 10' 6"	$100.00
9' to 9' 9"	95.00	10' 6" to 11'	105.00

12' Tandem 120.00

Splash Bottom — Deck Patches — Glass Fins — each $5.00 Extra

34195 Coast Highway Dana Point, California GYpsy 6-5222

Hobie Surfboards, Dana Point, California. Price list card. Courtesy of Buck Labadie/Artstuff. $100-150

Head Dip A maneuver used while riding the wave in which the surfer bends the head to touch the wave or white water.

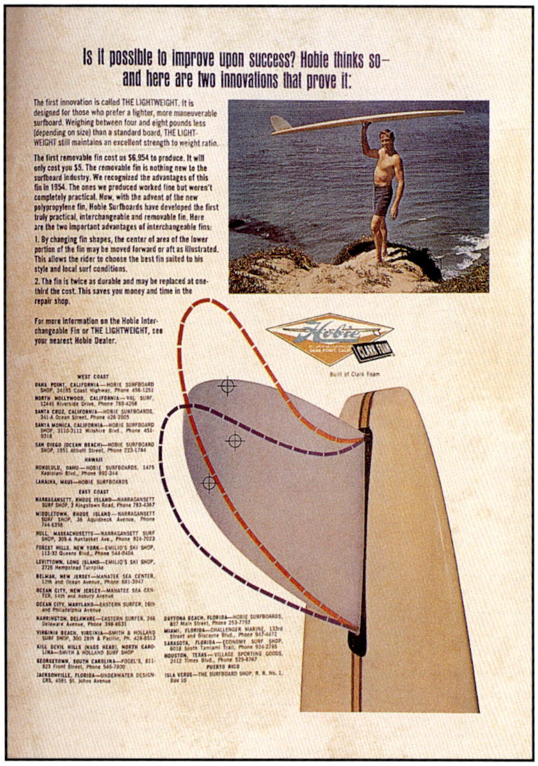

Vintage Advertisement. Mauna Kea Galleries, Kamuela, Hawaii.

Hobie Surfboards, Dana Point, California, Decal. Peter and Cathy Noble, Monterey, California. $40-60

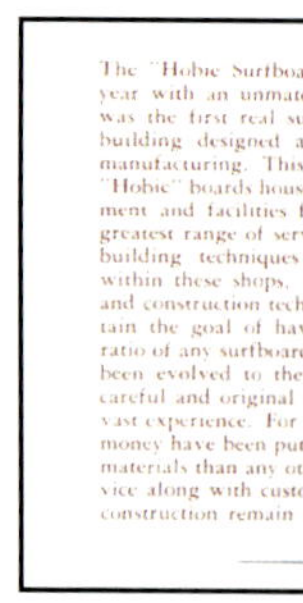

Gary Propper Model by Hobie, Patch. Peter and Cathy Noble, Monterey, California. $40-60

Promotional Flyer for the Hobie Gary Propper Model Surfboard. Circa mid-1960s. Mauna Kea Galleries, Kamuela, Hawaii. $100-150

Hobie Surfboards, Fold-out Business Card. Circa early 1960s. Peter and Cathy Noble, Monterey, California. $150-250

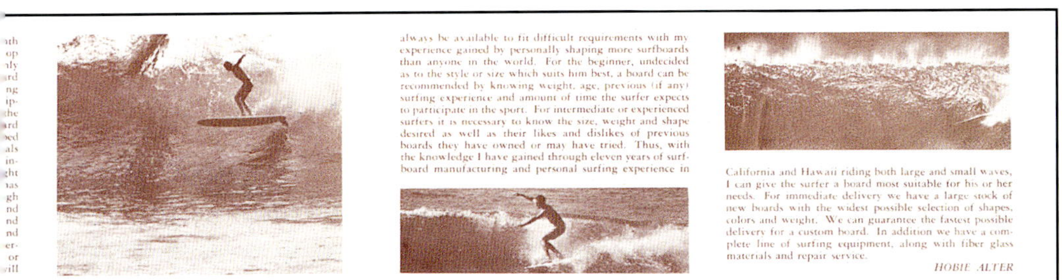

Promotional Flyer for the Hobie Gary Propper Model Surfboard. Circa mid-1960s. Mauna Kea Galleries, Kamuela, Hawaii. $100-150

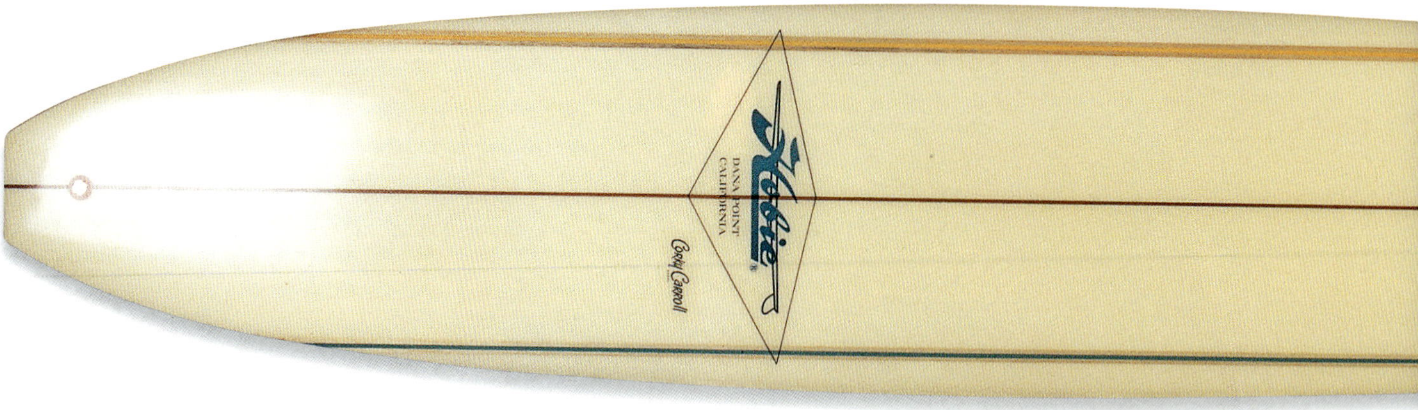

Hobie, Dana Point, California, Corky Carroll Model, 9'6". Three stringer, foam with redwood and balsa, circa 1967. Spencer and Annette Croul Collection. As shown: $2,000-3,000. Average: $600-900

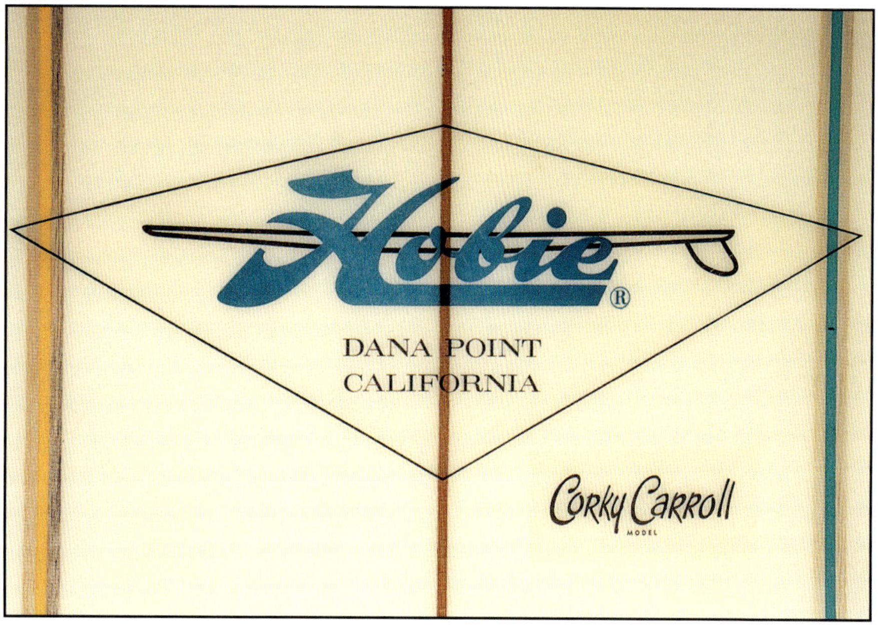

Surfer **Corky Carroll** today.

Outside the Third Dimension. A Jim Freeman film, circa 1964. The first attempt at a surf film in 3D. Courtesy of Buck Labadie/ Artstuff. $400-600

Yabba-dabba-doo A surfer's happy cry based on the 1960s cartoon character Fred Flintstone.

Outside the Third Dimension. A Jim Freeman film, circa 1964. The first attempt at a surf film in 3-D. Mauna Kea Galleries, Kamuela, Hawaii. $200-300

Outside the Third Dimension. Complete ticket stub. Mauna Kea Galleries, Kamuela, Hawaii. $60-90

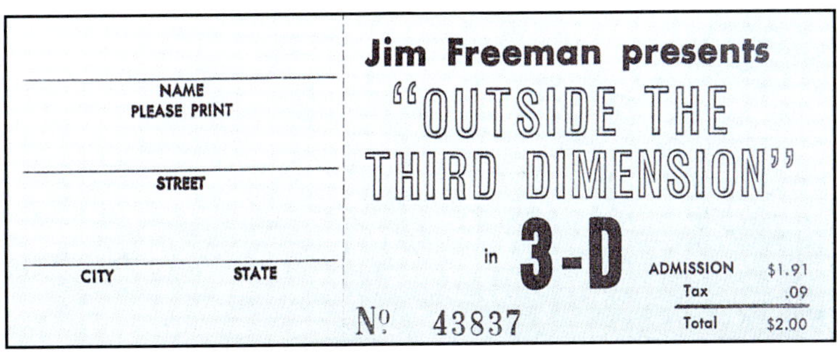

Hobie Surfboards Patch. Peter and Cathy Noble, Monterey, California. $30-40

Shooting the Pier The act of riding a wave between the pilings of a pier or wharf.

Vintage Advertisement. Mauna Kea Galleries, Kamuela, Hawaii.

Pier Shot – A&W Root Beer Company, Santa Monica, California. Restaurant premium. Peter and Cathy Noble, Monterey, California. $30-50

Popout An inexpensive mass-produced surfboard made in the early 1960s by molding foam and fiberglass matting together. Being heavy and weak, and involving very little hand work, these boards were abandoned fairly quickly. They proved to be a marketing and financial disaster.

Tiki Surf Board, 9'1". Single stringer, foam with redwood. A pop-out model made by Ventura Plastics in 1965 and sold for $69.95 by Sears and Roebuck. The original mold was possibly made by Tom Morey. Mint, never-used condition. Peter and Cathy Noble, Monterey, California. As shown: $800-1,200. Average: $400-600

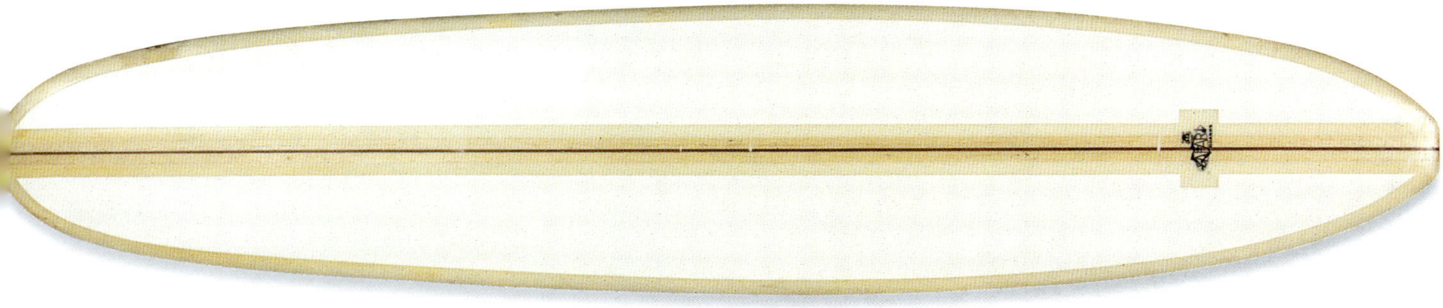

Safari Boards, Los Angeles, 9'4". Wedge t-bar stringer, foam with balsa and redwood, circa 1964. Produced by a small Santa Monica-based operation with an unusual logo and starburst fin design. Peter and Cathy Noble, Monterey, California. $800-1,200

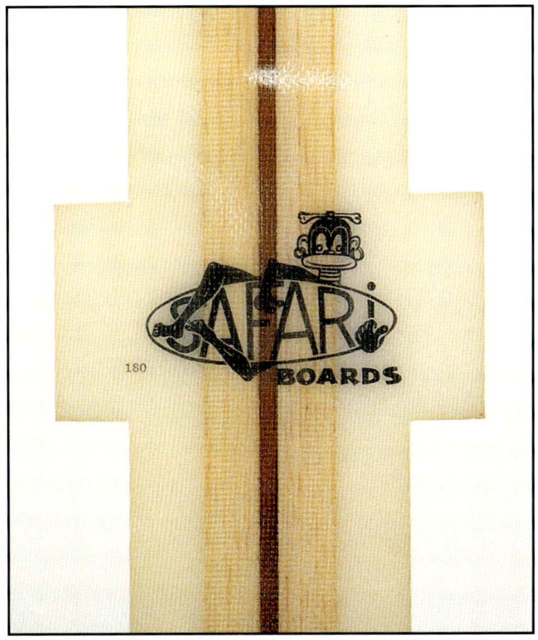

***Hot Surf Spots U.S.A.* Advertising Brochure.** By Capitol Records, circa mid-1960s. Mauna Kea Galleries, Kamuela, Hawaii. $100-150

Gordie Surfboards – Founded in the mid-1950s by Gordon Duane, he first started shaping balsa boards in 1955 in his parents' garage. In 1956, he opened his first shop under the Huntington Pier and operated there until his shop burned down in 1959. He then set up shop on Pacific Coast Highway in Huntington Beach. In 1957, he helped Harold Walker develop blanks later using Walker Foam exclusively in all his boards. His most famous model was his Hot Shape, which was an extremely well balanced board. One of his most unusual designs was the Assassin, which contains a small fin in the nose. An accomplished woodworker, he is well known for using very complicated stingers, tail blocks and wood fins in many of his designs. In 1962, his Gordie Surf Team won numerous contests; two of his more famous team riders were John Mayson and Danny Lenahan.

The Only Way to Travel - Gordie, Huntington Beach, California, Decal. Peter and Cathy Noble, Monterey, California. $80-120

Finest Quality
Custom Surfboards
FOR
27 YEARS
NEW AND USED BOARDS IN STOCK
Gordon Duane - Owner
13TH ST. AND PACIFIC COAST HWY
HUNTINGTON BEACH, CALIF.
536-6050

Gordie Surfboards, Huntington Beach, California, Business Card. Peter and Cathy Noble, Monterey, California. $50-70

Gordie Surf Boards, Huntington Beach, California, Decal. "The only way to travel." Peter and Cathy Noble, Monterey, California. $25-35

Gordie Surf Boards, Huntington Beach, Calif., 9'6". T-bar stringer, foam with balsa, circa mid-1960s. Hoffman Collection. $600-900

Gordie Surf Boards, Huntington Beach, California, Patch. "The only way to travel." Peter and Cathy Noble, Monterey, California. $25-35

Gordie Surf Boards, Huntington Beach, California, 9'6". Single stringer, foam with redwood, circa 1965. A boldly decorated board with classic hatchet fin. Peter and Cathy Noble, Monterey, California. $1,200-1,800

SURFER
BI-MONTHLY

THE MAGAZINE OF THE SURFER – FOR THE SURFER – AND BY THE SURFER. THE MOST COMPREHENSIVE UP-TO-DATE SURFING MAGAZINE IN THE WORLD. PUBLISHED AND EDITED BY WORLD-FAMOUS SURFER AND PHOTOGRAPHER, JOHN SEVERSON ■ AVAILABLE ON YOUR NEWSSTAND OR THROUGH SUBSCRIPTION (SAVE 50c OVER NEWSSTAND PRICE). $4.00 BRINGS SIX BIG ISSUES TO YOUR DOOR. WHY NOT SEND FOR ONE STARTING WITH THE NEXT ALL-TIME EDITION? BOX 1028B DANA POINT, CALIF.

Vintage Advertisement. Mauna Kea Galleries, Kamuela, Hawaii.

Gordie Surf Boards, Huntington Beach, California, Price List. Circa early 1960s. Mauna Kea Galleries, Kamuela, Hawaii. $100-150

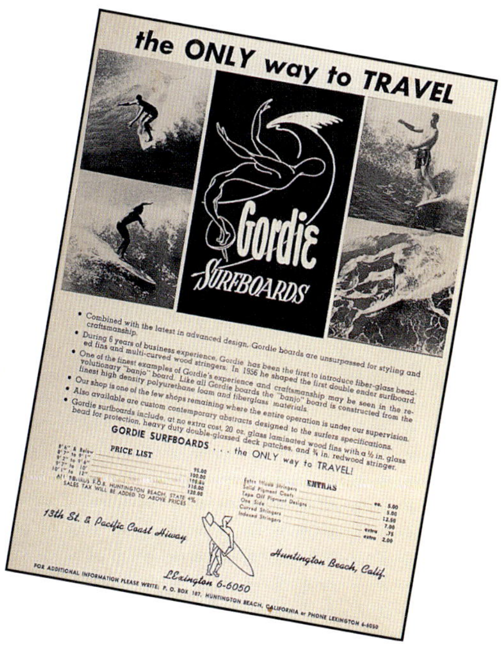

the ONLY way to TRAVEL

Gordie
SURFBOARDS

- Combined with the latest in advanced design, Gordie boards are unsurpassed for styling and craftsmanship.
- During 6 years of business experience, Gordie has been the first to introduce fiber-glass beaded fins and multi-curved wood stringers. In 1956 he shaped the first double ender surfboard.
- One of the finest examples of Gordie's experience and craftsmanship may be seen in the revolutionary "banjo" board. Like all Gordie boards the "banjo" board is constructed from the finest high density polyurethane foam and fiberglass materials.
- Our shop is one of the few shops remaining where the entire operation is under our supervision.
- Also available are custom contemporary abstracts designed to the surfers specifications.
- Gordie surfboards include, at no extra cost, 20 oz. glass laminated wood fins with a ½ in. glass bead for protection, heavy duty double-glassed deck patches, and ¾ in. redwood stringer.

GORDIE SURFBOARDS . . . the ONLY way to TRAVEL!

PRICE LIST

SALES TAX WILL BE ADDED TO ABOVE PRICES

EXTRAS

Solid Pigment Coats
Tape Off Pigment Designs
One Side
Curved Stringers
Indexed Stringers

13th St. & Pacific Coast Hiway

Huntington Beach, Calif.

LExington 6-6050

FOR ADDITIONAL INFORMATION PLEASE WRITE: P. O. BOX 187, HUNTINGTON BEACH, CALIFORNIA or PHONE LEXINGTON 6-6050

Gordie Surf Boards, Huntington Beach, California, Price List. Circa early 1960s. Mauna Kea Galleries, Kamuela, Hawaii. $100-150

Bing Surfboards – Founded in 1959 by Bing Copeland and Rick Stoner, their main shop was located in Hermosa Beach, California. Bing's masterpiece model was the David Nuuhiwa Noserider. Another popular model was made for big wave riding and was named the Bing Pipeliner. Rick Stoner later went his own way and started a company called Rick Surfboards. At its peak, the company had a wide network of dealers primarily located on the East Coast. Between the years 1964 and 1968, they produced over 3,000 boards a year.

Bing Surfboards Decal. Peter and Cathy Noble, Monterey, California. $80-120

Bing Boards. Folding price list business card. Rare. Peter and Cathy Noble, Monterey, California. $100-150

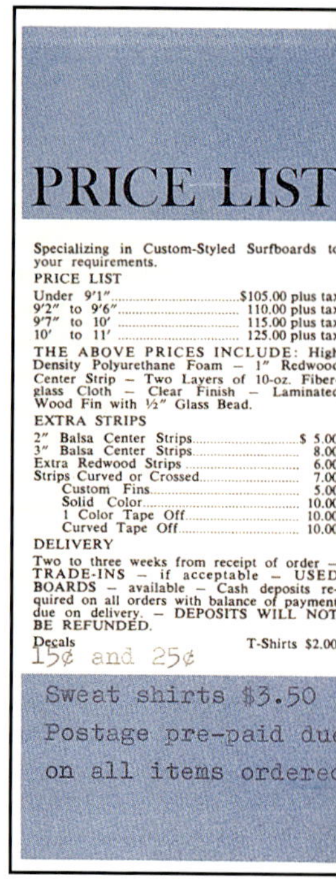
PRICE LIST

Specializing in Custom-Styled Surfboards to your requirements.

PRICE LIST

Under 9'1"	$105.00 plus tax
9'2" to 9'6"	110.00 plus tax
9'7" to 10'	115.00 plus tax
10' to 11'	125.00 plus tax

THE ABOVE PRICES INCLUDE: High Density Polyurethane Foam – 1" Redwood Center Strip – Two Layers of 10-oz. Fiberglass Cloth – Clear Finish – Laminated Wood Fin with ½" Glass Bead.

EXTRA STRIPS

2" Balsa Center Strips	$ 5.00
3" Balsa Center Strips	8.00
Extra Redwood Strips	6.00
Strips Curved or Crossed	7.00
Custom Fins	5.00
Solid Color	10.00
1 Color Tape Off	10.00
Curved Tape Off	10.00

DELIVERY

Two to three weeks from receipt of order – TRADE-INS – if acceptable – USED BOARDS – available – Cash deposits required on all orders with balance of payment due on delivery. – DEPOSITS WILL NOT BE REFUNDED.

Decals 15¢ and 25¢ T-Shirts $2.00

Sweat shirts $3.50
Postage pre-paid due
on all items ordered

Bing Surfboards, 10'0". Wide t-bar stringer, foam with balsa, circa early 1960s. Hoffman Collection. $600-900

David Nuuhiwa Noserider – In 1966, Bing Surfboards produced the first David Nuuhiwa model and a year later came out with the "light weight" model. This particular model is undoubtedly the winningest noserider ever produced and is still widely used in vintage surfboard competitions.

Bing Surfboards Decal. David Nuuhiwa noseriding model. Peter and Cathy Noble, Monterey, California. $150-250

Vintage Advertisement. Mauna Kea Galleries, Kamuela, Hawaii.

Hang Ten To ride so far forward on the nose of the board that the toes of both feet are hanging over the front end.

Bing Surfboards, David Nuuhiwa Light Weight Model, 10'0". Three stringer, foam with balsa and redwood, circa mid-1960s. Allan Seymour, Pacific Coast Vintage Surf Auctions. $1,200-1,800

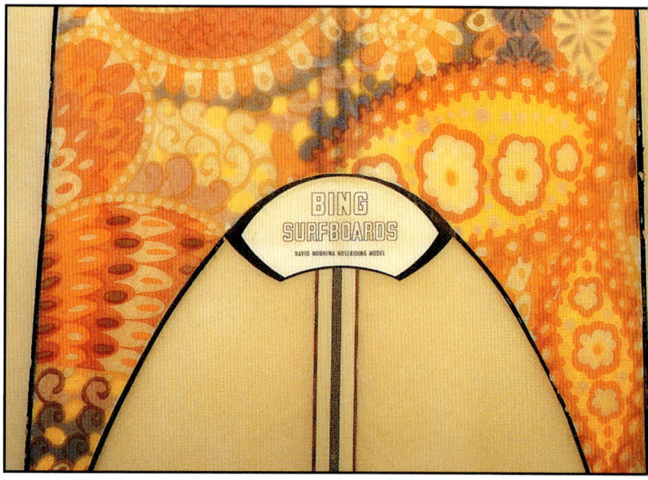

Bing Surfboards – David Nuuhiwa Noseriding Model, 9'8". Five stringer, foam with redwood and balsa, circa 1966-69. Board decoration influenced by the "Flower Power" movement of the late 1960s. Hoffman Collection. $1,200-1,800

Pull Out Ending a ride by steering the board through the back of the wave.

Continental Airlines Hawaii. Original artwork by Peter Max. Circa mid-1960s. Mauna Kea Galleries, Kamuela, Hawaii. $500-700

Psyche Out. A Walt Phillips film, circa 1962. Mauna Kea Galleries, Kamuela, Hawaii. $150-250

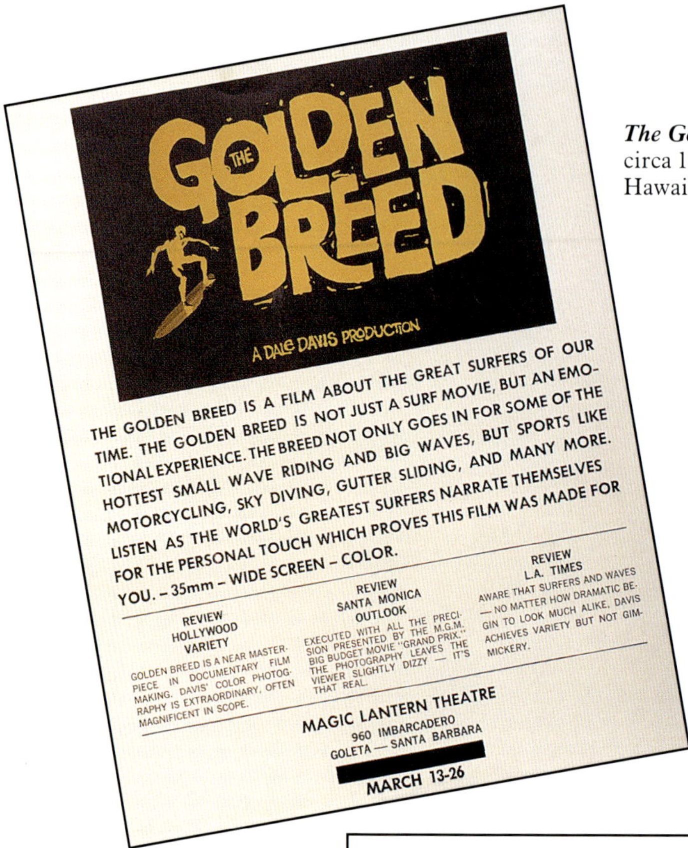

***The Golden Breed*.** A film by Dale Davis, circa 1968. Mauna Kea Galleries, Kamuela, Hawaii. $150-250

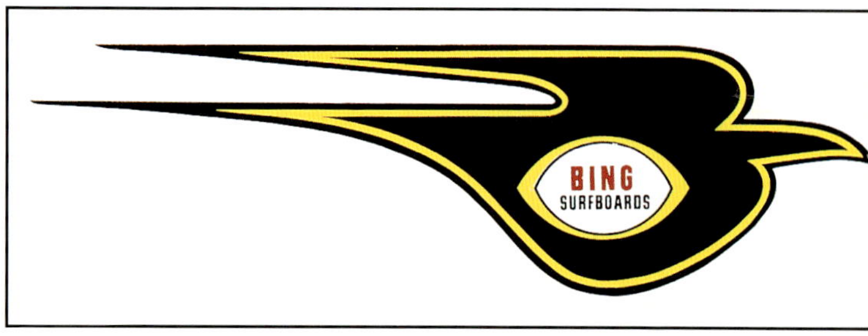

Bing Surfboards Decal. Peter and Cathy Noble, Monterey, California. $60-90

Bing, 12'0". Three stringer, big wave gun, foam with balsa, circa late 1960s. This was Flippy Hoffman's personal board last ridden at Kaena Point. Hoffman Collection. As shown: $5,000-7,000. Average: $2,500-3,500

Vintage Advertisement. Mauna Kea Galleries, Kamuela, Hawaii.

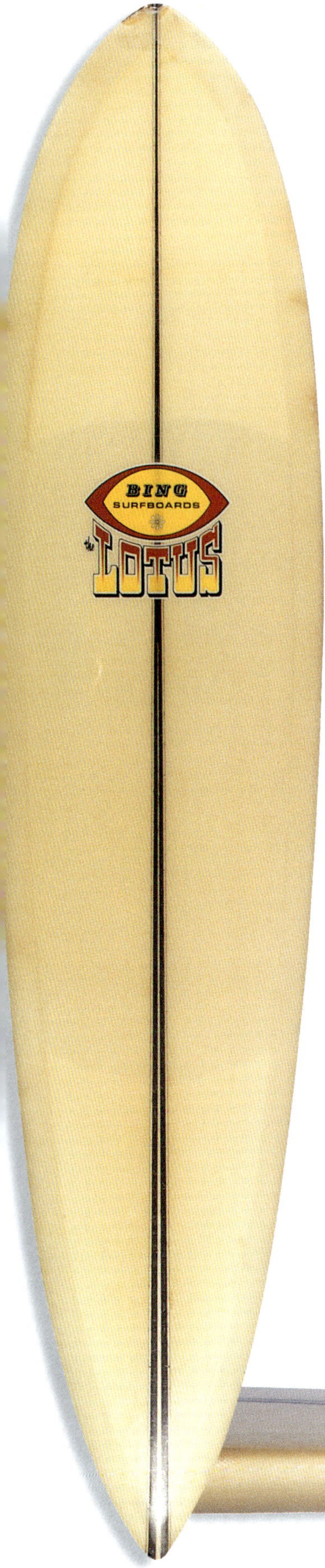

Bing Surfboard, The Lotus, 8'6". Tapered t-band stringer, foam with balsa, circa late 1960s. This was their first attempt at a semi-gun. Allan Seymour, Pacific Coast Vintage Surf Auctions. $1,200-1,800

Bing Surfboards, Hermosa Beach Business Card. Peter and Cathy Noble, Monterey, California. $40-60

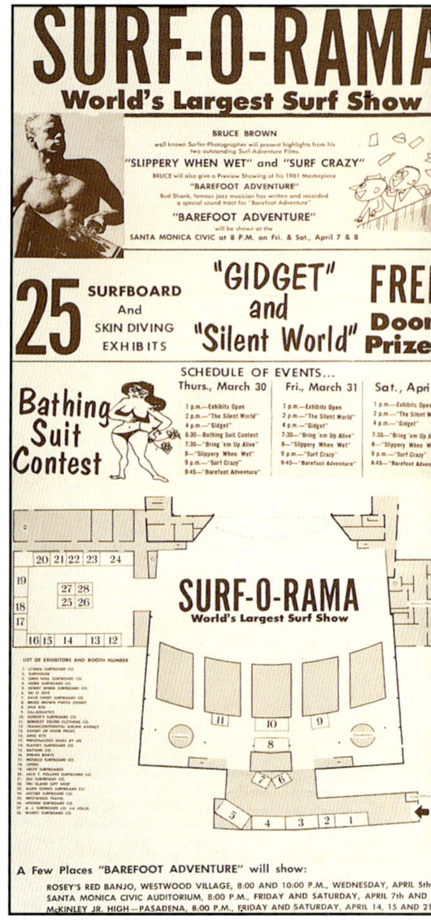

Surf-O-Rama World's Largest Surf Show. Circa 1961. Courtesy of Buck Labadie/Artstuff. $200-300

Bing Surfboards Decal. Peter and Cathy Noble, Monterey, California. $60-90

DON BROWN *presents*

Surf-O-Rama

WORLD'S LARGEST SURF SHOW

Don't Miss —
Bruce Brown's
"BAREFOOT ADVENTURE"
Santa Monica Civic Auditorium
8 p.m. Fri. & Sat., April 7 & 8

Adults	$1.91
Tax	.09
Total	$2.00

Surf-O-Rama Admission Ticket Stub. Presented by Don Brown, circa 1961. Courtesy of Buck Labadie/ Artstuff. $30-50

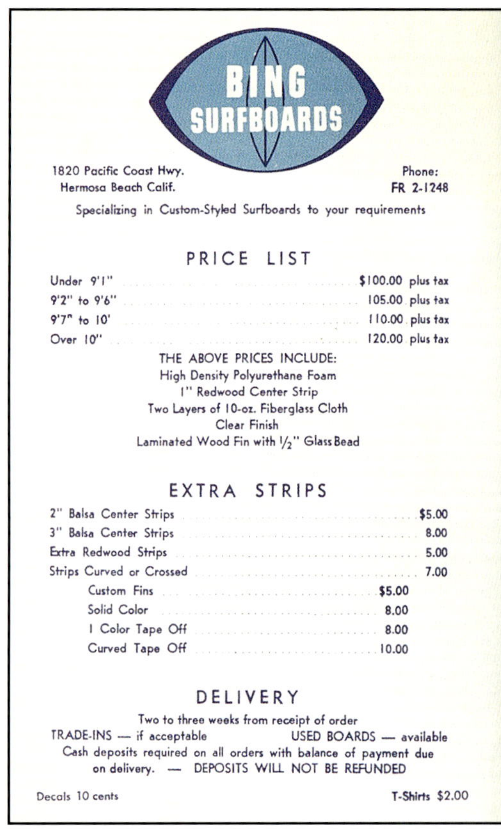

BING SURFBOARDS

1820 Pacific Coast Hwy.
Hermosa Beach Calif.

Phone:
FR 2-1248

Specializing in Custom-Styled Surfboards to your requirements

PRICE LIST

Under 9'1"	$100.00 plus tax
9'2" to 9'6"	105.00 plus tax
9'7" to 10'	110.00 plus tax
Over 10"	120.00 plus tax

THE ABOVE PRICES INCLUDE:
High Density Polyurethane Foam
1" Redwood Center Strip
Two Layers of 10-oz. Fiberglass Cloth
Clear Finish
Laminated Wood Fin with 1/2" Glass Bead

EXTRA STRIPS

2" Balsa Center Strips	$5.00
3" Balsa Center Strips	8.00
Extra Redwood Strips	5.00
Strips Curved or Crossed	7.00
Custom Fins	$5.00
Solid Color	8.00
1 Color Tape Off	8.00
Curved Tape Off	10.00

DELIVERY

Two to three weeks from receipt of order
TRADE-INS — if acceptable USED BOARDS — available
Cash deposits required on all orders with balance of payment due on delivery. — DEPOSITS WILL NOT BE REFUNDED

Decals 10 cents T-Shirts $2.00

Bing Surfboards, Hermosa Beach, California, Price List. Circa early 1960s. Courtesy of Buck Labadie/ Artstuff. $100-150

Bing Surfboards Patch. Peter and Cathy Noble, Monterey, California. $25-35

Acid Drop Dropping into a wave and having the bottom fall out, leaving the rider with a sense of weightlessness and often helplessness.

Surfin' Wild. A Grant Rohloff film, circa 1962. Mauna Kea Galleries, Kamuela, Hawaii. $150-250

Men Who Ride Mountains. A Grant Rohloff film, circa 1963. Mauna Kea Galleries, Kamuela, Hawaii. $200-300

Out of Control. A Grant Rohloff film, circa 1962. Mauna Kea Galleries, Kamuela, Hawaii. $150-250

For Surfers Only. A Grant Rohloff film, circa 1964. Mauna Kea Galleries, Kamuela, Hawaii. $150-250

Surfin' Wild. A film by Grant Rohloff, circa 1962. Mauna Kea Galleries, Kamuela, Hawaii. $150-250

Too Hot to Handle. A Grant Rohloff film, circa 1961. Mauna Kea Galleries, Kamuela, Hawaii. $150-250

Harbour Surfboards – Founded in 1959 by Rich Harbour in Seal Beach, California, he started shaping boards at 16 in his parents' garage. He produced some of the most classic and popular models of all time, including the Rich Chew Banana, Trestle Special and the Cheater. The Cheater is his most sought after model and was designed and tested by Mark Martinson.

Harbour Surfboards, Seal Beach, California, Decal. Peter and Cathy Noble, Monterey, California. $40-60

Surfboards by Harbour, Seal Beach Patch. Peter and Cathy Noble, Monterey, California. $20-30

Surfboards by Harbour, Seal Beach, 9'4". Wide single stringer, foam with balsa, circa mid-1960s. Banana model. Allan Seymour, Pacific Coast Vintage Surf Auctions. $800-1,200

ot Dog A broad term used to describe both surfers nd boards used in fancy, trick-style surfing maneu-ers; a person showing a great deal of skill in the surf oing fancy turns, walking on the nose, etc.

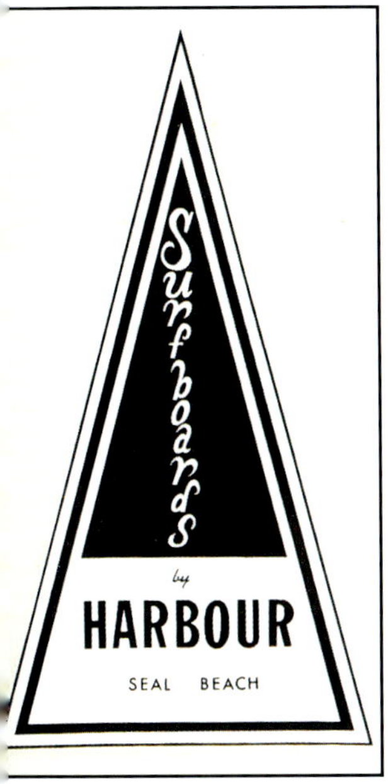

Surfboards by Harbour, Seal Beach Decal. Peter and Cathy Noble, Monterey, California. $40-60

urfboards by Harbour, Seal Beach Patch. Peter and Cathy Noble, Monterey, California. $15-25

Hot Dog on a Stick. A Bill Stromberg film, circa 1962. Courtesy of Buck Labadie/ Artstuff. $200-300

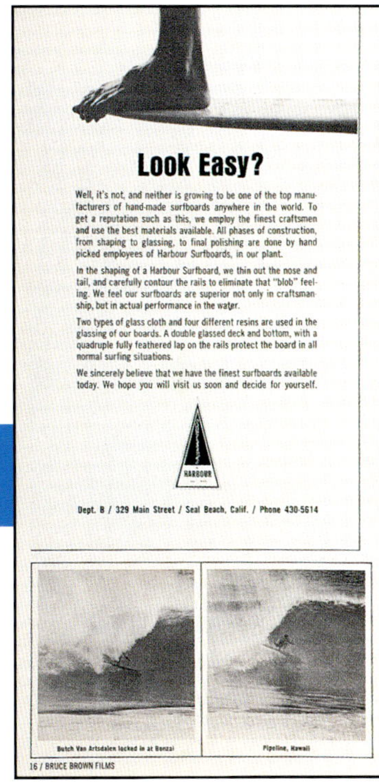

Vintage Advertisement. Mauna Kea Galleries, Kamuela, Hawaii.

Toes on the Nose Riding the surfboard in a hang five or hang ten situation.

Hot Dog on a Stick. A Bill Stromberg film, featuring "Dynomotion." Circa 1962. Mauna Kea Galleries, Kamuela, Hawaii. $300-500

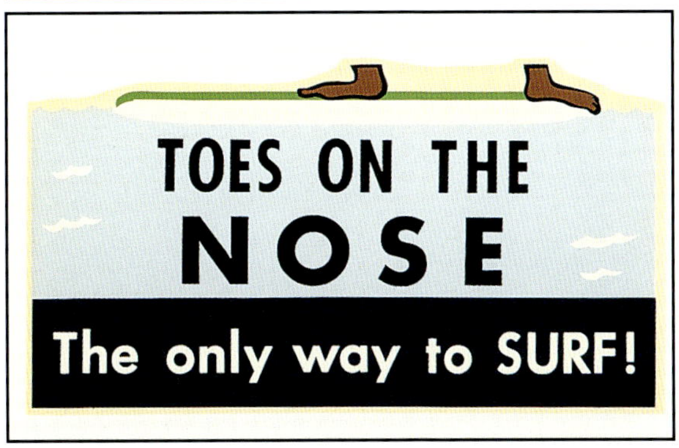

TOES ON THE NOSE, The only way to SURF! Decal. Peter and Cathy Noble, Monterey, California. $150-250

Hang Ten Decal. Peter and Cathy Noble, Monterey, California. $30-50

Hang Ten – A&W Root Beer Company, Santa Monica, California. Restaurant premium. Peter and Cathy Noble, Monterey, California. $60-90

***Surfer* Magazine**

John Severson started *Surfer* magazine as a way to distribute surfing images to the public. The idea began with the *Surf Fever* program with individual black and white photos being sold to moviegoers. From there, it evolved into a small program of about 100 images, then grew into a quarterly publication, the first of which sold 5,000 copies. Eventually the newsstands encouraged production of this magazine. With *Surfer*, John Severson set the standards for surfing magazines with stunning issues, great photography, graphics and art. *Surfer* is the undisputed King of all the vintage magazines and is still being published over 40 years later.

Year	Issue	Value
1960	Vol. 1, No. 1	$400-600 (10,000 copies issued)
1973	Reprint	$30-50
1983	Reprint	$15-25
1961	Vol. 2, No. 1	The first Murphy issue. $800-1,200 (5,000 copies issued)
	Vol. 2, No. 2	$400-600 (7,500 copies issued)
	Vol. 2, No. 3	$300-500 (10,000 copies issued)
	Vol. 2, No. 4	$200-300 (18,000 copies issued)
1962	Vol. 3, No. 1	$150-250 (50,000 copies issued)
	Vol. 3, No. 2	$100-150 First bi-monthly issue.
	Vol. 3, No. 3	$150-250
	Vol. 3, No. 4	$100-150
	Vol. 3, No. 5	$100-150
1963	Vol. 4, No. 1	$100-150
	Vol. 4, No. 2	$120-180
	Vol. 4, No. 3	$100-150
	Vol. 4, No. 4	$100-150
	Vol. 4, No. 5	$100-150
	Vol. 4, No. 6	$100-150
1964	Vol. 5, No. 1	$80-120
	Vol. 5, No. 2	$80-120
	Vol. 5, No. 3	$80-120
	Vol. 5, No. 4	$80-120
	Vol. 5, No. 5	$80-120
1965	Vol. 5, No. 6	$80-120
	Vol. 6, No. 1	$80-120
	Vol. 6, No. 2	$80-120
	Vol. 6, No. 3	$80-120
	Vol. 6, No. 4	$80-120
	Vol. 6, No. 5	$80-120
1966	Vol. 6, No. 6	$80-120
	Vol. 7, No. 1	$40-60
	Vol. 7, No. 2	$40-60
	Vol. 7, No. 3	$40-60
	Vol. 7, No. 4	$40-60
	Vol. 7, No. 5	$40-60
1967	Vol. 7, No. 6	$40-60
	Vol. 8, No. 1	$40-60
	Vol. 8, No. 2	$40-60
	Vol. 8, No. 3	$40-60
	Vol. 8, No. 4	$40-60
	Vol. 8, No. 5	$40-60
1968	Vol. 8, No. 6	$40-60
	Vol. 9, No. 1	$40-60
	Vol. 9, No. 2	$40-60
	Vol. 9, No. 3	$40-60
	Vol. 9, No. 4	$40-60
	Vol. 9, No. 5	$40-60
1969	Vol. 9, No. 6	$30-50
	Vol. 10, No. 1	$30-50
	Vol. 10, No. 2	$30-50
	Vol. 10, No. 3	$30-50
	Vol. 10, No. 4	$30-50
	Vol. 10, No. 5	$30-50

Complete sets of *Surfer* magazine from the first issue to the latest have a value of $4,000-6,000.

***Surfer* Magazine Promotional Calendar, 1962.** A great image of Ricky Grigg surfing at Waimea Bay, Hawaii. Courtesy of Buck Labadie/Artstuff. $150-250

The Surfer Magazine – A John Severson Production Decal. Peter and Cathy Noble, Monterey, California. $60-90

Promotional Flyer for John Severson's Surfing Photo Book *The Surfer*. Circa 1960. Courtesy of Buck Labadie/Artstuff. $400-600

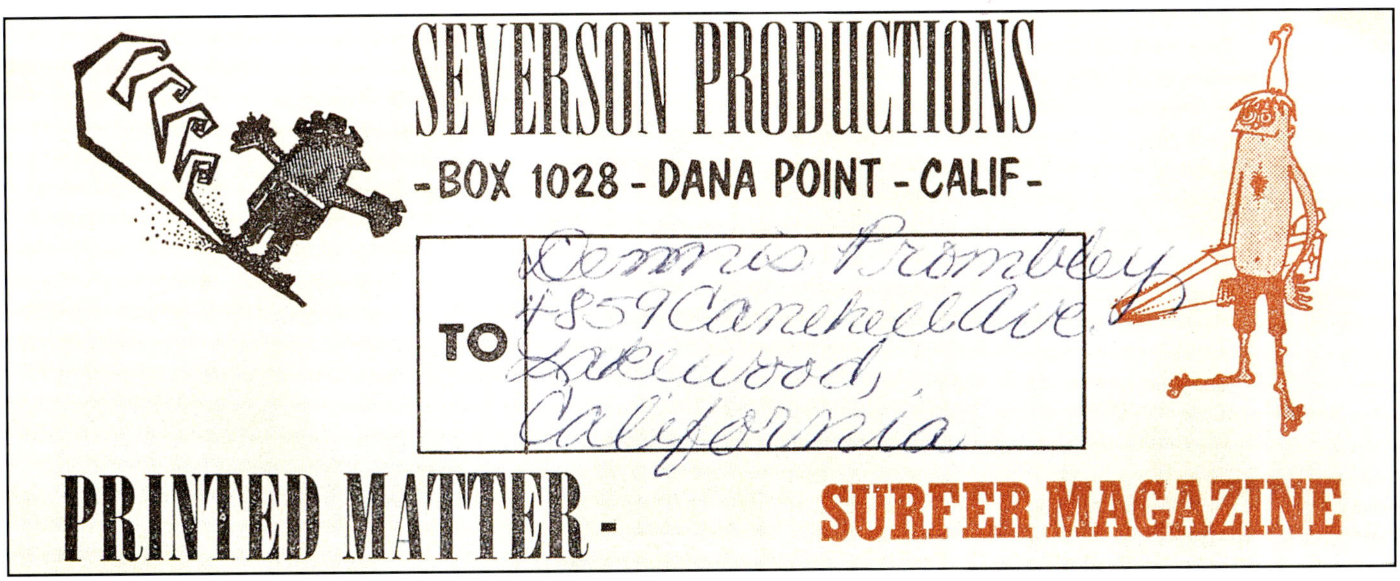

Address Label for *Surfer* Magazine, Severson Productions, Dana Point, California. Circa 1960. Courtesy of Buck Labadie/Artstuff. $20-30

Murphy The cartoon character created by Rick Griffin typifying the characterization of a typical gremmie. Debuted in 1961 in the second issue of *Surfer* magazine.

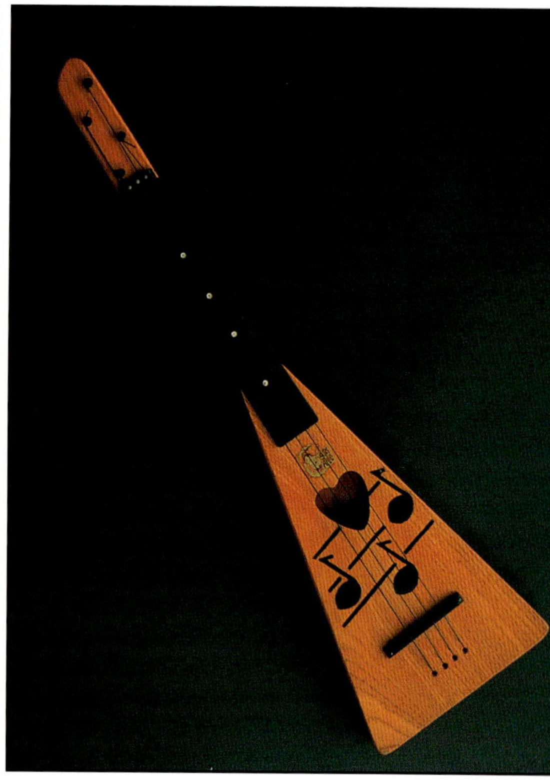

A Murphy Surf-A-Lele. A rare example of the short-lived production of a ukulele inspired by Rick Griffin's cartoon character Murphy, circa 1963. Courtesy of Mark and Cindy Fragale. $400-600

Surfer **Magazine, 1961, vol. 2, no. 1**. The first Murphy issue, 5,000 copies issued. Mauna Kea Galleries, Kamuela, Hawaii. $800-1200

Murph the Surf The surfer-turned-jewel-thief Jack Murphy, who, along with his accomplice, stole the Star of India sapphire from the American Museum of Natural History in 1964.

Murphy Beer Stein. Sold by mail order through *Surfer* magazine in the 1960s. Inspired by Rick Griffin's cartoon character Murphy. *Cowabunga!* on opposite side of stein. Courtesy of Mark and Cindy Fragale. $200-300

The ***Surfer*** **Magazine Decal.** Rick Griffin Murphy cartoon character, circa 1963. Peter and Cathy Noble, Monterey, California. $200-300

Surf Safari. A John Severson Studios film, circa 1959. Courtesy of Buck Labadie/Artstuff. $300-500

Surf Safari. A John Severson Studios film, circa 1959. Courtesy of Buck Labadie/Artstuff. $400-600

John Severson Productions, Dana Point, California. John Severson's personal card. Courtesy of Buck Labadie/Artstuff. $100-150

Severson Productions, Dana Point, California. John Severson's personal card. Peter and Cathy Noble, Monterey, California. $100-150

Surf Fever. A John Severson film, circa 1960. Mauna Kea Galleries, Kamuela, Hawaii. $300-500

Promotional Card for *Surf Fever*. A John Serverson Production, circa 1960. Courtesy of Buck Labadie/Artstuff. $80-120

***Surf Fever* Admission Ticket Stub.** A John Severson film, circa 1960. Courtesy of Buck Labadie/Artstuff. $30-50

Promotional Two-Sided Flyer for *Surf Fever*. A John Severson film, circa 1960. Rare. Mauna Kea Galleries, Kamuela, Hawaii. $300-500

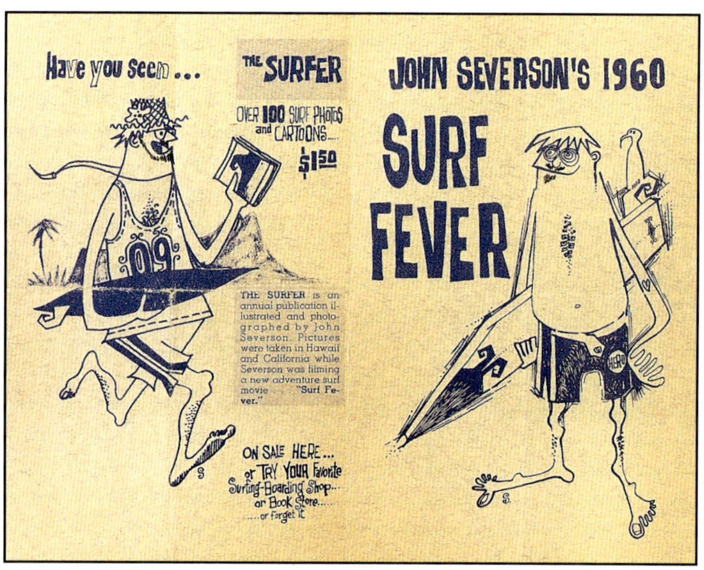

Rare John Severson Flyer for *Surf Fever*. Circa 1960. Courtesy of Buck Labadie/Artstuff. $500-700

Surfing Movies – Surf Hi-Lights of *Surf Safari* and *Surf Fever* along with *Big Wednesday*. Films by John Severson, circa 1962. A rare multi-venue surf poster. Courtesy of Buck Labadie/Artstuff. $400-600

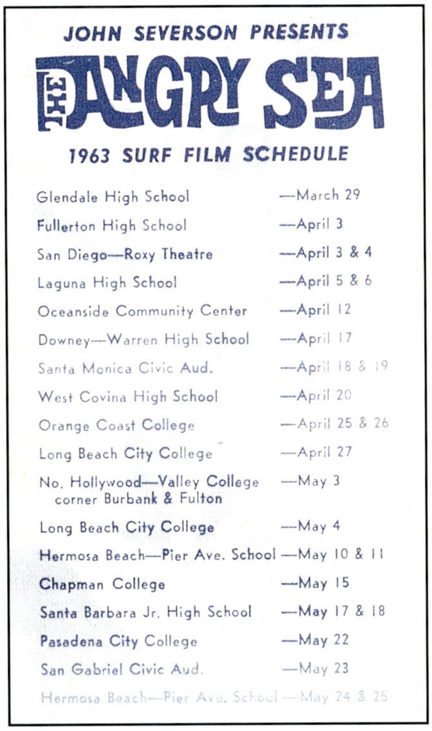

JOHN SEVERSON PRESENTS

THE ANGRY SEA

1963 SURF FILM SCHEDULE

Glendale High School	—March 29
Fullerton High School	—April 3
San Diego—Roxy Theatre	—April 3 & 4
Laguna High School	—April 5 & 6
Oceanside Community Center	—April 12
Downey—Warren High School	—April 17
Santa Monica Civic Aud.	—April 18 & 19
West Covina High School	—April 20
Orange Coast College	—April 25 & 26
Long Beach City College	—April 27
No. Hollywood—Valley College corner Burbank & Fulton	—May 3
Long Beach City College	—May 4
Hermosa Beach—Pier Ave. School	—May 10 & 11
Chapman College	—May 15
Santa Barbara Jr. High School	—May 17 & 18
Pasadena City College	—May 22
San Gabriel Civic Aud.	—May 23
Hermosa Beach—Pier Ave. School	—May 24 & 25

John Severson Presents *The Angry Sea*. 1963 surf film schedule. Peter and Cathy Noble, Monterey, California. $80-120

***Big Wednesday* Admission Ticket Stub.** A John Severson film, circa 1961. Courtesy of Buck Labadie/Artstuff. $30-50

Bowl A bowl-shaped feature on a wave face, often caused by reef contours.

Promotional Postcard for *Big Wednesday*. A John Severson film, circa 1961. Mauna Kea Galleries, Kamuela, Hawaii. $60-90

***Big Wednesday*.** A John Severson film, circa 1961. Mauna Kea Galleries, Kamuela, Hawaii. $300-500

Backdoor The rider takes off to one side or behind the peak in order to go the full length of the section of the wave where the lip usually throws first.

Promotional Flyer for *Going My Wave* with John Severson. An interesting promotional piece from 1962 offering for sale a subscription to *Surfer* magazine as well as various posters and surf movies. Courtesy of Buck Labadie/Artstuff. $300-500

Color Surf Movie *Going My Wave* with John Severson, 1962, Decal. Peter and Cathy Noble, Monterey, California. $200-300

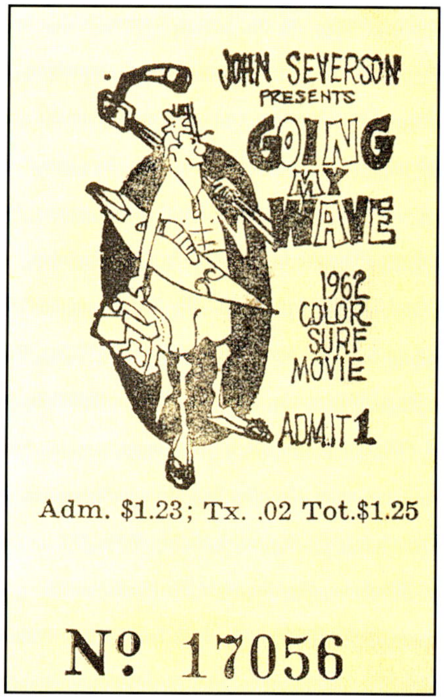

***Going My Wave* Admission Ticket Stub.** A John Severson film, circa 1962. Courtesy of Buck Labadie/Artstuff. $30-50

Promotional Postcard for *Going My Wave*. A John Severson film, circa 1962. Mauna Kea Galleries, Kamuela, Hawaii. $60-90

The Angry Sea. A John Severson film, circa 1963. Mauna Kea Galleries, Kamuela, Hawaii. $200-300

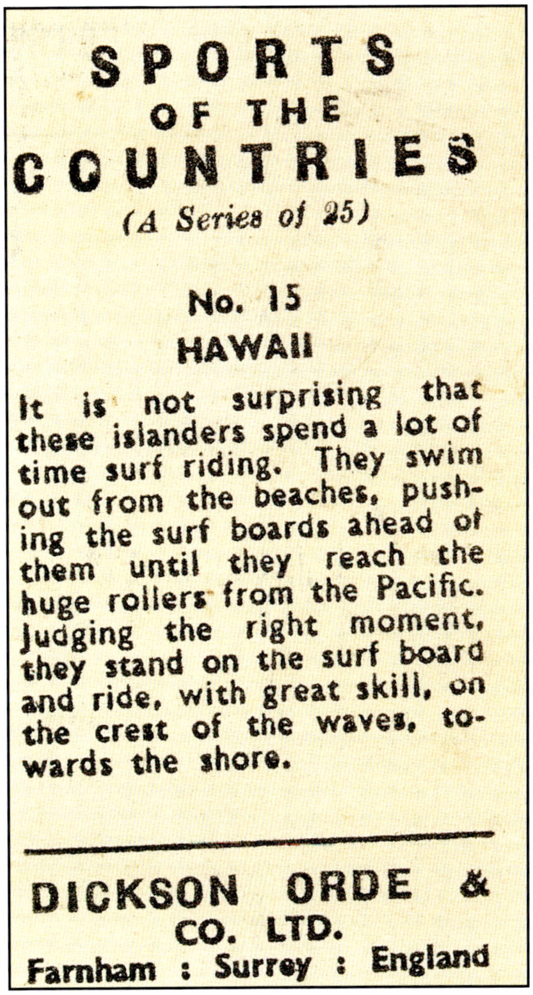

SPORTS OF THE COUNTRIES

(A Series of 25)

No. 15

HAWAII

It is not surprising that these islanders spend a lot of time surf riding. They swim out from the beaches, pushing the surf boards ahead of them until they reach the huge rollers from the Pacific. Judging the right moment, they stand on the surf board and ride, with great skill, on the crest of the waves, towards the shore.

DICKSON ORDE & CO. LTD.

Farnham : Surrey : England

English Cigarette Premium, 1962.
SPORTS of the COUNTRIES
(A Series of 25)
No. 15

HAWAII

It is not surprising that these islanders spend a lot of time surf riding. They swim out from the beaches, pushing the surf boards ahead of them until they reach the huge rollers from the Pacific. Judging the right moment, they stand on the surf board and ride, with great skill, on the crest of the waves, toward the shore.

DICKSON ORDE & CO. LTD.
Farnham : Surrey : England

Mauna Kea Galleries, Kamuela, Hawaii. $25-35

United Airlines Hawaii. Circa 1962. Mauna Kea Galleries, Kamuela, Hawaii. $250-350

Yater Surfboards, Santa Barbara, 9'8". A classic spoon that became famous and synonymous with Rincon. This board is a double 10 oz. volan with a wedge t-band (redwood, balsa, redwood). Early Yaters were very similar to Velzy's and had a slightly tan tint due to the type of resin he used. John Eichert, of Ike Surfboards, was his early glasser. The spoon name originated from the spooned out nose, which was Bob Simmons idea. The fin is polypropylene from Morey Pope, and the tail block is of high-density foam. Peter and Cathy Noble, Monterey, California. $1,200-1,800

Blown Off When the wind lifts a surfer right out of the wave he or she was attempting to ride.

Vintage Advertisement. Mauna Kea Galleries, Kamuela, Hawaii.

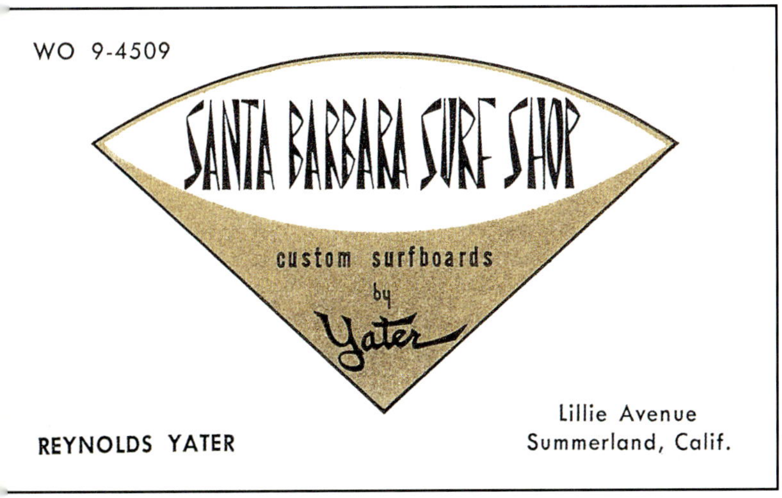

Santa Barbara Surf Shop, Custom Surfboards by Yater, Summerland, California. Reynolds Yater's personal card. Peter and Cathy Noble, Monterey, California. $100-150

Santa Barbara Surf Shop, Surfboards by Yater Decal. Peter and Cathy Noble, Monterey, California. $80-120

Reynolds Yater today

Hodad Most often used in a derogatory manner by surfers to describe a non-surfer or a surfer who rarely goes into the water but acts as if he is "God's gift" to the sport. Sometimes used to describe an unknown surfer in the lineup.

Promotional Flyer for Surfboards by Sweeney, North Long Beach, California. Circa early 1960s. Courtesy of Buck Labadie/ Artstuff. $250-350

Fiberglass Jungle. A Dale Davis film, circa late 1960s. Courtesy of Buck Labadie/Artstuff. $150-250

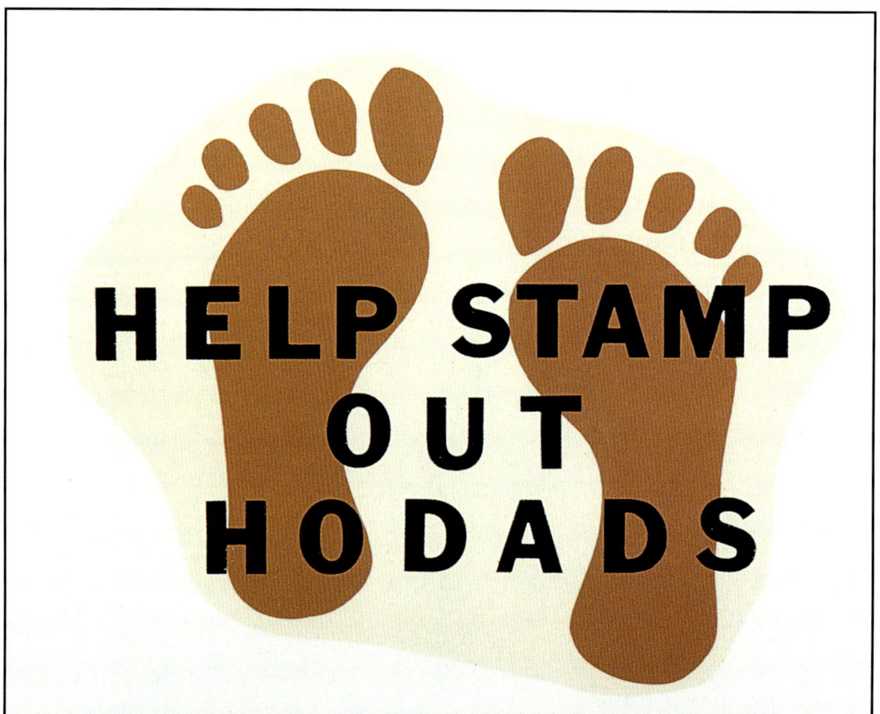

Help Stamp Out Hodads Decal. Peter and Cathy Noble, Monterey, California. $80-120

Cowabunga! Often shouted, it is a surfer's expression of joy popularized in the 1960s. The originator of the cry was legendary Chief Thunderthud (played by Bill Lecornec) of *The Howdy Doody Show*, which aired on television in the 1950s.

Wipe Out Ho-Dads, Sea Cross Surfboards, Burbank, Decal. Peter and Cathy Noble, Monterey, California. $200-300

Spinning Boards. A Bud Browne film, circa 1961. Mauna Kea Galleries, Kamuela, Hawaii. $200-300

Gun Ho. A Bud Browne film, circa 1963. Mauna Kea Galleries, Kamuela, Hawaii. As shown $200-300. Average $150-250

Critical The condition when the wave is about to break.

Vintage Advertisement. Mauna Kea Galleries, Kamuela, Hawaii.

Custom Boards by Haut Decal. Peter and Cathy Noble, Monterey, California. $80-120

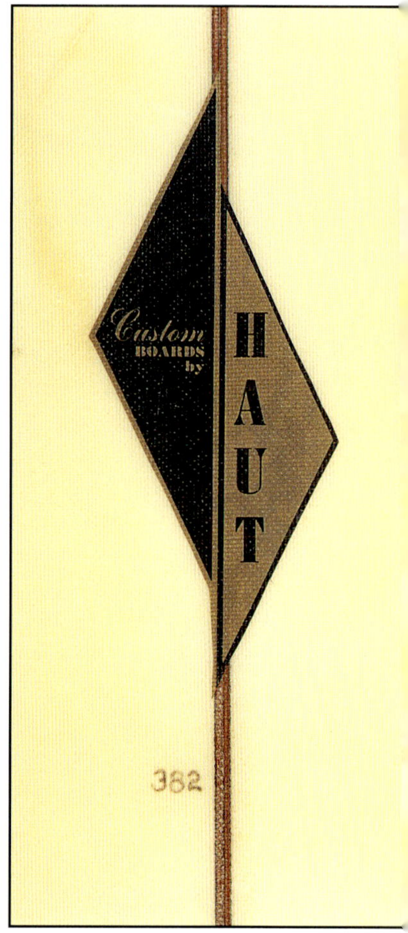

Custom Boards by Haut, 10'0". Single stringer, foam with redwood, circa 1966. This board was found under a rental house in Watsonville, California, about 15 years ago, and is thought to have come from the Pleasure Point area. Doug Haut was obviously influenced by the Morey Pope and the Con wing nose models, which were probably custom boards in that age of nose riders. Haut was a major player in the Santa Cruz market. His original operation on the east side of Santa Cruz burned down. His present operation is the Santa Cruz Surf Shop. Peter and Cathy Noble, Monterey, California. $600-900

Free and Easy. A Greg Macgillivray and Jim Freeman film, Santa Ana, California. Peter and Cathy Noble, Monterey, California. $40-60

Barge A clunky or unusually large or heavy surfboard.

Promotional Booklet for the Movie *Free and Easy*. A Magillivray and Freeman film, circa 1967. Mauna Kea Galleries, Kamuela, Hawaii. $250-350

Getting Worked When the waves – whether through a wipeout or similar situation– put the surfer into a "spin cycle."

Fin Box A channel that the fin can slide or fit into.

Jacobs, 10'4". T-bar stringer, foam with balsa, circa early 1960s. Hoffman Collection. $600-900

Jacobs Surfboards – Originally in partnership with Dale Velzy, Harold "Hap" Jacobs opened his own shop in Hermosa Beach, California, in 1959. In the 1960s, he had one of the best surf teams ever formed, with Donald Takayama, Rick Irons, Robert August, Lance Carson, Steve Dabney, Sparky Hudson and Kemp Aaberg, among others. One of his most popular and famous models was the Donald Takayama, produced in 1965, and the Lance Carson Signature model, produced in 1966. In 1965, he also produced the short-lived Duke Kahanamoku Pop Out model.

Left: ***The Performers.*** A Greg Macgillivray film, circa 1965. Courtesy of Buck Labadie/Artstuff. $120-180

Right: ***The Performers.*** A Greg Macgillivray film, circa 1965. Courtesy of Buck Labadie/ Artstuff. $120-180

Pacific Coast Surfboards by Dale Velzy Decal. Prototype with working notes to printer. Peter and Cathy Noble, Monterey, California. $150-250

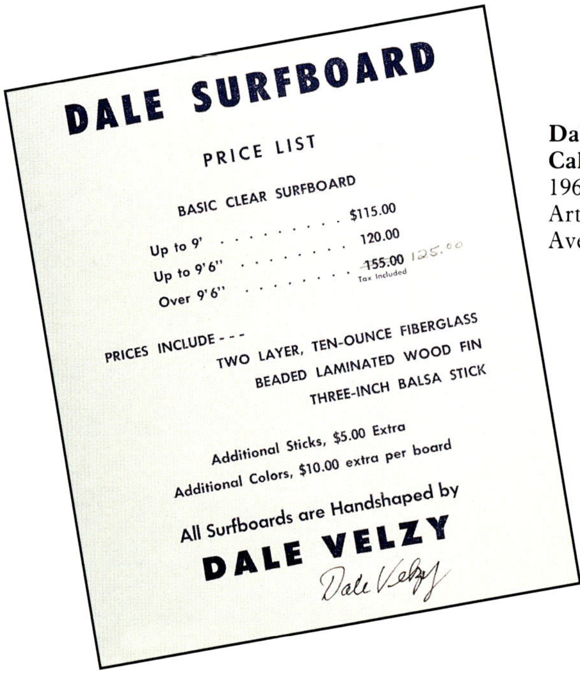

Dale Surfboard, Newport Beach, California, Price List. Circa early 1960s. Courtesy of Buck Labadie/ Artstuff. As shown: $250-350. Average: $120-180

Promotional Flyer for Surfboards by Velzy. Circa early 1960s. Courtesy of Buck Labadie/ Artstuff. As shown: $300-500 Average: $150-250

Promotional Flyer for Custom Surfboards by Velzy, San Clemente, California. Circa late 1950s. Courtesy of Buck Labadie/ Artstuff. $150-250

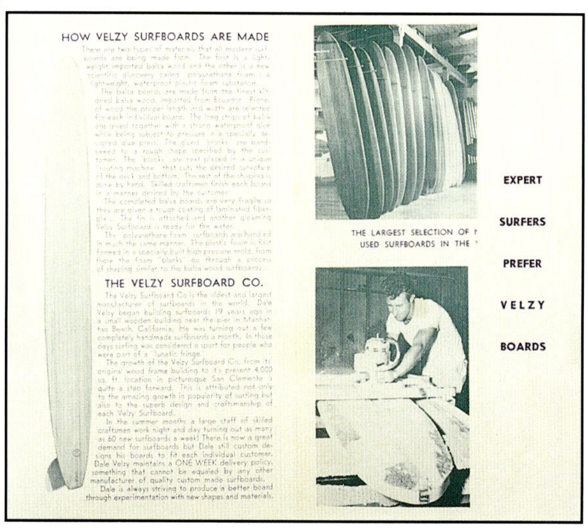

Boxy Sharp edges on the sides of a surfboard, as opposed to smooth, rounded edges or rails.

Surf Boards by Velzy and Jacobs Decal. Peter and Cathy Noble, Monterey, California. $80-120

Pacific Coast Surfboards by Dale, Decal. Peter and Cathy Noble, Monterey, California. $100-150

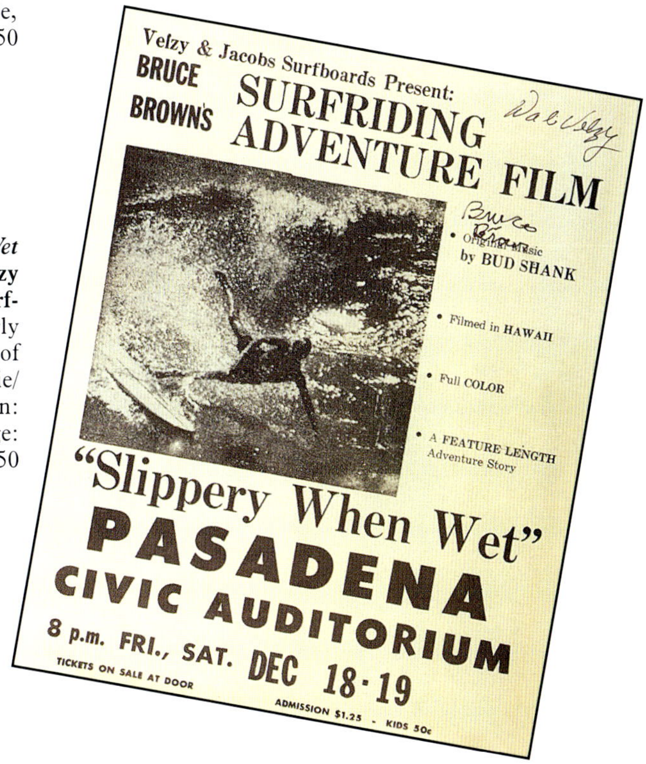

***Slippery When Wet* Sponsored by Velzy & Jacobs Surfboards.** Circa early 1960s. Courtesy of Buck Labadie/ Artstuff. As shown: $500-700. Average: $250-350

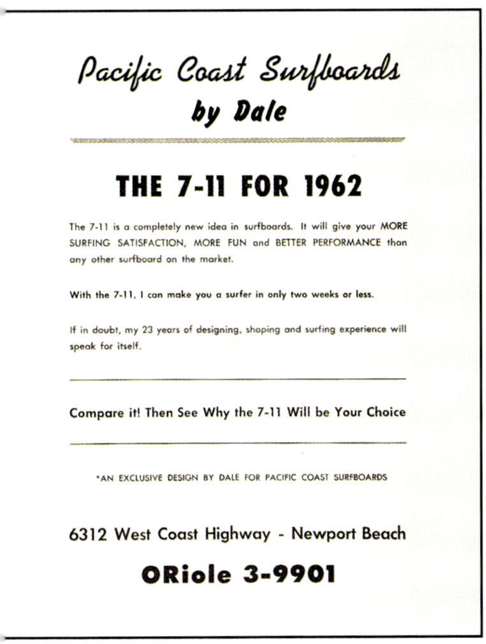

Promotional Flyer for Pacific Coast Surfboards by Dale. Circa early 1960s. Courtesy of Buck Labadie/Artstuff. $100-150

Promotional Flyer for Pacific Coast Surfboards by Dale. Circa early 1960s. Courtesy of Buck Labadie/ Artstuff. As shown: $200-300. Average: $100-150

Crazing Hairline cracks on the surface or below the surface of fiberglass laminates. They originate from a multitude of sources, including excessive heat while curing.

Jacobs Decal. Peter and Cathy Noble, Monterey, California. $40-60

Vintage Advertisement. Mauna Kea Galleries, Kamuela, Hawaii.

Vintage Advertisement. Mauna Kea Galleries, Kamuela, Hawaii.

Surfboard by Jacobs, 9'8". Multi-stringer, balsa with foam. Purchased in 1965 on Long Island, New York, by the Thorpe family as a high school graduation gift for their son. This board was surfed only twice due to a bad automobile accident that kept him out of the Viet Nam war. Mauna Kea Galleries, Kamuela, Hawaii. $1,200-1,800

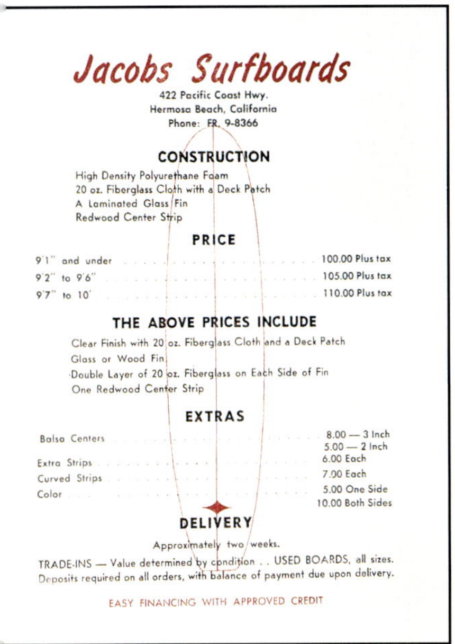

Jacobs Surfboards

422 Pacific Coast Hwy.
Hermosa Beach, California
Phone: FR. 9-8366

CONSTRUCTION

High Density Polyurethane Foam
20 oz. Fiberglass Cloth with a Deck Patch
A Laminated Glass Fin
Redwood Center Strip

PRICE

9'1" and under	100.00 Plus tax
9'2" to 9'6"	105.00 Plus tax
9'7" to 10'	110.00 Plus tax

THE ABOVE PRICES INCLUDE

Clear Finish with 20 oz. Fiberglass Cloth and a Deck Patch
Glass or Wood Fin
Double Layer of 20 oz. Fiberglass on Each Side of Fin
One Redwood Center Strip

EXTRAS

Balsa Centers	8.00 — 3 Inch 5.00 — 2 Inch
Extra Strips	6.00 Each
Curved Strips	7.00 Each
Color	5.00 One Side 10.00 Both Sides

DELIVERY

Approximately two weeks.

TRADE-INS — Value determined by condition . . USED BOARDS, all sizes.
Deposits required on all orders, with balance of payment due upon delivery.

EASY FINANCING WITH APPROVED CREDIT

Jacobs Surfboards, Hermosa Beach, California, Price List. Circa early 1960s. Courtesy of Buck Labadie/ Artstuff. $80-120

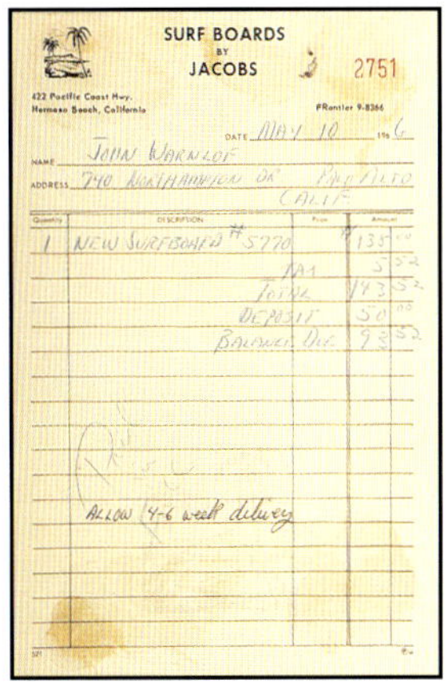

SURF BOARDS BY JACOBS 2751

422 Pacific Coast Hwy.
Hermosa Beach, California
FRontier 9-8366

DATE May 10 196 6
NAME John Warnlof
ADDRESS 740 Northampton Dr Palo Alto Calif.

Quantity	Description	Price	Amount
1	New Surfboard #5770		135 00
	Tax		5 52
	Total		143 52
	Deposit		50 00
	Balance Due		93 52

Allow 4-6 week delivery

Jacobs, 9'10". Wide t-bar stringer, foam with balsa, circa 1966. Mint, never surfed, with original receipt for $138. Peter and Cathy Noble, Monterey, California. As shown: $2,500-3,500. Average: $600-900

Jacobs, 10'0". Three stringer team riding board, foam with redwood, circa 1966-67. Hoffman Collection. $800-$1,200

Surf Boards by Jacobs, Hermosa Beach, California, Business Card. Peter and Cathy Noble, Monterey, California. $40-60

Surfboards by Jacobs, Patch. Peter and Cathy Noble, Monterey, California. $25-35

Vintage Advertisement. Mauna Kea Galleries, Kamuela, Hawaii.

Promotional Flyer for Rick's Ric-Shaw. Circa early 1960s. Courtesy of Buck Labadie/Artstuff. $100-150

Promotional Flyer for Lakewood Cycle and Surf Shop, Long Beach, California. Circa early 1960s. Courtesy of Buck Labadie/Artstuff. $100-150

Impact Zone The area directly in front of breaking waves where the wave breaks first.

Surf Boards by Jacobs, Decal. Peter and Cathy Noble, Monterey, California. $60-90

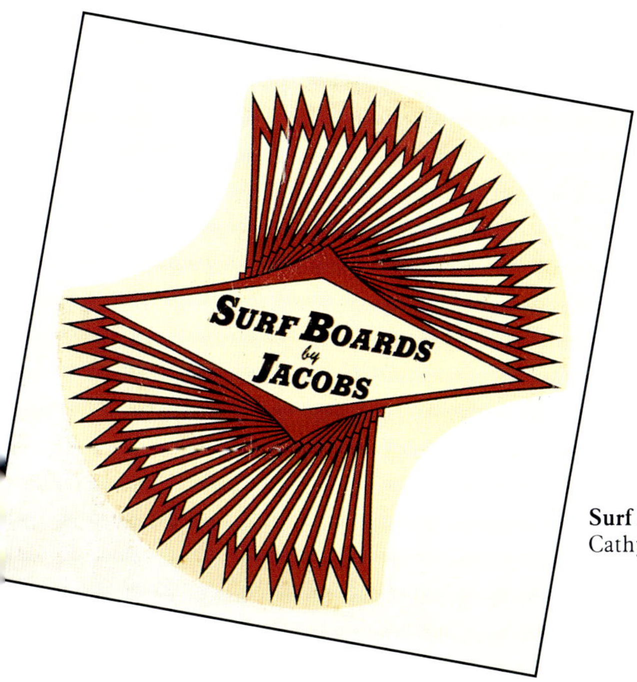

Surf Boards by Jacobs, Decal. Peter and Cathy Noble, Monterey, California. $80-120

***Reef* Magazine, August 1960.** Rare issue featuring the death of Bob Simmons. Peter and Cathy Noble, Monterey, California. $400-600

Second Annual Pacific Coast Mixed Tadem Surfing Championships, Dana Point Chamber of Commerce. Circa 1962. Courtesy of Buck Labadie/ Artstuff. $200-300

The Best of *Surf Mania* and *Sunset Surf Craze*. A Walt Phillips film, circa 1962. Even though the original movies were released in 1960, Walt Phillips re-released parts of these two films and combined them with his current film "Psyche Out" in this year. Mauna Kea Galleries, Kamuela, Hawaii. $200-300

Follow That Surf. A Bill Singer film, circa 1963. Mauna Kea Galleries, Kamuela, Hawaii. $150-250

The Nu-Pike and the American Cancer Society Present Summer Surf Stomp in Person Dick Dale and Del-Tones. Circa 1964. Courtesy of Buck Labadie/ Artstuff. $250-350

Dick Dale

Known as the "King of the Surf Guitar," he was the originator of the "surf sound" in 1958-59. With his band the Del-Tones, he had numerous hits, including *Let's Go Trippin'*, in 1961.

Duke Model Longboard. Made in the mid-1960s by Nash, 44 inches. This rare board is made of koa wood and birch and stenciled with a portrait of Duke along with a vignette of Duke surfing. The board shown is in exceptional condition. Ed and Randi Economy Collection. As shown: $3,000-5,000. Average: $1,200-1,800.

Original Photograph of Duke Kahanamoku and Admirer. Circa early 1960s. Waikiki Beach. Mauna Kea Galleries, Kamuela, Hawaii. $60-90

Duke Model Skateboard. Made in the mid-1960s by Nash, 22 inches. All known examples have been found in Hawaii. The board shown is in exceptional condition. Ed and Randi Economy Collection. As shown: $800-1,200 Average: $400-600

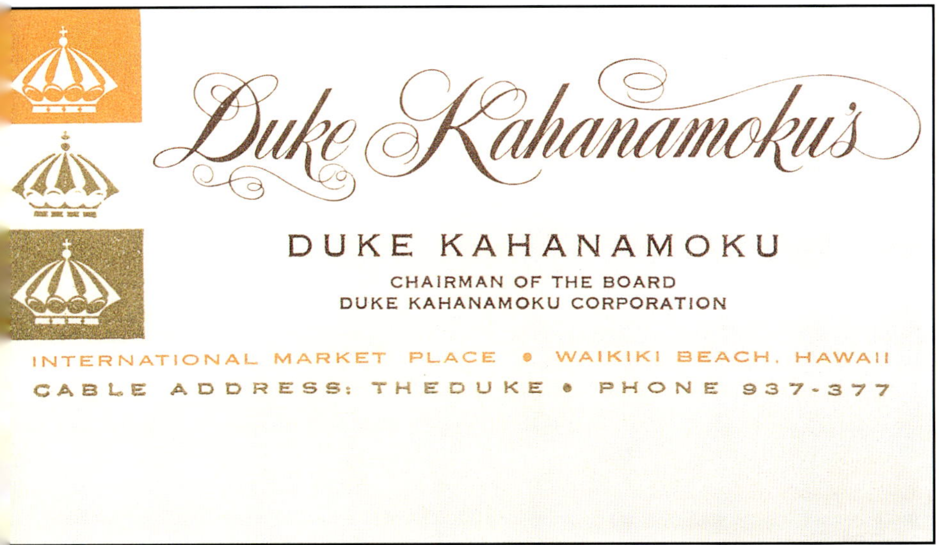

Duke Kahanamoku. Personal business card of the Duke for his corporation located in the International Marketplace, Waikiki Beach. Mid-1960s. Ed and Randi Economy Collection. $300-500

Vintage Advertisement. Mauna Kea Galleries, Kamuela, Hawaii.

Pair of Duke Kahanamoku Aloha Shoes with Box. Circa mid-1960s. Made for a very short time period. Each pair came with an official membership card in The Duke Fan Club. Rare. Ed and Randi Economy Collection. $1,500-2,500. Shoes without box: $800-1,200 mint condition

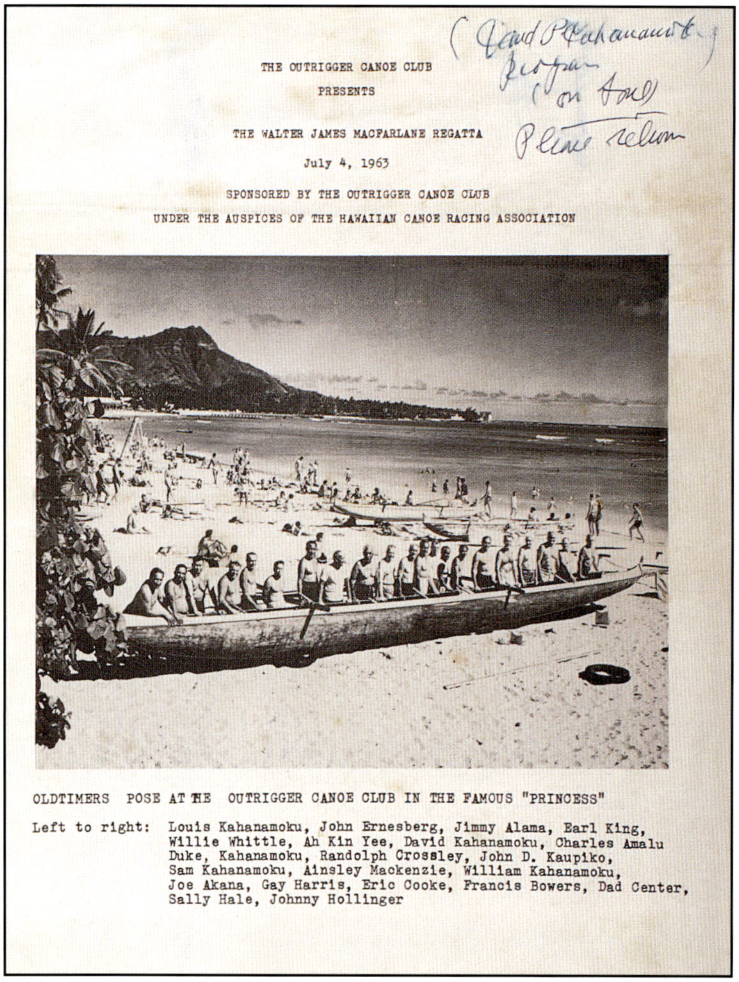

THE OUTRIGGER CANOE CLUB
PRESENTS

THE WALTER JAMES MACFARLANE REGATTA

July 4, 1963

SPONSORED BY THE OUTRIGGER CANOE CLUB
UNDER THE AUSPICES OF THE HAWAIIAN CANOE RACING ASSOCIATION

OLDTIMERS POSE AT THE OUTRIGGER CANOE CLUB IN THE FAMOUS "PRINCESS"

Left to right: Louis Kahanamoku, John Ernesberg, Jimmy Alama, Earl King, Willie Whittle, Ah Kin Yee, David Kahanamoku, Charles Amalu Duke, Kahanamoku, Randolph Crossley, John D. Kaupiko, Sam Kahanamoku, Ainsley Mackenzie, William Kahanamoku, Joe Akana, Gay Harris, Eric Cooke, Francis Bowers, Dad Center, Sally Hale, Johnny Hollinger

The Walter James MacFarlane Regatta, July 4, 1963, Souvenir Program. Sponsored by the Outrigger Canoe Club under the auspices of the Hawaiian Canoe Racing Association. A rare item featuring surfing old-timers in front of the famous canoe "The Princess." This program is autographed by David Kahanamoku. Mauna Kea Galleries, Kamuela, Hawaii. As shown: $300-500. Average: $150-250

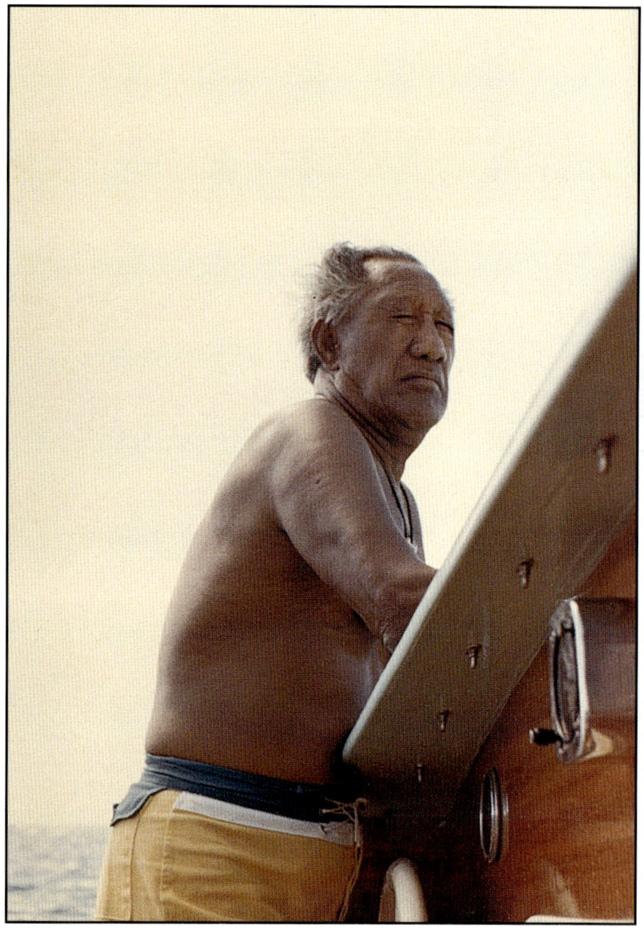

Original Photograph of David Kahanamoku on his boat. Circa 1960s. Mauna Kea Galleries, Kamuela, Hawaii. $80-120

Pan Am Promotional Flyer. Circa 1960s. *Duke Kahanamoku with the officers of the world famous Duke Kahanamoku Surf Club, International Market Place, Waikiki Beach, Hawaii.*
From left to right: Paul Strauch, Jr., Joey Cabell, The Duke, Fred Hemmings, and Butch Van Artsdalen. Mauna Kea Galleries, Kamuela, Hawaii. $120-180

Duke Kahanamoku Best All-Around Surfer Award, United States Surfboard Championships, Huntington Beach, California. Won in 1965 by Mike Doyle. Ed and Randi Economy Collection. $1,800-2,400

Ricky Grigg's Passport for The Duke Contest, 1967. Ed and Randi Economy Collection. $600-900

Duke Invitational Surfing Championship Trophy. Presented in 1968 to Charlie Galanto in Hawaii. Ed and Randi Economy Collection. $1,200-1,800

Duke Kahanamoku Best All-Around Surfer Award, United States Surfboard Championships, Huntington Beach, California. Won in 1966 by Corky Carroll. Ed and Randi Economy Collection. $1,800-2,400

Patch from the contest. Ed and Randi Economy Collection. $80-120

Author, at left, with **Corky Carroll** today.

Duke Kahanamoku, 9'8". Multi-stringer, redwood and balsa pop out model with outstanding wood fin. Circa 1965. Produced by Harold "Hap" Jacobs. Mauna Kea Galleries, Kamuela, Hawaii. As shown $2,000-3,000

"In Hawaii we greet friends, loved ones and strangers alike, with Aloha, which means love. Aloha is the key word to the universal spirit of real hospitality, which makes Hawaii renowned as the world's center of understanding and fellowship. Try meeting or leaving people with Aloha. You'll be surprised by their reaction. I believe it and it is my creed.

Aloha to you.

Duke Paoa Kahanamoku"

Original Photograph of Duke Kahanamoku. Circa 1963. A photo showing a relaxed Duke judging the Huntington Beach surf contest. Ed and Randi Economy Collection. $80-120

***International Surfing* Magazine, August/September 1966.** Special collectors issue with Duke Kahanamoku cover. Considered the most desirable of this magazine's short run. Mauna Kea Galleries, Kamuela, Hawaii. $200-300

Prices listed below for the following issues of this magazine:

1964- Volume 1. No. 1.: $150-250

1965- All issues: $80-120

1966- All issues from this year were produced in an oversized format: $150-250

1967- 1969 - All issues: $40-60

Blown Out When very high winds misshape the waves and make them virtually unrideable.

South Coast Surfboards, San Diego, California, 10'6". Five stringer, foam with redwood and balsa, circa 1965. Extremely high-density foam used in its construction. Peter and Cathy Noble, Monterey, California. $800-1,200

Foam Blank Gordon "Grubby" Clark is the person most responsible for perfecting the basic block of foam from which a surfboard is shaped.

Cat on a Hot Foam Board. A Bud Browne film, circa 1959. Mauna Kea Galleries, Kamuela, Hawaii. $200-300

Promotional Flyer for JJ Moon Competition Surf Team. Circa mid-1960s. Courtesy of Buck Labadie/Artstuff. $250-350

JJ Moon Competition Surf Team Decal. Peter and Cathy Noble, Monterey, California. $100-150

Holden Surfboards, Long Beach, California, 9'4". Wide t-bar stringer, foam with balsa, circa 1962. Unusual caricature graphics that were influenced by the Casper the Friendly Ghost cartoon series. Peter and Cathy Noble, Monterey, California. $800-1,200

Barney A poor surfer, derived from the cartoon character Barney Rubble.

Face Plant A wipeout term with its origin in skateboarding.

Pacific Beach Surf Shop. Peter and Cathy Noble, Monterey, California. $60-90

Egg Roll A derogatory 1960s term referring to a novice.

Decals

Wipe Out. Peter and Cathy Noble, Monterey, California. $10-20

Surf Shoppe, Huntington Beach. Peter and Cathy Noble, Monterey, California. $150-250

Surfer Boy, Sea Cross, Burbank. Peter and Cathy Noble, Monterey, California. $120-180

Pray for Surf. Peter and Cathy Noble, Monterey, California. $100-150

"I'm stoked – I've been to Jack's Surf Shop in Huntington Beach!" Peter and Cathy Noble, Monterey, California. $150-250

Hansen Surf Shop — Founded in 1961 by Don Hansen in Cardiff, California. He used Clark Foam exclusively in all his designs and was well known for his beautiful wood tail blocks and stringers. An avid surfer himself, Don was well known as a great tandem surfer. His first signature board was the Mike Doyle model, which had two versions: a pintail and a square tail; both were very popular. His most successful model was his 50/50, which was his concept for both noseriding and maneuverability. This model sold in huge numbers. Hansen had numerous dealers on the East Coast and Texas along with Surfline in Hawaii. Among some of his other famous team riders were Mike Doyle, Rusty Miller and Dickey Moon.

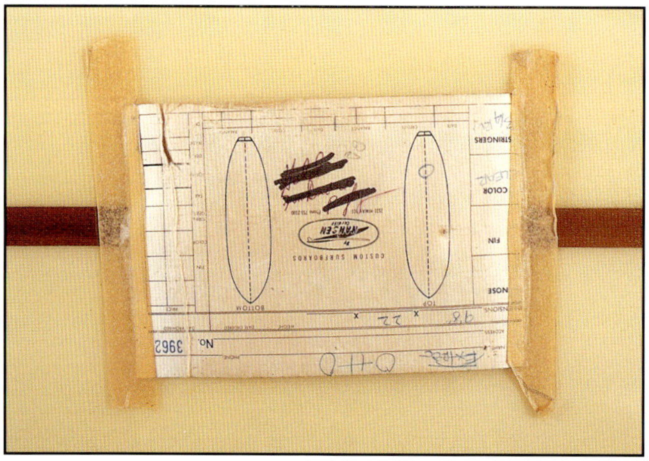

Hansen-Cardiff, 9'8". Single stringer board, foam with redwood. Rare mint condition board with original work order attached. Peter and Cathy Noble, Monterey, California. As shown: $2,500-3,500. Average condition: $600-900

Vintage Advertisement. Mauna Kea Galleries, Kamuela, Hawaii.

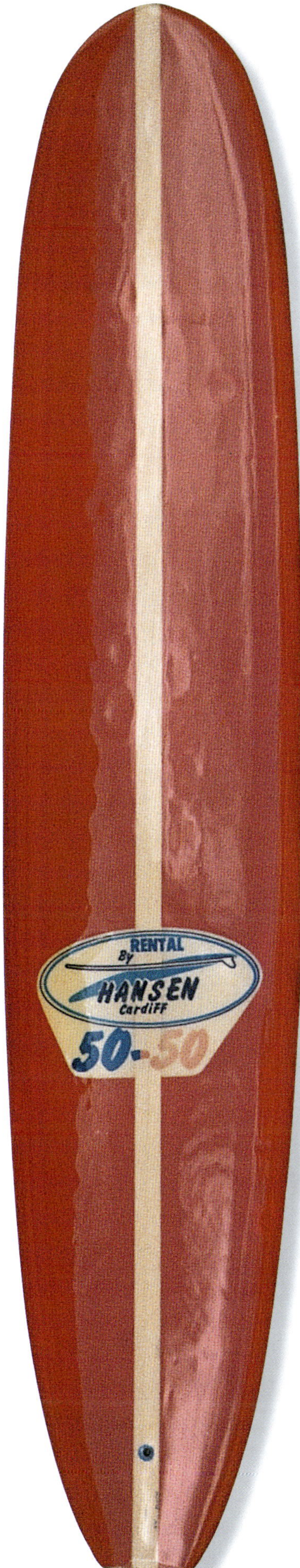

Fifty-Fifty Rental by Hansen - Cardiff, 9'10". Wide single stringer, foam with balsa, circa 1963. A great example of a board that was produced in large numbers for the rental market. Courtesy of Mark and Cindy Fragale. As shown: $1,200-1,800. Average: $500-700

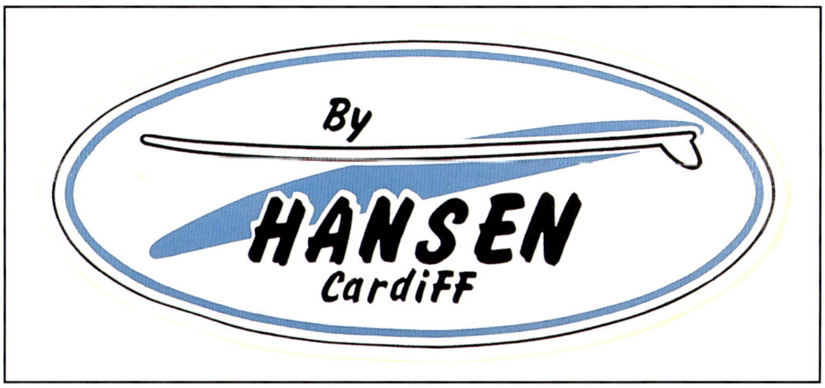

By Hansen-Cardiff Decal. Peter and Cathy Noble, Monterey, California. $60-90

Point Break A surf area where the waves wrap around a point or promontory and peel as they break.

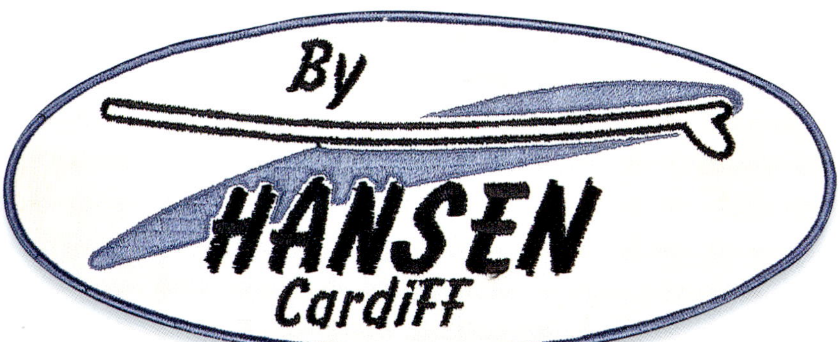

By Hansen - Cardiff Patch. Peter and Cathy Noble, Monterey, California. $15-25

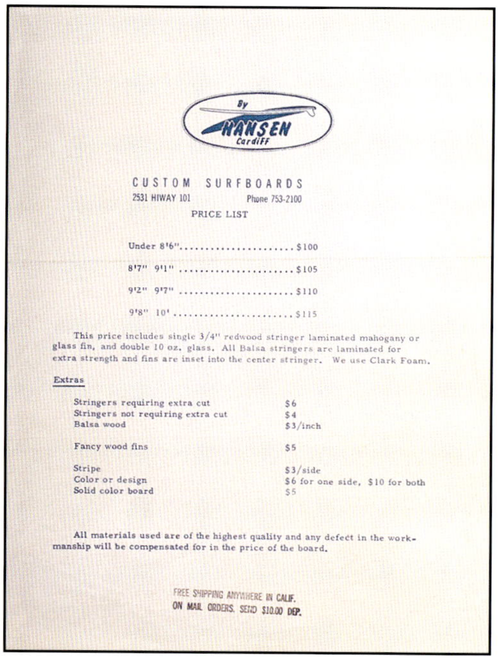

By HANSEN Cardiff

CUSTOM SURFBOARDS
2531 HIWAY 101 Phone 753-2100

PRICE LIST

Under 8'6"....................... $100

8'7" 9'1" $105

9'2" 9'7" $110

9'8" 10' $115

This price includes single 3/4" redwood stringer laminated mahogany or glass fin, and double 10 oz. glass. All Balsa stringers are laminated for extra strength and fins are inset into the center stringer. We use Clark Foam.

Extras

Stringers requiring extra cut	$6
Stringers not requiring extra cut	$4
Balsa wood	$3/inch
Fancy wood fins	$5
Stripe	$3/side
Color or design	$6 for one side, $10 for both
Solid color board	$5

All materials used are of the highest quality and any defect in the workmanship will be compensated for in the price of the board.

FREE SHIPPING ANYWHERE IN CALIF.
ON MAIL ORDERS. SEND $10.00 DEP.

Hansen - Cardiff Custom Surfboards, Cardiff, California, Price List. Circa early 1960s. Mauna Kea Galleries, Kamuela, Hawaii. $100-150

By Hansen, Patch. Peter and Cathy Noble, Monterey, California. $10-15

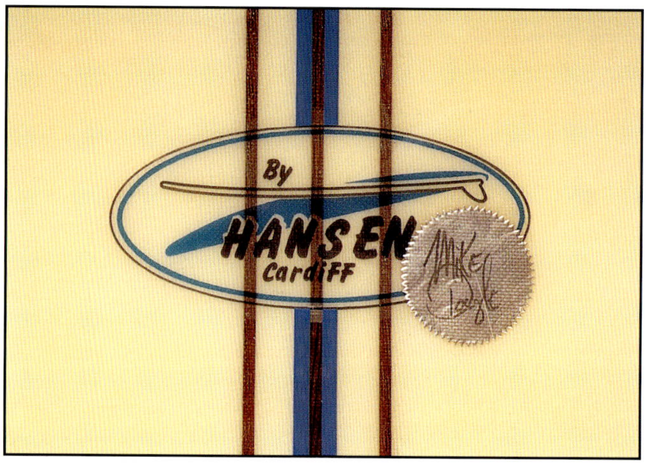

Hansen-Cardiff, California, 9'6". Three stringer, foam with redwood, circa 1967. Original cost new was $168. Spencer and Annette Croul Collection. As shown $1,200-1,800. Average $600-900

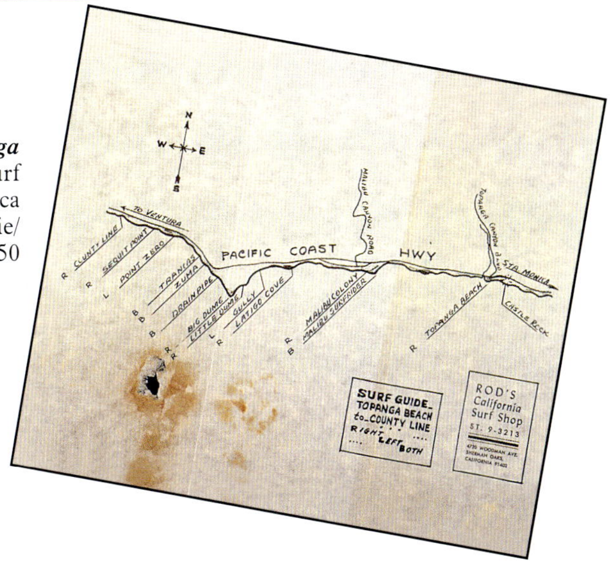

Promotional *Surf Guide to Topanga Beach*. Issued by Rod's California Surf Shop, Sherman Oaks, California, circa late 1960s. Courtesy of Buck Labadie/ Artstuff. $30-50

By Hansen, Decal. Peter and Cathy Noble, Monterey, California. $40-60

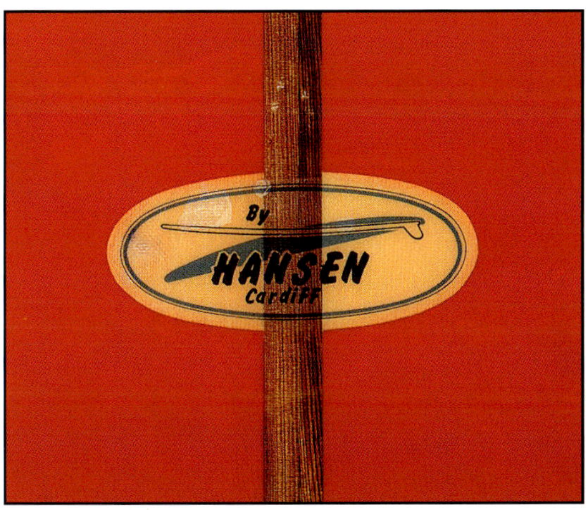

Hansen Surfboards, 10'11". Wide single stringer, big wave gun, foam with redwood, circa 1967. Mike Doyle's personal board. A unique piece of big wave surfing history. Ed and Randi Economy Collection. As shown: $8,000-12,000. Average: $4,000-6,000

Bruce Brown Films Catalog. Circa 1960s. Mauna Kea Galleries, Kamuela, Hawaii. $150-250

Water Logged. A Bruce Brown film, circa 1963. Mauna Kea Galleries, Kamuela, Hawaii. $200-300

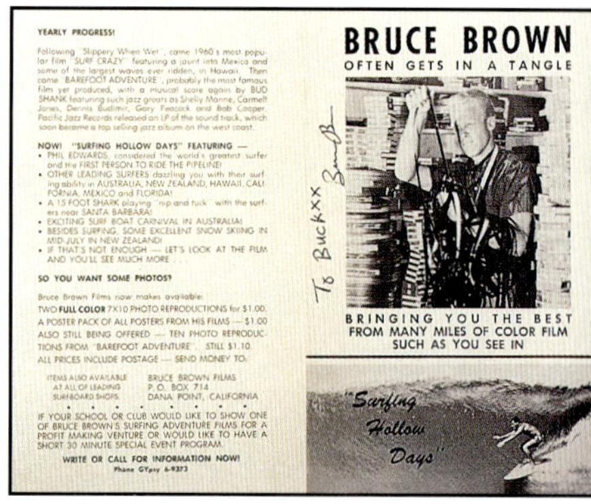

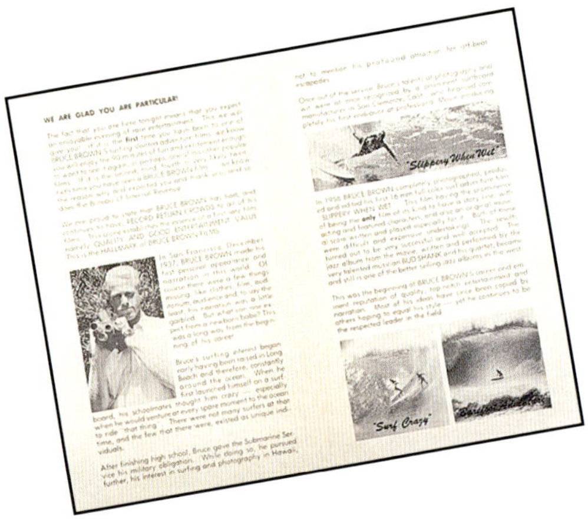

Promotional Flyer for Bruce Brown Films. Circa 1962. Courtesy of Buck Labadie/Artstuff. As shown: $150-250. Average: $100-150

Promotional Postcard for *Surfing Hollow Days*. A Bruce Brown film, circa 1962. Courtesy of Buck Labadie/Artstuff. As shown: $80-120. Average: $40-60

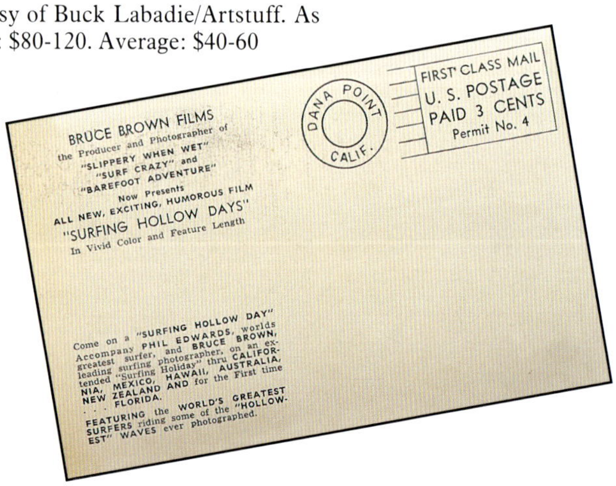

***Slippery When Wet* and *Surf Crazy* Admission Ticket Stub.** A Bruce Brown film, circa 1961. Courtesy of Buck Labadie/Artstuff. $30-50

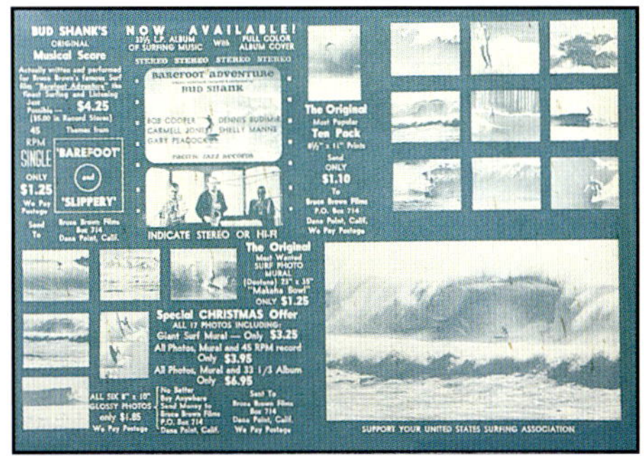

***Surfing Hollow Days*.** A Bruce Brown film, circa 1962. Mauna Kea Galleries, Kamuela, Hawaii. $200-300

Promotional Holiday Postcard for Bruce Brown Films. Circa 1961. Courtesy of Buck Labadie/Artstuff. $80-120

Bumpy Very choppy water, usually due to wind or a change in the tide.

Hickey Custom Surfboards, San Francisco, 9'10". Five stringer, foam with redwood and balsa, circa 1966. Bold, knifey rails, this board was glassed by Jack O'Neill. Peter and Cathy Noble, Monterey, California. $600-900

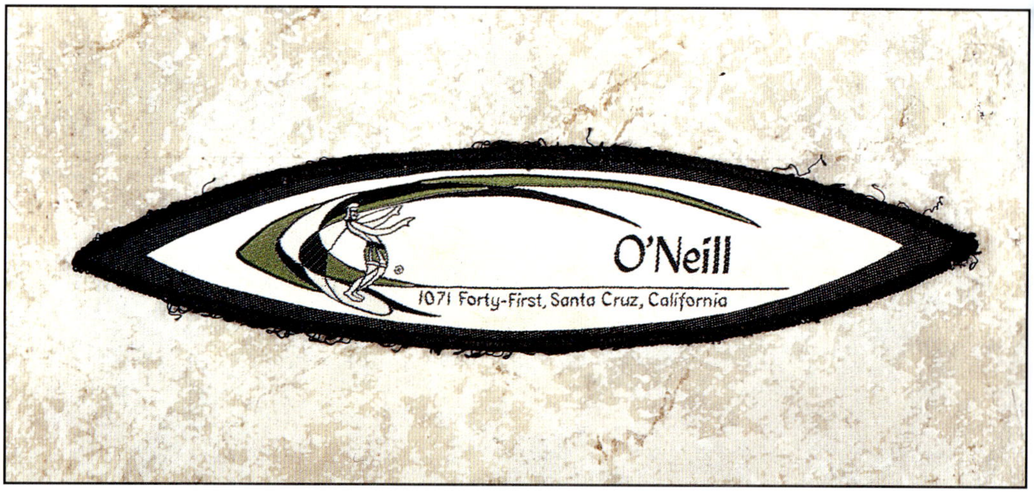

O'Neill, Santa Cruz Patch. Peter and Cathy Noble, Monterey, California. $30-50

O'Neill's Surf Shop, Santa Cruz, California, 9'6". Three stringer, foam with redwood and balsa, circa 1965. This stock surfboard was $145 when new. At this point in O'Neill's career he was blowing his own foam cores. He later went back to Clark Foam. Peter and Cathy Noble, Monterey, California. $600-900

Tubed The much-sought-after act of riding inside the hollow section of the wave. Often referred to as "being barreled."

O'Neill's Surf Shop, Santa Cruz, California, Decal. Blue design. Peter and Cathy Noble, Monterey, California. $80-120

O'Neill's Surf Shop, San Francisco-Santa Cruz, California, Decal. Green design. Peter and Cathy Noble, Monterey, California. $60-90

O'Neill, Santa Cruz, California, Decal. Peter and Cathy Noble, Monterey, California. $80-120

O'Neill's Surf Shop, Santa Cruz, California, Decal. Black design. Peter and Cathy Noble, Monterey, California. $60-90

George Downing, 10'6". Wide single stringer, big wave gun, foam with redwood, circa 1960. This historic board is one of ten shaped by big wave surfer George Downing and was his personal board. Stripes on fin were used to identify boards that went out to sea as these were pre-leash days. This was a common occurrence at Sunset Beach in the early 1960s. Ed and Randi Economy Collection. $12,000-18,000

Pipeline. A Bruce Gibson film, circa 1963. Mauna Kea Galleries, Kamuela, Hawaii. $100-150

North Shore The famous Hawaiian surf spots of Haleiwa, Waimea, Pupukea, Pipeline and Sunset on the island of Oahu.

Pipeline. A Walt Phillips film featuring the best of *Once Upon a Wave* and *Ride on the Wild Side*, circa 1964. Mauna Kea Galleries, Kamuela, Hawaii. $150-250

O'Neill, Santa Cruz, Intruder, 10'2". Three stringer, foam with redwood, circa mid-1960s. Allan Seymour, Pacific Coast Vintage Surf Auctions. $800-1,200

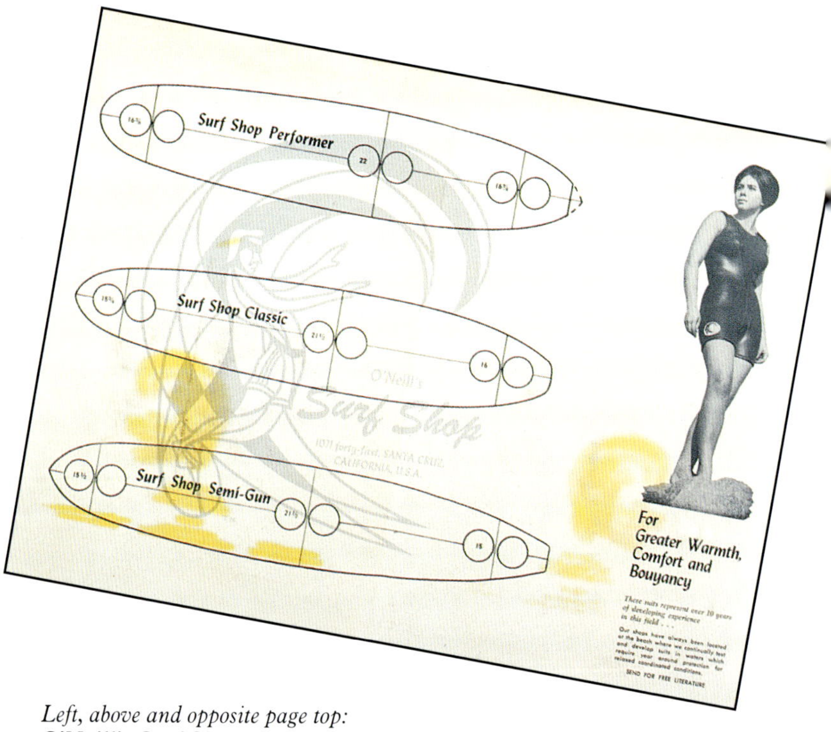

Left, above and opposite page top:
O'Neill's Surf Shop, Santa Cruz, California, Price List. Circa mid-1960s. Peter and Cathy Noble, Monterey, California. $150-250

Surf Wax

A mainstay of modern surfing. The actual story of how wax evolved is an interesting one and was related by Alfred Gallant - who appears to be the first person ever to have used wax on a board - in a letter to the editor in the March/April 1999 issue of *Longboard Magazine*. Following is an excerpt:

In 1935 I started surfing at Palos Verdes Cove. In those days we made our own surfboards. We made them 11' or 12' long, of redwood or red cedar and varnished them spreading sand on the top when the varnish was still wet so that our feet wouldn't slip.

One night I came home from the Cove and walked across the living room floor and my feet would almost stick on the wooden floors. My mother had waxed the floors with liquid wax.

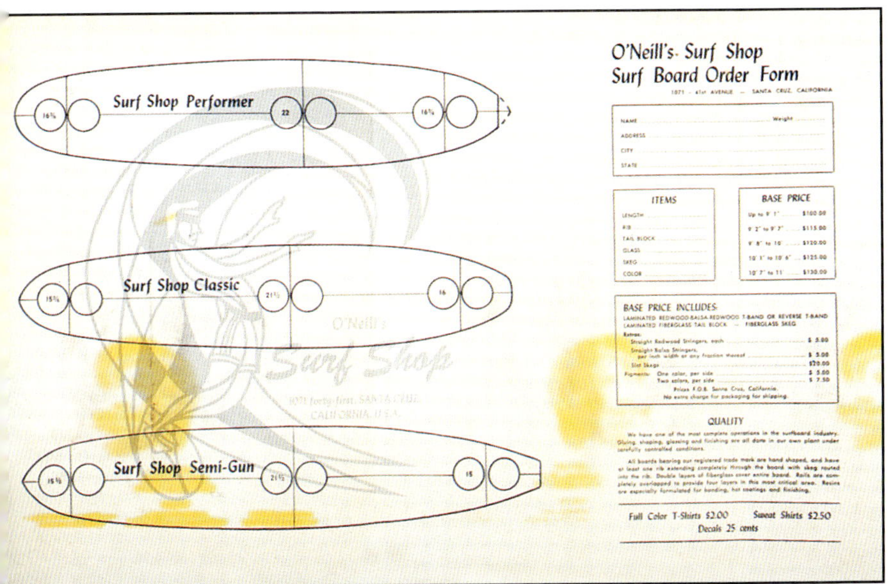

When I left to go to the Cove the next morning, I took the bottle of wax and put it on my board. When surfing, my feet just almost stuck on the board. It worked fine.

When I got home that night my mother was screaming at me. She said, "Where's the floor wax?" I told her we put it on the surfboards so our feet wouldn't slip on the board. Then mom said, "Use the stuff we use on the top of the jam jars." When my mom made the jam she would melt the wax and put it on top of the jam in the jars to preserve it. It acted like a cover so the jam wouldn't get sour. It was paraffin.

The next day I took the wax (paraffin) and put it on my board and all the other guys boards. That's how it started. We then removed the sand and re-varnished the boards so the sand would be gone and the wax was there.

In those days we were kneeling on the boards when paddling out. Our knees would get sore and sometimes bleed. With the wax on the board, the bleeding didn't happen. My knees show little bumps where the bleeding took place.

My surfing buddies were among: John H. (Doc) Ball, Leroy Grannis, Fenton Scholes and Bud Morrissey. In those days there were only about fifty surfers in Southern California. Our surfing places included Malibu, Hermosa Beach, Redondo Beach, the entrance to Newport Harbor, San Onofre, and other spots. The boards in those days weighed about 125 pounds.

That was how waxing on the boards got started.

Vintage Advertisement. Mauna Kea Galleries, Kamuela, Hawaii.

Surf Mania. A Walt Phillips film, circa 1960. Mauna Kea Galleries, Kamuela, Hawaii. $150-250

Promotional Flyer for Walt Phillips Productions. Circa early 1960s. This promotional flyer has a vast array of products from surf posters costing 10 cents to professionally shot 8mm rolls of film depicting surfing for $5.98. Courtesy of Buck Labadie/ Artstuff. $200-300

Walt Phillips Productions, Hermosa Beach, California. Walt Phillips' personal card, circa early 1960s. Courtesy of Buck Labadie/Artstuff. $100-150

Walt Phillips Productions. Film company decal. Peter and Cathy Noble, Monterey, California. $100-150

Banzai! A holdover Japanese term from World War II used by surfers as a yell when they shoot the curl.

Surf Dance. A summer film festival of Grant Rohloff films, including *Surfing Wild*, *North Swell* and *Out of Control*, featuring the music of the Pharoahs, circa 1964. Mauna Kea Galleries, Kamuela, Hawaii. $200-300

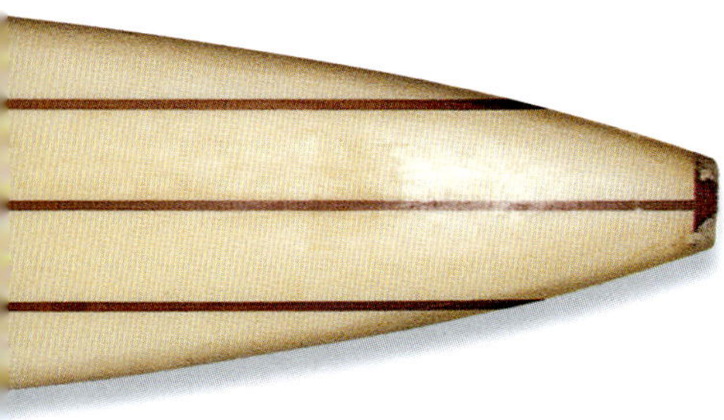

Pat Curren, Newport Beach, 11'8". Three stringer, big wave gun, foam with redwood, circa 1960. This Waimea gun belonged to Dr. Jim Bleautu, who surfed 30'-40' waves with it in Hawaii. According to Jim, it was the ultimate surfboard. His main concern was to get out of the way after the drop! Jim took the board to San Francisco in the early 1960s while attending medical school, where it was rarely used. The board was then stored for 30 years. Many shapers today attribute the hard rail on the tail to modern shaping, however, it was a standard feature on the guns of the 1960s. Today, big wave guns are achieving cult status among collectors because they are so rare. Peter and Cathy Noble, Monterey, California. As shown: $6,000-9,000. Average: $2,500-3,500

Surfboards by Yount, Santa Cruz, Decal. Peter and Cathy Noble, Monterey, California. $80-120

Surfboards by Yount, Santa Cruz, 10'0". Single stringer, foam with redwood, circa 1964. This board was produced for about three years. Peter and Cathy Noble, Monterey, California. $600-900

The Living Curl. A Jamie Budge film, circa mid-1960s. Mauna Kea Galleries, Kamuela, Hawaii. $200-300

So-Cal Surfing News. Published by Gordon Bright for one year only in 1963.

Vol. 1, No. 1	$200-300
Vol. 1, No. 2	$150-250
Vol. 1, No. 3	$150-250

Surf Hi-Lights – '59 & '60 *Surf Safari* and *Surf Fever*. A John Severson film, circa 1960. A great image showing Mickey Munoz doing the Quasimoto, a hot dog riding stance that he invented. This stance is performed by riding on the nose of the board in a crouched, hunchback position, with one arm stretched forward and the other stretched to the rear. The term derives from the character Quasimodo, the hunchback of the title of Victor Hugo's novel *The Hunchback of Notre Dame.* Mauna Kea Galleries, Kamuela, Hawaii. $300-500

United States Surfing Association Patch. Peter and Cathy Noble, Monterey, California. $25-35

United States Surfing Association, 1964, Decal. Peter and Cathy Noble, Monterey, California. $60-90

United States Surfing Association, 1966, Decal. Peter and Cathy Noble, Monterey, California. $60-90

Surfboards Miami, Adventurers Dive and Surf, 9'8". Five stringer with unusual s-shaped offset stringer, foam with redwood and balsa, circa mid-1960s. Unusual use of a surfboard. Allan Seymour, Pacific Coast Vintage Surf Auctions. $600-900

Bottom Turn A classic turning maneuver used after the rider has made the drop and turns back onto the face of the wave.

Walk on the Wet Side. A Dale Davis film, circa 1963. Mauna Kea Galleries, Kamuela, Hawaii. $150-250

Strictly Hot. A Dale Davis film, circa 1964. Mauna Kea Galleries, Kamuela, Hawaii. $150-250

Out of Control. A Grant Rohloff film, circa 1962. Mauna Kea Galleries, Kamuela, Hawaii. $150-250

Chuck Dent Surfboards, Seal Beach, California, 10'2". Three stringer, foam with redwood, circa early 1960s. Hoffman Collection. $600-900

Vintage Advertisement. Mauna Kea Galleries, Kamuela, Hawaii.

Vintage Advertisement. Mauna Kea Galleries, Kamuela, Hawaii.

Los Angeles Surf Fair Sponsored by KRLA Radio and Surf Guide Magazine. Circa 1963. Mauna Kea Galleries, Kamuela, Hawaii. $100-150

Con Surfboards – Founded by Con Colburn in Santa Monica, California, in 1959, the mainstay of his early business was repairing old boards; he later switched to producing boards using Clark foam and 10-ounce cloth. He is credited with being one of the first to put stringers and tail blocks into high-density Clark foam. He produced several types of boards, but his most famous signature model was his C.C. model. He also experimented with a substance sold under the name of Con-Trol, which was sprayed on the board to prevent slipping. In 1959, he is credited with introducing the first noserider model ever produced in a joint effort with George Bartell.

Surf House, Santa Monica, California, Decal. Con logo. Peter and Cathy Noble, Monterey, California. $60-90

Con Surf Boards. 8x10 promotional glossy. Peter and Cathy Noble, Monterey, California. $40-60

Surf Boards by Con, 9'10". Serial number 583, circa 1963. Purchased from the Con store in Santa Monica, California. It was stored until 1987, when it was removed from the box. Mint and never ridden. Wide t-bar stringer, foam with balsa. Peter and Cathy Noble, Monterey, California. As shown: $3,000-5,000. Average: $600-900

Shaper A person who shapes the foam blanks into surfboards.

Con Competition Team T-shirt. Mid-1960s. Peter and Cathy Noble, Monterey, California. $40-60

Con Surf Boards Patch. Peter and Cathy Noble, Monterey, California. $15-25

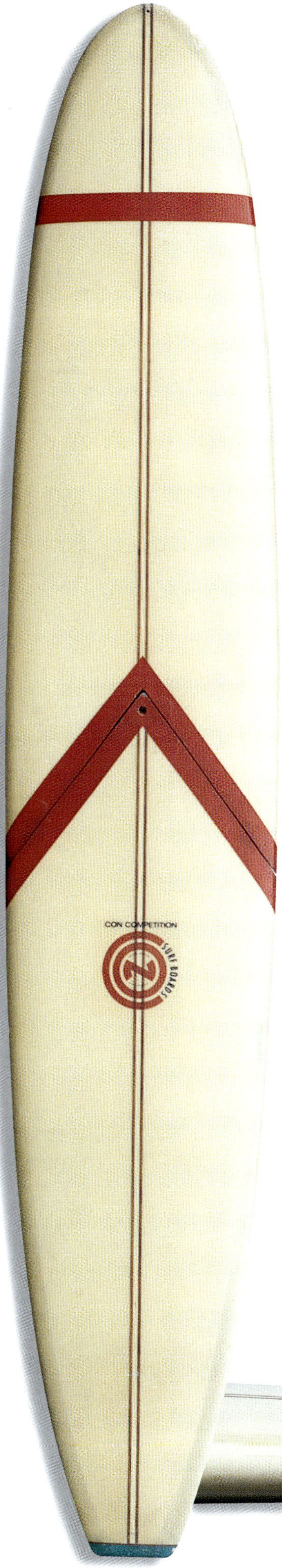

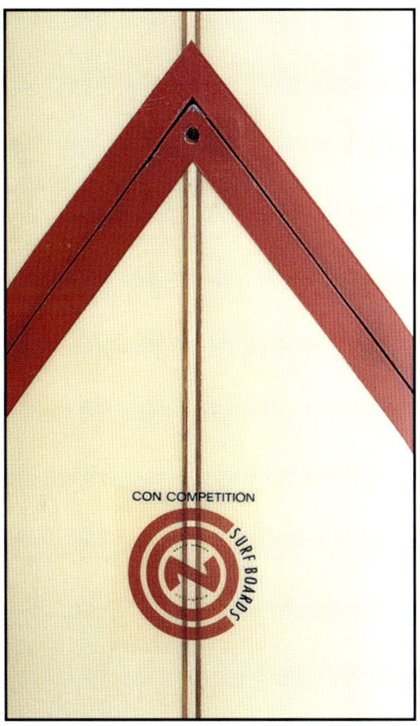

Con Surf Boards, Santa Monica, California, 9'6". Three stringer, high-density foam with redwood and balsa, circa 1966. This is one of 12 surfboards Con Colburn produced as a multi board, a two-part board held together by two pins. The board was finished down to the gloss coat, then put into a special jig to be cut in half in a wedge configuration. A resin mold was used to form the joining surfaces (a male/female groove setup). When the joining surfaces were finished, the board was gloss coated. Con used this board as a demo board, and there are photos of Mike Ballard surfing with it at Topanga Canyon. Multi Board was based in Pasadena, California, and the other manufacturers who tried the Multi Board concept were: Hobie, which produced about two dozen; Gordon & Smith, believed to have made two; and Con. The concept was to be able to put the board in the front seat of a VW, but the idea didn't sell, although, according to Con, the board surfed very well. Peter and Cathy Noble, Monterey, California. As shown: $3,500-4,500. Average: $2,000-3,000

Con Surf Boards, Santa Monica, California. Con Colburn's personal card. Peter and Cathy Noble, Monterey, California. $60-90

Vintage Advertisement. Mauna Kea Galleries, Kamuela, Hawaii.

Surf House, Surf Boards by Con, Santa Monica, California, Business Card. Peter and Cathy Noble, Monterey, California. $40-60

Con Surfboards Patch. Peter and Cathy Noble, Monterey, California. $15-25

Con Surf Boards, Santa Monica, California, Decal. Peter and Cathy Noble, Monterey, California. $60-90

Surfboards, Santa Monica, California, Decal. An unusual Con working prototype with handwritten notes to printer in margins. Peter and Cathy Noble, Monterey, California. $200-300

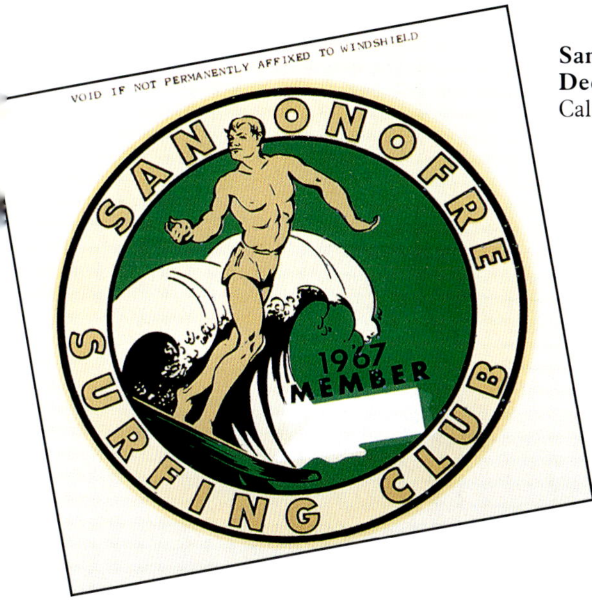

San Onofre Surfing Club 1967 Member Decal. Peter and Cathy Noble, Monterey, California. $60-90

Wind & Sea Surfboards Decal. Peter and Cathy Noble, Monterey, California. $40-60

Woody – A&W Root Beer Company, Santa Monica, California. Restaurant premium. Peter and Cathy Noble, Monterey, California. $60-90

***Car Craft*, July 1963.** Special Woody edition. Courtesy of Buck Labadie/Artstuff. $80-120

Bruce Brown's Personal San Onofre Surfing Club Membership Card and Decal, 1975. An unusual grouping of items. Mauna Kea Galleries, Kamuela, Hawaii. $200-300

Weber Surfboards – Without a doubt, the most famous and recognizable surfing figure in the 1960s, he opened his first shop in Venice, California, in 1960. He is credited with having produced the most popular surfboards of all time: The Feather, The Performer and The Stylist. At one time, among his team riders were Nat Young, David Nuuhiwa and Donald Takayama.

Surf Boards by Dewey Weber Business Card. Courtesy of Buck Labadie/Artstuff. $40-60

Surf Boards by Dewey Weber, 9'8". Three stringer, foam with balsa and redwood, circa early 1960s. Allan Seymour, Pacific Coast Vintage Surf Auctions. $600-900

Dewie Weber Surfboards Grand Opening Advertising Flyer. Two-sided flyer featuring photographs of Donald Takayama, Dewie Weber and Harold Iggy, circa early 1960s. Courtesy of Buck Labadie/Artstuff. $300-500

Surf Boards by Dewey Weber Decal. Peter and Cathy Noble, Monterey, California. $60-90

Weber Feather Decal. Peter and Cathy Noble, Monterey, California. $60-90

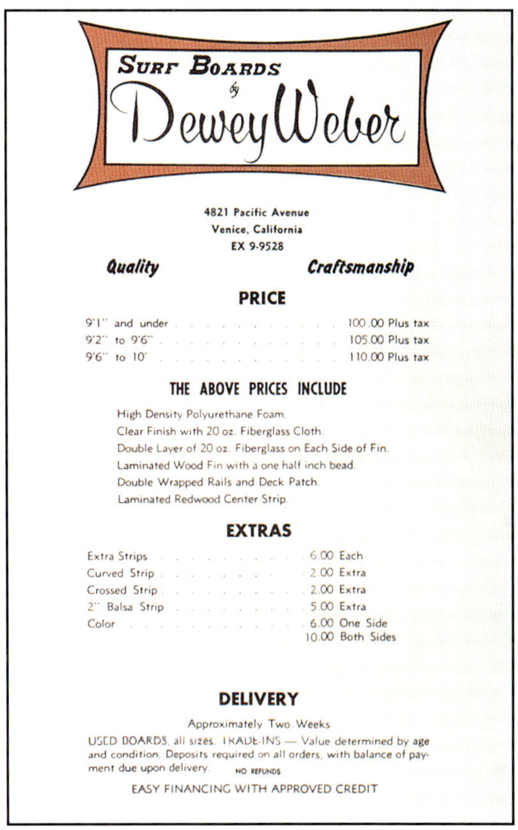

SURF BOARDS
by
Dewey Weber

4821 Pacific Avenue
Venice, California
EX 9-9528

Quality Craftsmanship

PRICE

9'1" and under	100.00 Plus tax
9'2" to 9'6"	105.00 Plus tax
9'6" to 10'	110.00 Plus tax

THE ABOVE PRICES INCLUDE

High Density Polyurethane Foam.
Clear Finish with 20 oz. Fiberglass Cloth.
Double Layer of 20 oz. Fiberglass on Each Side of Fin.
Laminated Wood Fin with a one half inch bead.
Double Wrapped Rails and Deck Patch.
Laminated Redwood Center Strip.

EXTRAS

Extra Strips	6.00 Each
Curved Strip	2.00 Extra
Crossed Strip	2.00 Extra
2" Balsa Strip	5.00 Extra
Color	6.00 One Side 10.00 Both Sides

DELIVERY

Approximately Two Weeks
USED BOARDS, all sizes. TRADE-INS — Value determined by age and condition. Deposits required on all orders, with balance of payment due upon delivery. NO REFUNDS
EASY FINANCING WITH APPROVED CREDIT

Surf Boards by Dewey Weber, Venice, California, Price List. Circa early 1960s. Courtesy of Buck Labadie/Artstuff. $100-150

Weber Performer – Over 4,000 boards were made by Dewey Weber in 1966, and this model forever changed the way surfboards were marketed, thanks to his skills in promotion. A wide and thin board with a full nose, the key success and selling point was the "turn fin," which today is referred to as a hatchet fin.

Vintage Advertisement. Mauna Kea Galleries, Kamuela, Hawaii.

Weber Performer, 9'10". Single stringer, foam with redwood, circa 1966, with hatchet fin. The Weber Performer was dubbed the "Potato Chip" because it was thin and wide. Peter and Cathy Noble, Monterey, California. $1,200-1,800

Hang Five To ride so far forward on the nose of the board that the toes of one foot hang over the front end.

Weberperformer Decal. Peter and Cathy Noble, Monterey, California. $50-70

Vintage advertisement. Mauna Kea Galleries, Kamuela, Hawaii.

Weber Performer, 10'2". T-band three stringer, foam with balsa and redwood, Wonderbolt hatchet fin, circa 1967. Allan Seymour, Pacific Coast Vintage Surf Auctions. $2,000-3,000

Surf Boards by Dewey Weber, 11'1". Three stringer, big wave gun, foam with balsa and redwood, checkerboard balsa and redwood fin, circa 1964-65. This was Flippy Hoffman's personal board used at Makaha. Hoffman Collection. As shown: $6,000-9,000. Average: $3,000-5,000

Dropping In A dreaded condition occurring when an discourteous surfer takes off on a breaking wave in front of a surfer already launched, thus refusing to give the right-of-way to the surfer already on the wave.

1966 Hawaiian Surfing Guide **Magazine, Volume 1 No. 1, December, 1965.** Published by Red Dot Publishing Co. in Honolulu, this short-lived production attempted to feature Hawaiian surfing, showing maps of the various surf spots and promoting the Makaha contest. Mauna Kea Galleries, Kamuela, Hawaii. $200-300

Classic Quality and Performance

SURF BOARDS
BY
LARRY FELKER

21050 Ventura Blvd.
Woodland Hills, Calif.

Phone
340-4555

QUALITY–PERFORMANCE

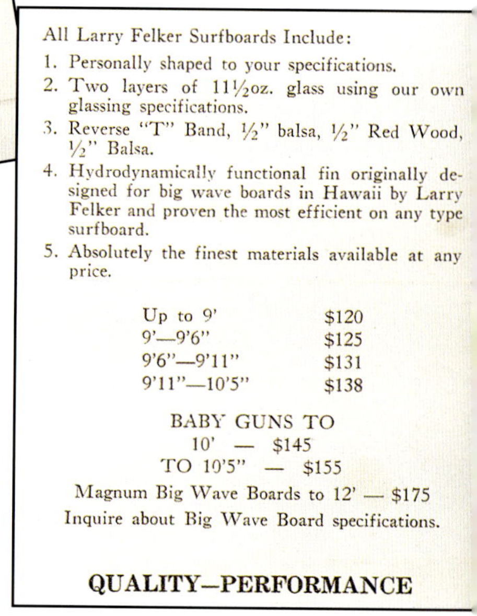
All Larry Felker Surfboards Include:

1. Personally shaped to your specifications.
2. Two layers of 11½oz. glass using our own glassing specifications.
3. Reverse "T" Band, ½" balsa, ½" Red Wood, ½" Balsa.
4. Hydrodynamically functional fin originally designed for big wave boards in Hawaii by Larry Felker and proven the most efficient on any type surfboard.
5. Absolutely the finest materials available at any price.

Up to 9'	$120
9'—9'6"	$125
9'6"—9'11"	$131
9'11"—10'5"	$138

BABY GUNS TO
10' — $145
TO 10'5" — $155

Magnum Big Wave Boards to 12' — $175

Inquire about Big Wave Board specifications.

QUALITY–PERFORMANCE

Surf Boards by Larry Felker, Woodland Hills, California. Folding price list business card. Rare. Peter and Cathy Noble, Monterey, California. $100-150

Larry Felker, Hermosa Beach, 10'6". Three stringer, big wave gun, foam with redwood, circa 1963. Larry Felker was considered to be one of the best shapers around by top surfers at Malibu. This board was originally shaped for movie maker Hal Jepsen. Ed and Randi Economy Collection. As shown: $6,000-9,000. Average: $3,000-5,000

Made for 8' and up, I've got memories. I've ridden big waves on it at Malibu, Rincon, Cojo and Steamer Lane in California. I took it to Hawaii twice, 1963 and 1964, and rode Makaha, Laniakea, Pipeline and Sunset. I've tried it on smaller waves, but it really doesn't work except to go fast down the line. It's hard to turn unless there's major juice. Hal Jepsen, 1994

Grommet A 1960s Australian term for a young surfer. Synonymous with "Gremmie."

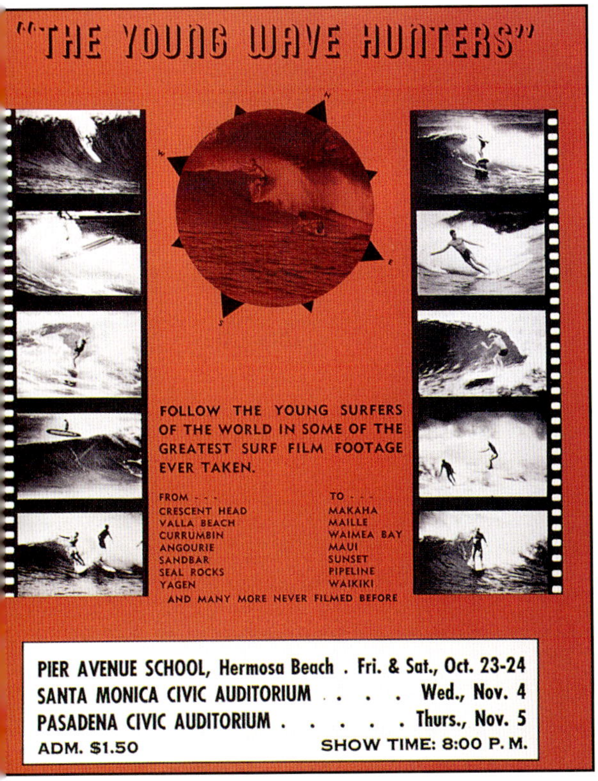

The Young Wave Hunters. A Bob Evans film shot in both Australia and Hawaii, circa 1964. Mauna Kea Galleries, Kamuela, Hawaii. $150-250

Australian Surf Shop Decal. Peter and Cathy Noble, Monterey, California. $40-60

Foamie An Australian term used for surfboards made of foam.

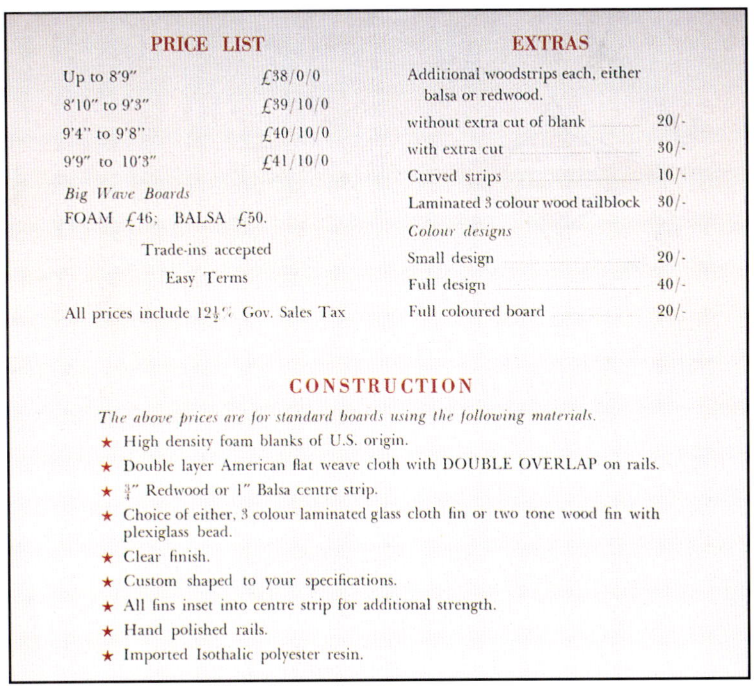

PRICE LIST

Up to 8'9"	£38/0/0
8'10" to 9'3"	£39/10/0
9'4" to 9'8"	£40/10/0
9'9" to 10'3"	£41/10/0

Big Wave Boards
FOAM £46; BALSA £50.

Trade-ins accepted
Easy Terms

All prices include 12½% Gov. Sales Tax

EXTRAS

Additional woodstrips each, either balsa or redwood.	
without extra cut of blank	20/-
with extra cut	30/-
Curved strips	10/-
Laminated 3 colour wood tailblock	30/-
Colour designs	
Small design	20/-
Full design	40/-
Full coloured board	20/-

CONSTRUCTION

The above prices are for standard boards using the following materials.

★ High density foam blanks of U.S. origin.
★ Double layer American flat weave cloth with DOUBLE OVERLAP on rails.
★ ¾" Redwood or 1" Balsa centre strip.
★ Choice of either, 3 colour laminated glass cloth fin or two tone wood fin with plexiglass bead.
★ Clear finish.
★ Custom shaped to your specifications.
★ All fins inset into centre strip for additional strength.
★ Hand polished rails.
★ Imported Isothalic polyester resin.

Bennett Surfboards, Brookvale, Australia, Price List. Circa early 1960s. Mauna Kea Galleries, Kamuela, Hawaii. $80-120

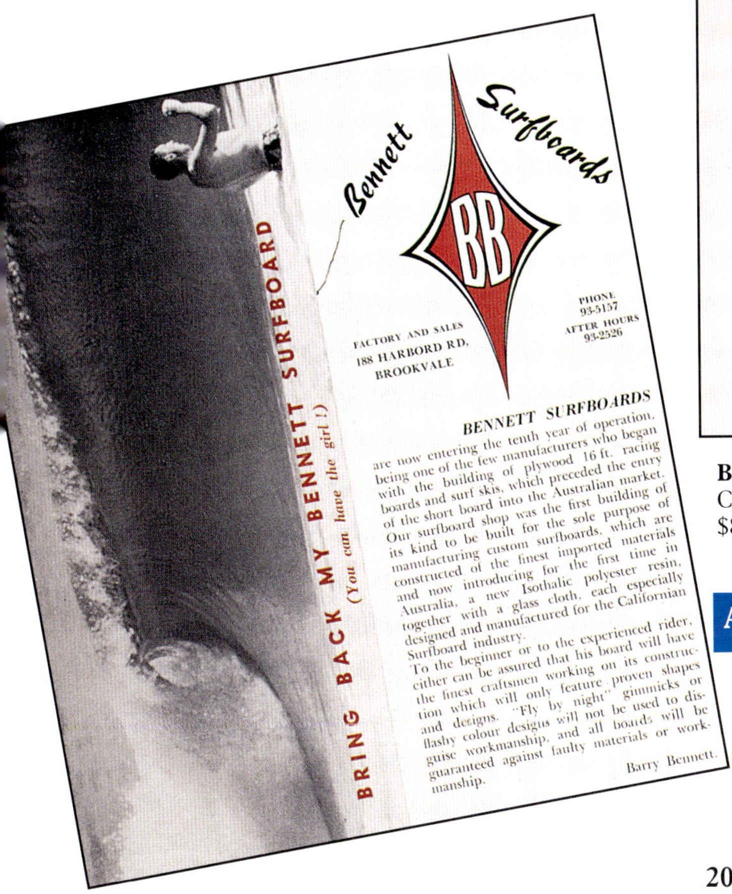

Aggro An Australian slang term for aggressive behavior.

Background: **A Photographic Print of Kimo Hollenger, Waimea Bay, Hawaii.** A photo by John Severson, circa early 1960s. Mauna Kea Galleries, Kamuela, Hawaii. As shown autographed: $80-120. Average: $30-50

Galt Custom. Peter and Cathy Noble, Monterey, California. $80-120

Vagabond Custom Surfboards. Peter and Cathy Noble, Monterey, California. $100-150

Decals

Surfboards by Ernie Tanaka. Peter and Cathy Noble, Monterey, California. $100-150

Surfboards by Phil, Downey, California. Peter and Cathy Noble, Monterey, California. $100-150

Malibu Custom Surfboards, Malibu Plastics Inc., 1971. Peter and Cathy Noble, Monterey, California. $40-60

Roberts Surf Shop. Peter and Cathy Noble, Monterey, California. $80-120

Surf Boards by Jack Haley, Seal Beach, California. Peter and Cathy Noble, Monterey, California. $80-120

Channel Islands Surfboards, Ventura-Santa Barbara. Peter and Cathy Noble, Monterey, California. $80-120

Paul Hunt Surfboards. Peter and Cathy Noble, Monterey, California. $80-120

Decals

Inland Surf Shop, Downey, California. Peter and Cathy Noble, Monterey, California. $100-150

Makaha Surf & Ski, Skateboards, Santa Monica, California. Peter and Cathy Noble, Monterey, California. $80-120

Scofield Surfboards, Santa Cruz, California. Peter and Cathy Noble, Monterey, California. $80-120

Phil Edwards. Peter and Cathy Noble, Monterey, California. $100-150

Surfboards by Tucker, Balboa Island, Newport Surfing Center. Peter and Cathy Noble, Monterey, California. $60-90

South Bay Surf Shop – Custom by Deese. Peter and Cathy Noble, Monterey, California. $100-150

Olympic Surf Boards. Peter and Cathy Noble, Monterey, California. $80-120

Surfboard sur mesure, Barland-Biarritz, Bayonne, France. Peter and Cathy Noble, Monterey, California. $60-90

Completely Custom Islander Surfboards. Peter and Cathy Noble, Monterey, California. $80-120

Clifford George Surfboards, Santa Barbara. Peter and Cathy Noble, Monterey, California. $80-120

Surfboards by Challenger Decal. "The means that make good surfers great surfers!" Peter and Cathy Noble, Monterey, California. $60-90

Dynamite. A Buzz Bailey film, circa 1962. Mauna Kea Galleries, Kamuela, Hawaii. $100-150

Surfboards by Challenger, 9'6". Three stringer, foam with redwood and balsa, circa mid-1960s. Unusual checkerboard design on deck by Knowles and Man. Hoffman Collection. $800-1,200

Taking Gas A troublesome situation that usually ends in a wipeout.

Dell Comic Book - *Beach Blanket Bingo*. Circa 1965. Courtesy of Buck Labadie/Artstuff. $60-90

Nite Fighter – A&W Root Beer Company, Santa Monica, California. Restaurant premium. Peter and Cathy Noble, Monterey, California. $30-50

Hot Dogger – A&W Root Beer Company, Santa Monica, California. Restaurant premium. Peter and Cathy Noble, Monterey, California. $60-90

Wipe-Out – A&W Root Beer Company, Santa Monica, California. Restaurant premium. Peter and Cathy Noble, Monterey, California. $60-90

Crest The highest point of any wave before it breaks.

Promotional Flyer for Custom Surfboards by Shooll, Harbor City, Calfornia. Circa mid-1960s. Courtesy of Buck Labadie/Artstuff. $100-150

Fred Hemmings, Jr., Design 1, 9'7". Single stringer, foam with redwood, circa late 1960s. Hoffman Collection. $1,000-1,500

House of Paipo Kneeboard, 4'5". Foam rails, glass deck, circa late 1960s. Allan Seymour, Pacific Coast Vintage Surf Auctions. $600-900

Once Upon a Wave. A Walt Phillips film, circa 1963. Courtesy of Buck Labadie/Artstuff. $120-180

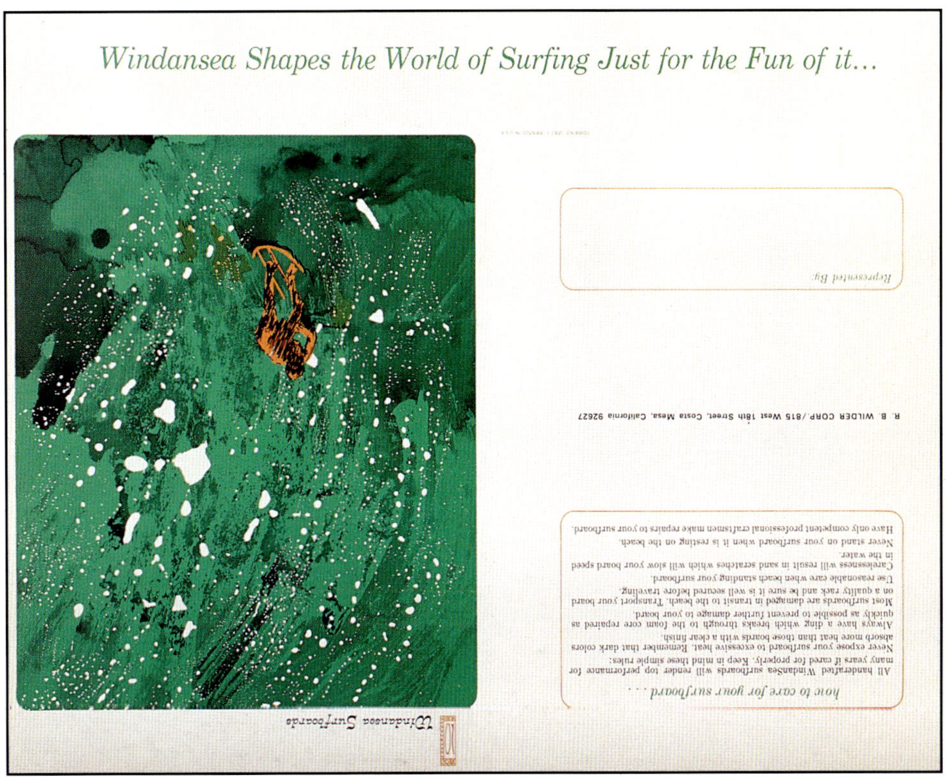

Wind and Sea Surfboards Advertising Book Cover. Circa late 1960s/early 1970s. Mauna Kea Galleries, Kamuela, Hawaii. $30-50

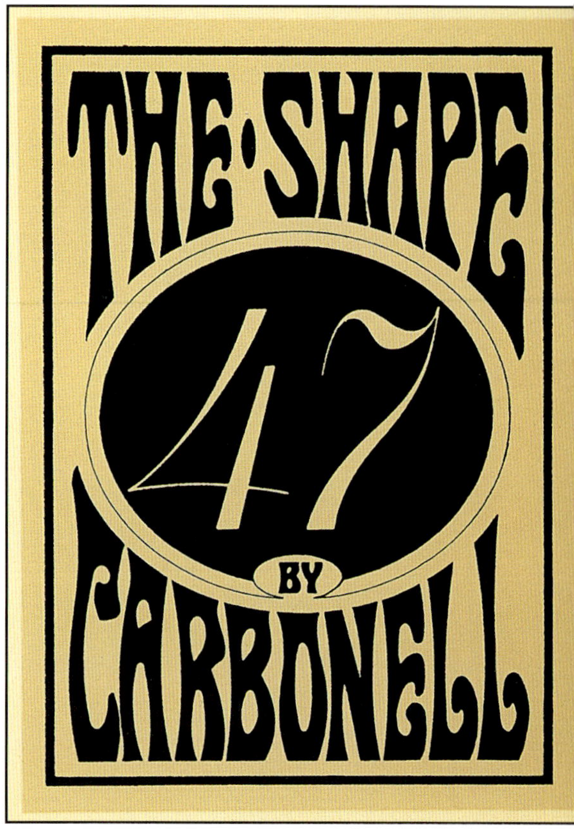

The Shape 47 by Carbonell Decal. Peter and Cathy Noble, Monterey, California. $80-120

Carbonelle Surfboards, Seal Beach, California, 9'9". Two stringer, foam with redwood, circa 1967. Mark Carbonelle was a shaper for Gordie and shaped this board for himself. Nose was highly influenced by Morey Pope designs. Peter and Cathy Noble, Monterey, California. $800-1,200

***For Men Only*, July 1969.** Issued with the True Book Bonus *The Hell Surfers - A weirdo gang of thrill-seekers on a sin and crime rampage...* Courtesy of Buck Labadie/Artstuff. $60-90

Carbonell Surfboards, Seal Beach, California, Decal. Peter and Cathy Noble, Monterey, California. $60-90

Carbonell Surf Shop, Long Beach, Decal. Peter and Cathy Noble, Monterey, California. $80-120

Wardy Surfboards, Laguna Beach and Pasadena, California, Business Card. Peter and Cathy Noble, Monterey, California. $50-70

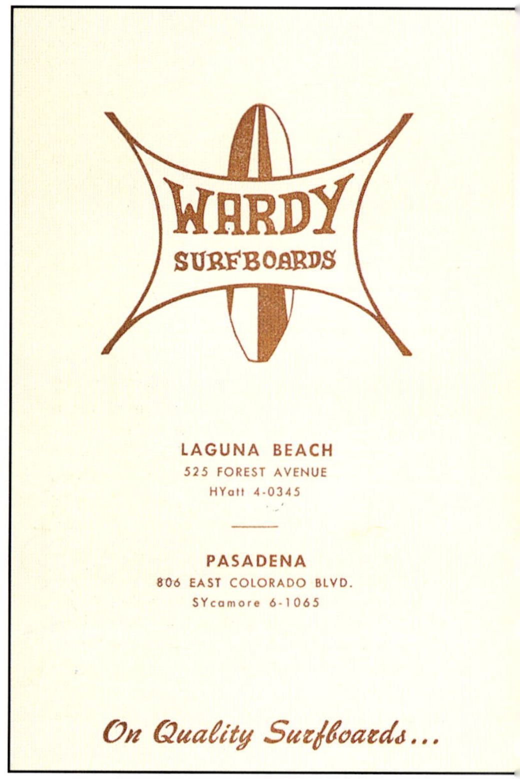

Wardy Surfboards, Laguna Beach and Pasadena, California, Business Card. Peter and Cathy Noble, Monterey, California. $30-50

Wardy Surfboard, 9'6". Balsa, circa mid-1960s. Peter and Cathy Noble, Monterey, California. $1,200-1,800

Wardy Surfboards, Laguna Beach, California, Decal. White background design. Peter and Cathy Noble, Monterey, California. $80-120

Wardy Surfboards, Hawaii, Decal. Peter and Cathy Noble, Monterey, California. $120-180

Wardy Surfboards, Laguna Beach, California, Decal. Gold background design. Peter and Cathy Noble, Monterey, California. $80-120

Wardy Surf Boards Patch. Peter and Cathy Noble, Monterey, California. $20-30

Wardy Surfboards Decal. Clarence Clubfoot character. Peter and Cathy Noble, Monterey, California. $150-250

Wardy Surfboards, Laguna Beach, California, Decal. Peter and Cathy Noble, Monterey, California. $80-120

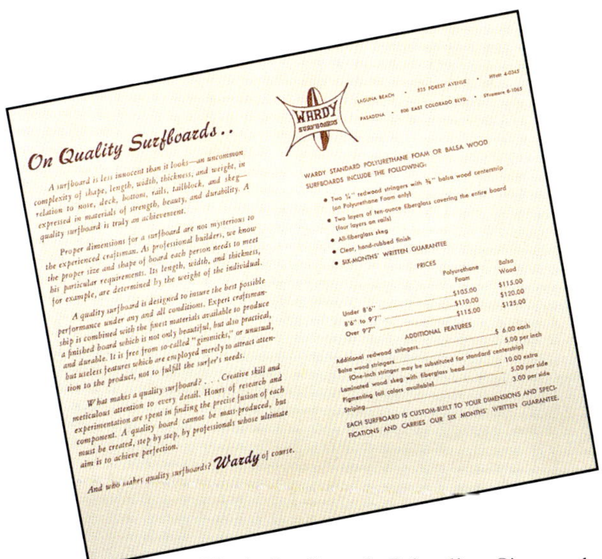

On Quality Surfboards . .

A surfboard is less innocent than it looks—an uncommon complexity of shape, length, width, thickness, and weight, in relation to nose, deck, bottom, rails, tailblock, and skeg—expressed in materials of strength, beauty, and durability. A quality surfboard is truly an achievement.

Proper dimensions for a surfboard are not mysterious to the experienced craftsman. As professional builders, we know the proper size and shape of board each person needs to meet his particular requirements. Its length, width, and thickness, for example, are determined by the weight of the individual.

A quality surfboard is designed to insure the best possible performance under any and all conditions. Expert craftsmanship is combined with the finest materials available to produce a finished board which is not only beautiful, but also practical, and durable. It is free from so-called "gimmicks," or unusual, but useless features which are employed merely to attract attention to the product, not to fulfill the surfer's needs.

What makes a quality surfboard? . . . Creative skill and meticulous attention to every detail. Hours of research and experimentation are spent in finding the precise fusion of each component. A quality board cannot be mass-produced, but must be created, step by step, by professionals whose ultimate aim is to achieve perfection.

And who makes quality surfboards? ***Wardy*** *of course.*

WARDY SURFBOARDS

LAGUNA BEACH • 525 FOREST AVENUE • HYatt 4-0345
PASADENA • 806 EAST COLORADO BLVD. • SYcamore 6-1065

WARDY STANDARD POLYURETHANE FOAM OR BALSA WOOD SURFBOARDS INCLUDE THE FOLLOWING:

- Two ¼" redwood stringers with ⅜" balsa wood centerstrip (on Polyurethane Foam only)
- Two layers of ten-ounce fiberglass covering the entire board (four layers on rails)
- All-fiberglass skeg
- Clear, hand-rubbed finish
- SIX-MONTHS' WRITTEN GUARANTEE

PRICES

	Polyurethane Foam	Balsa Wood
Under 8'6"	$105.00	$115.00
8'6" to 9'7"	$110.00	$120.00
Over 9'7"	$115.00	$125.00

ADDITIONAL FEATURES

Additional redwood stringers	$ 6.00 each
Balsa wood stringers	5.00 per inch
(One-inch stringer may be substituted for standard centerstrip)	
Laminated wood skeg with fiberglass bead	10.00 extra
Pigmenting (all colors available)	5.00 per side
Striping	3.00 per side

EACH SURFBOARD IS CUSTOM-BUILT TO YOUR DIMENSIONS AND SPECIFICATIONS AND CARRIES OUR SIX MONTHS' WRITTEN GUARANTEE.

Wardy Surfboards Price list. Circa early 1960s. Peter and Cathy Noble, Monterey, California. $80-120

Surfboards by Olson, Santa Cruz, Decal. Peter and Cathy Noble, Monterey, California. $80-120

Surfboards by Olson, Santa Cruz, 10'6". Two stringer board, balsa with redwood. This unusual balsa wood board was shaped especially for the owner, who provided the wood for construction. Peter and Cathy Noble, Monterey, California. $2,000-3,000

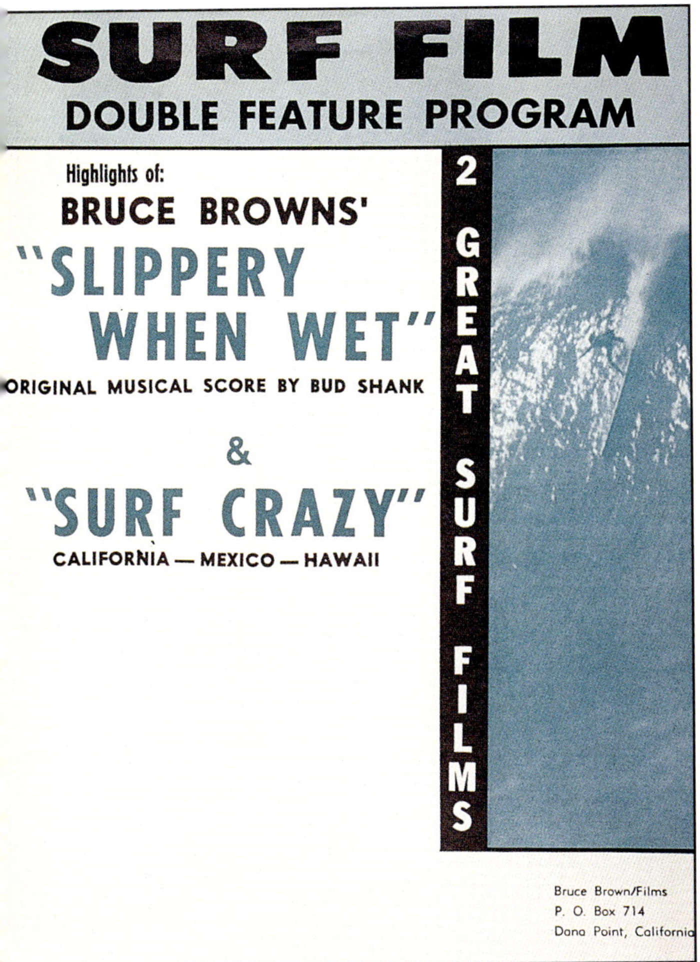

Over the Falls The dreaded position of being trapped in the plunging lip of a wave and hurled to the bottom.

Double Feature Program for *Slippery When Wet* and *Surf Crazy*. Bruce Brown films, circa late 1950s/early 1960s. Courtesy of Buck Labadie/ Artstuff. $150-250

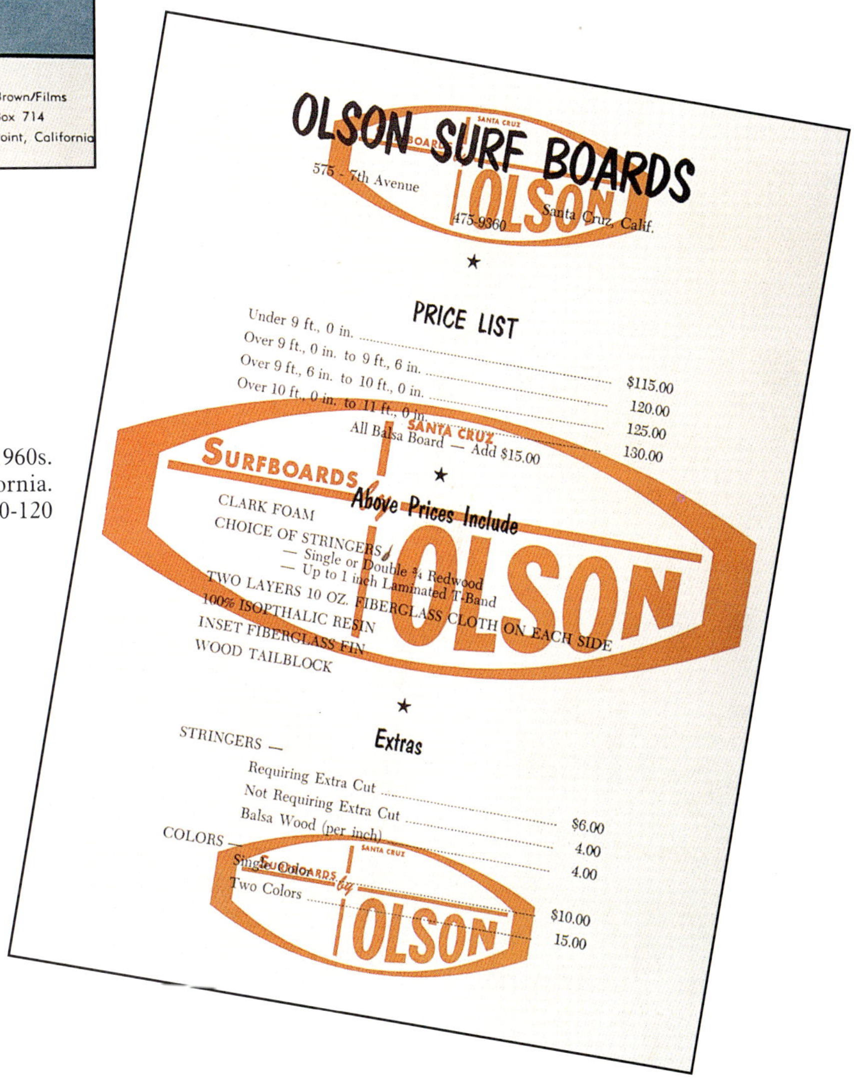
OLSON SURF BOARDS

575 - 7th Avenue 475-9360 Santa Cruz, Calif.

★

PRICE LIST

Under 9 ft., 0 in.	$115.00
Over 9 ft., 0 in. to 9 ft., 6 in.	120.00
Over 9 ft., 6 in. to 10 ft., 0 in.	125.00
Over 10 ft., 0 in. to 11 ft., 0 in.	130.00

All Balsa Board — Add $15.00

★

Above Prices Include

CLARK FOAM
CHOICE OF STRINGERS
— Single or Double ¾ Redwood
— Up to 1 inch Laminated T-Band
TWO LAYERS 10 OZ. FIBERGLASS CLOTH ON EACH SIDE
100% ISOPTHALIC RESIN
INSET FIBERGLASS FIN
WOOD TAILBLOCK

★

Extras

STRINGERS —

Requiring Extra Cut	$6.00
Not Requiring Extra Cut	4.00
Balsa Wood (per inch)	4.00

COLORS —

Single Color	$10.00
Two Colors	15.00

Olson Surf Boards Price List. Circa early 1960s. Peter and Cathy Noble, Monterey, California. $80-120

Decals

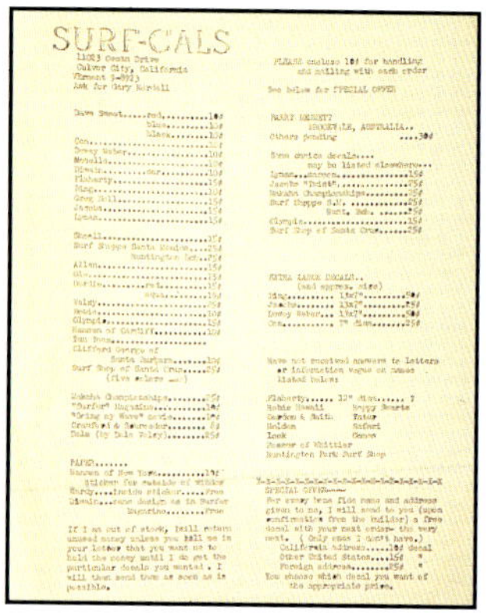

Surf-Cals. Circa early 1960s. Unusual price list for decals. Peter and Cathy Noble, Monterey, California. $120-180

The Trestle Special. Peter and Cathy Noble, Monterey, California. $60-90

The Spoiler Lightweight by Oceanside, Cocoa, Florida. Peter and Cathy Noble, Monterey, California. $60-90

Surfer Bi-Monthly. Peter and Cathy Noble, Monterey, California. $30-50

Surfboards from the Skag, Hermosa Beach, California. Peter and Cathy Noble, Monterey, California. $100-150

Bilbo Surfboards, Swansea, Wales. Peter and Cathy Noble, Monterey, California. $40-60

Lyman Surf Boards. Peter and Cathy Noble, Monterey, California. $100-150

Matador Surfboards. Peter and Cathy Noble, Monterey, California. $80-120

Lightning Bolt Surfboards. Peter and Cathy Noble, Monterey, California. $80-120

Surfing Illustrated. Magazine decal. Peter and Cathy Noble, Monterey, California. $60-90

Surfrider, Hialeah, Florida. Peter and Cathy Noble, Monterey, California. $60-90

ISF/USSA World Surfing Championships, San Diego, California, 1966. Peter and Cathy Noble, Monterey, California. $100-150

Birdwell Beach Britches. "Birdie" image. Peter and Cathy Noble, Monterey, California. $100-150

Custom Rick Surfboards. Peter and Cathy Noble, Monterey, California. $100-150

Surf Board House, Hialeah, Florida. Peter and Cathy Noble, Monterey, California. $60-90

Surfboards by Shore, Hermosa Beach. Peter and Cathy Noble, Monterey, California. $60-90

Wardy. Highly stylized design. Peter and Cathy Noble, Monterey, California. $80-120

Surf Photos by Grannis. Peter and Cathy Noble, Monterey, California. $100-150

Web Surf Shop, Walters of Ship Bottom & Cranford, New Jersey. Peter and Cathy Noble, Monterey, California. $80-120

Custom Built Surfboards by Johnny, Galveston, Texas. Peter and Cathy Noble, Monterey, California. $80-120

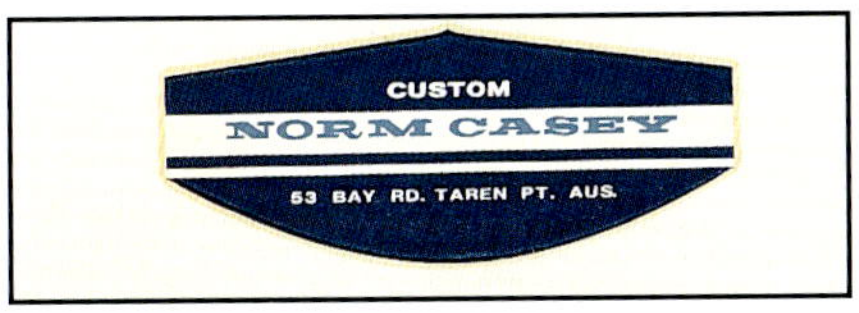

Custom Norm Casey, Australia. Peter and Cathy Noble, Monterey, California. $40-60

Surfari, Malibu, California. Peter and Cathy Noble, Monterey, California. $100-150

Collier Custom Surfboards. Peter and Cathy Noble, Monterey, California. $40-60

On The Beach Surf Shop, Monterey, California. Peter and Cathy Noble, Monterey, California. $80-120

Surfboards by Travis. Peter and Cathy Noble, Monterey, California. $40-60

Surfboards by Jeffrey Dale, Santa Ana. Peter and Cathy Noble, Monterey, California. $80-120

Decals

Austin-Baird Custom Surfboards, Surfside, California. Peter and Cathy Noble, Monterey, California. $80-120

Kick Out To pull out of a wave when riding by kicking or putting pressure on the tail section with the back foot resulting in the lifting of the nose out of the water and back over the crest.

Surfboards Hawaii, Patch. Peter and Cathy Noble, Monterey, California. $30-50

Surfboards Hawaii, Haleiwa, Hawaii, 11'0". Four-stringer, foam with redwood. An early example of a Dick Brewer shaped big wave gun, circa early 1960s. This board was previously owned by Condi Kalhoun. Hoffman Collection. As shown: $8,000-12,000. Average: $4,000-6,000.

Surfboards Hawaii – Founded by John Trent in the early 1960s, he spent most of his early shaping career in Hawaii, later moving to Encinitas, California. In 1965, at the peak of his production, he produced over 1,300 boards, primarily due to the big wave prowess of many of his team riders, who included Buzzy Trent, Fred Hemmings, Dick Brewer, Fred Van Dyke, Ricky Grigg and Butch Van Artsdalen, among others.

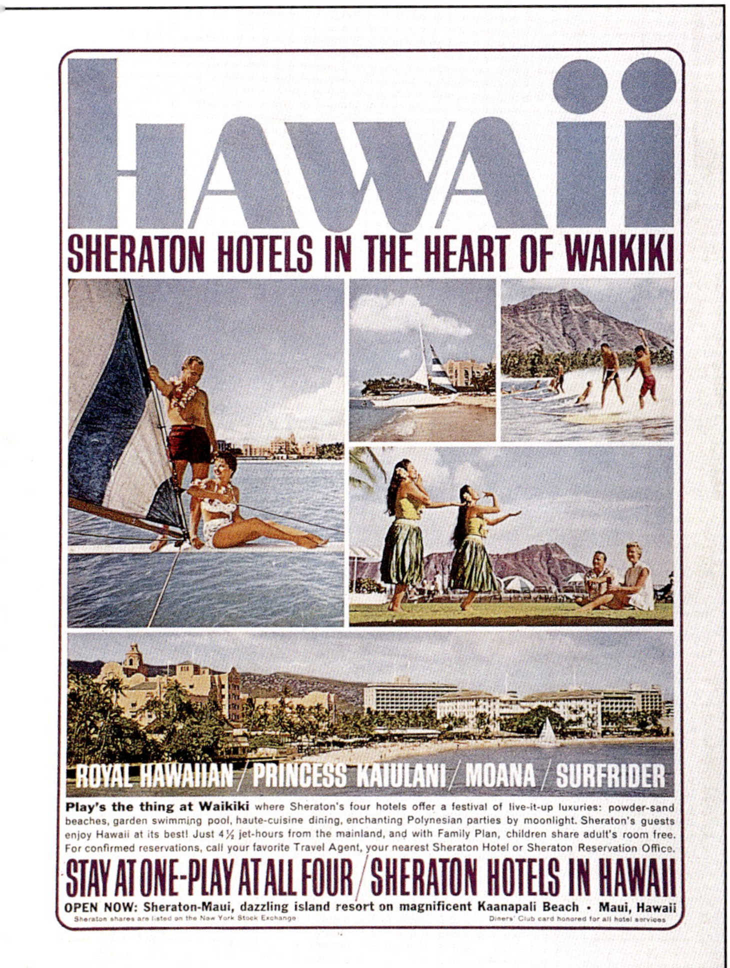

Vintage Advertisement. Mauna Kea Galleries, Kamuela, Hawaii.

Vintage Advertisement. Mauna Kea Galleries, Kamuela, Hawaii.

Surfboards Hawaii, Model A, 10'0". Tapered three stringer, foam with redwood, circa mid-1960s. Allan Seymour, Pacific Coast Vintage Surf Auctions. $600-900

Surfboards Hawaii, Haleiwa, Hawaii, 11'0". Three stringer, big wave gun, foam with redwood, circa mid-1960s. Hoffman Collection. $3,000-5,000

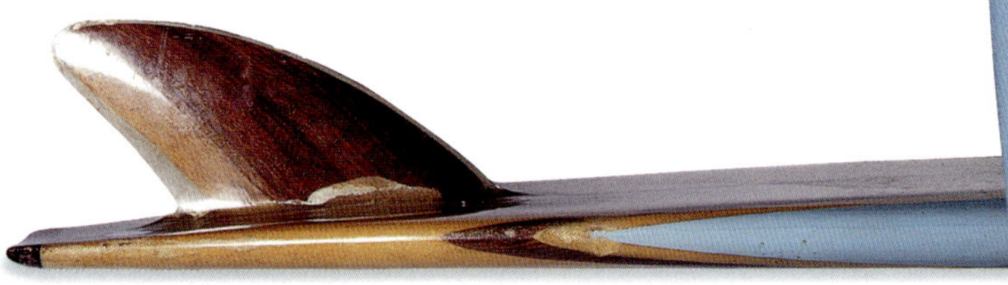

Vintage Advertisement. Mauna Kea Galleries, Kamuela, Hawaii.

Surfboards Hawaii, Haleiwa, Hawaii, Encinitas, California, Decal. Peter and Cathy Noble, Monterey, California. $80-120

Surfboards Hawaii, Haleiwa, Hawaii – Encinitas, California, 10'0". A rare mint condition board purchased new in 1965 by the previous owner, who never put it in the water but put it on top of his maroon Porsche to look cool. Also, this board was used in a 1992 United Airlines ad. Peter and Cathy Noble, Monterey, California. As shown: $4,000-6,000. Average: $800-1,200

Patches

Vintage Advertisement. Mauna Kea Galleries, Kamuela, Hawaii.

Greg Noll Surf Boards. Peter and Cathy Noble, Monterey, California. $30-50

Wardy. Peter and Cathy Noble, Monterey, California. $15-25

Baja Surf Club, Ensenada, Mexico. Peter and Cathy Noble, Monterey, California. $20-30

Wind & Sea Surfboards. Peter and Cathy Noble, Monterey, California. $25-35

Custom Surfboards by Bunger. Peter and Cathy Noble, Monterey, California. $30-50

Birdie. Peter and Cathy Noble, Monterey, California. $25-35

Joey Cabell Custom Surfboards. Peter and Cathy Noble, Monterey, California. $25-35

Custom Surfboards by Bunger. Peter and Cathy Noble, Monterey, California. $15-25

Caster Surfboards. Peter and Cathy Noble, Monterey, California. $15-25

Kanvas by Katin, Custom Surf Trunks, Surfside, California. Peter and Cathy Noble, Monterey, California. $25-35

Oceanside Custom, Cocoa, Florida. Peter and Cathy Noble, Monterey, California. $8-12

Patches

Custom Rick Surfboards. Peter and Cathy Noble, Monterey, California. $25-35

Steamer Lane Surf Club. Peter and Cathy Noble, Monterey, California. $15-25

Vintage Advertisement. Mauna Kea Galleries, Kamuela, Hawaii.

Walmar Productions Inc., Surfside, California. Walt Phillips personal card. Peter and Cathy Noble, Monterey, California. $80-120

Business Cards

Surf House, Santa Monica, California. Con Colburn's personal card. Peter and Cathy Noble, Monterey, California. $100-150

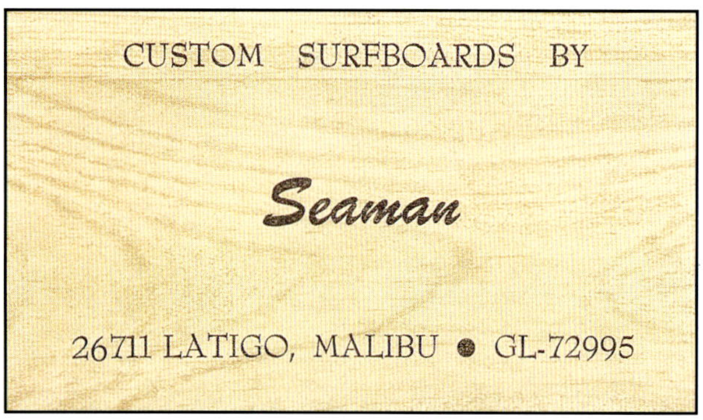

Seaman, Malibu, California. Peter and Cathy Noble, Monterey, California. $50-70

Surfboards by Rosser, Whittier, California. Courtesy of Buck Labadie/ Artstuff. $50-70

Surfboards by Grasman & Brooks, Lakewood, California. Courtesy of Buck Labadie/Artstuff. $40-60

Business Cards

Official Program for the United States Surfboard Championships 1967, Huntington Beach, California. Mauna Kea Galleries, Kamuela, Hawaii. $120-180

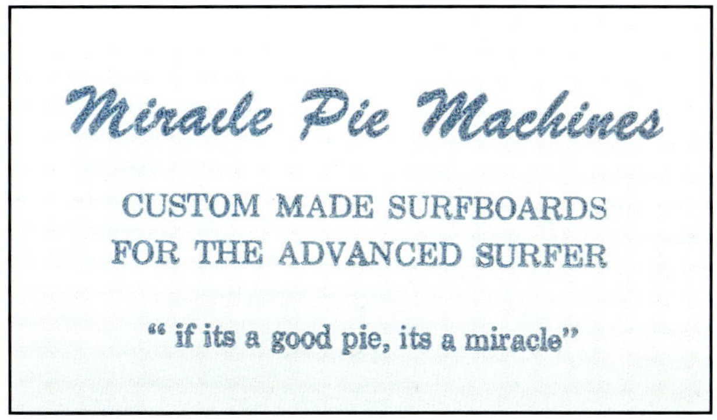

Miracle Pie Machines. Custom Made Surfboards For The Advanced Surfer, "if its a good pie, its a miracle". Peter and Cathy Noble, Monterey, California. $80-120

Valley Surf Shop, Burbank, California. Peter and Cathy Noble, Monterey, California. $60-90

Church Surfboards – Tracking Machines. Inner space probing zappers also available. Peter and Cathy Noble, Monterey, California. $100-150

Jack Pollard, Venice. Fiber glassing, surf boards & repairs. Folding price list business card. Rare. Peter and Cathy Noble, Monterey, California. $80-120

Surfboard Repair Specialist, Hermosa Beach, California. Peter and Cathy Noble, Monterey, California. $30-50

G & S Surfboards – Started by Larry Gordon and Floyd Smith in their garage in 1959, they have one of the longest and most talented histories in the industry, opening their first shop in San Diego, California, in 1960. Among their most famous models are the Stock, Mike Hynson and the Hynson Gun. In 1965, they turned out over 3,000 boards with 1,500 of them being the Mike Hynson red fin model. Today their main office still is located at the site of their original shop.

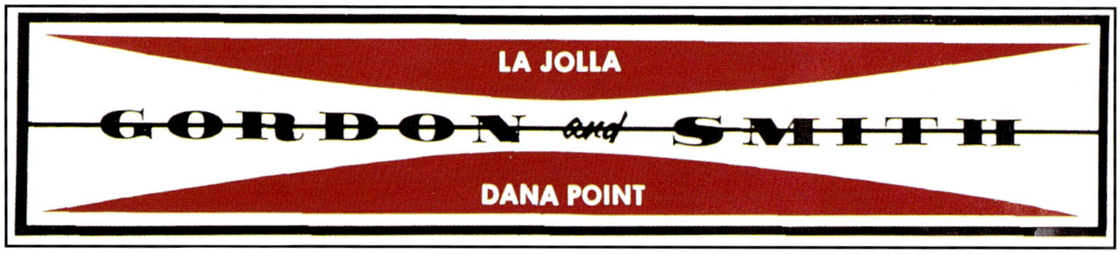

Gordon and Smith, La Jolla – Dana Point, Decal. Peter and Cathy Noble, Monterey, California. $60-90

Gordon & Smith Custom Surfboards, 9'8". Three stringer, foam with redwood, glass tailblock, circa mid-1960s. Allan Seymour, Pacific Coast Vintage Surf Auctions. $800-1,200

Vintage Advertisement. Mauna Kea Galleries, Kamuela, Hawaii.

Gordon & Smith, 9'8". Three stringer, foam with redwood. Original owner bought this board new in 1966, surfed it once, and left for Viet Nam. This is the first generation of the Mike Hynson model. Peter and Cathy Noble, Monterey, California. $800-1,200

Gordon & Smith Custom Surfboards Decal. Peter and Cathy Noble, Monterey, California. $60-90

Gordon & Smith, Mike Hynson Model, 9'8". Three stringer, foam with redwood, circa mid-1960s. Allan Seymour, Pacific Coast Vintage Surf Auctions. $600-900

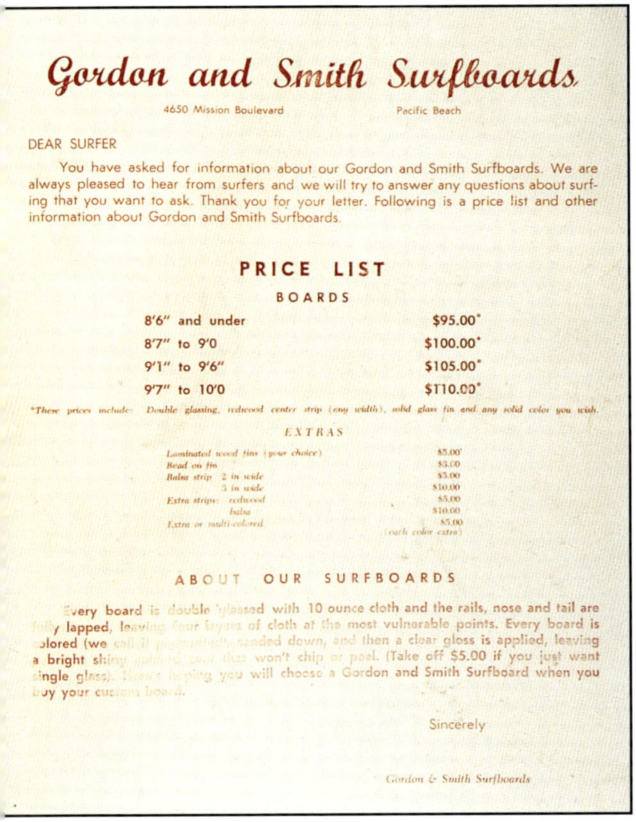

Gordon and Smith Surfboards

4650 Mission Boulevard Pacific Beach

DEAR SURFER

You have asked for information about our Gordon and Smith Surfboards. We are always pleased to hear from surfers and we will try to answer any questions about surfing that you want to ask. Thank you for your letter. Following is a price list and other information about Gordon and Smith Surfboards.

PRICE LIST

BOARDS

8'6" and under	$95.00*
8'7" to 9'0	$100.00*
9'1" to 9'6"	$105.00*
9'7" to 10'0	$110.00*

*These prices include: Double glassing, redwood center strip (any width), solid glass fin and any solid color you wish.

EXTRAS

Laminated wood fins (your choice)		$5.00
Bead on fin		$3.00
Balsa strip	2 in wide	$5.00
	3 in wide	$10.00
Extra strips:	redwood	$5.00
	balsa	$10.00
Extra or multi-colored		$5.00 (each color extra)

ABOUT OUR SURFBOARDS

Every board is double glassed with 10 ounce cloth and the rails, nose and tail are fully lapped, leaving four layers of cloth at the most vulnerable points. Every board is colored (we call it pigmented), sanded down, and then a clear gloss is applied, leaving a bright shiny colored coat that won't chip or peel. (Take off $5.00 if you just want single glass). Here's hoping you will choose a Gordon and Smith Surfboard when you buy your custom board.

Sincerely

Gordon & Smith Surfboards

Gordon and Smith Surfboards, Pacific Beach, California, Price List. Circa early 1960s. Courtesy of Buck Labadie/Artstuff. $100-150

GORDON & SMITH SURFBOARDS

PHOTO BY BRUCE BROWN

PRICE LIST

8'6" and under	$ 95.00
8'7" to 9'0"	100.00
9'1" to 9'6"	105.00
9'7" to 10'0"	110.00

These prices include: Hand shaping by Mike Hynson or Larry Gordon, in redwood or balsa center strip, double 10-oz. glassing with Deck Patch, solid glass fin, and our guarantee of perfect craftsmanship.

EXTRAS

Laminated wood fins (your choice)
Bead of fin
Balsa strip 2" wide
3" wide
1 ½" wide
Extra strips: redwood
balsa
Extra or multi-colored

$ 5.00
3.00
5.00
10.00
2.50
5.00
10.00
5.00
(each color extra)

ABOUT OUR SURFBOARDS

The reason Gordon & Smith Surfboards are considered the finest surfboards made today is seen with the first glance at their quality. First of all, a G & S is always made to your EXACT specifications. There are always perfect strips (never routed). Every G & S made is double glassed, plus a deck patch. These reasons, plus our standards of the best materials and craftsmanship, enable us to give you the best for your money. We also stand behind our surfboards 100%.

Gordon and Smith Surfboards, Pacific Beach, California, Price List. Circa early 1960s. Courtesy of Buck Labadie/Artstuff. $150-250

Gordon & Smith Patch. Peter and Cathy Noble, Monterey, California. $20-30

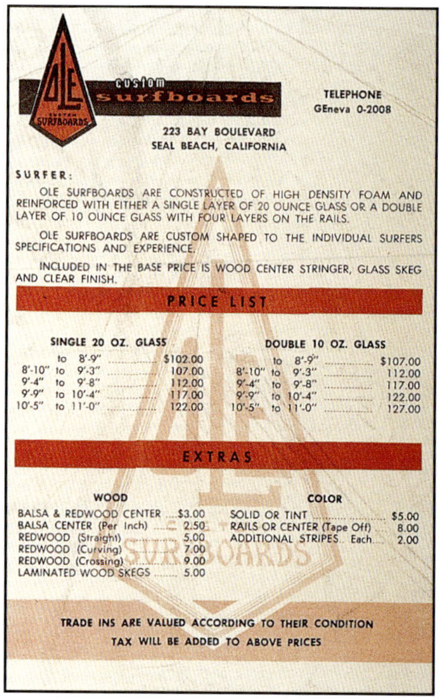

custom surfboards

OLE CUSTOM SURFBOARDS

TELEPHONE
GEneva 0-2008

223 BAY BOULEVARD
SEAL BEACH, CALIFORNIA

SURFER:

OLE SURFBOARDS ARE CONSTRUCTED OF HIGH DENSITY FOAM AND REINFORCED WITH EITHER A SINGLE LAYER OF 20 OUNCE GLASS OR A DOUBLE LAYER OF 10 OUNCE GLASS WITH FOUR LAYERS ON THE RAILS.

OLE SURFBOARDS ARE CUSTOM SHAPED TO THE INDIVIDUAL SURFERS SPECIFICATIONS AND EXPERIENCE.

INCLUDED IN THE BASE PRICE IS WOOD CENTER STRINGER, GLASS SKEG AND CLEAR FINISH.

PRICE LIST

SINGLE 20 OZ. GLASS		DOUBLE 10 OZ. GLASS	
to 8'-9"	$102.00	to 8'-9"	$107.00
8'-10" to 9'-3"	107.00	8'-10" to 9'-3"	112.00
9'-4" to 9'-8"	112.00	9'-4" to 9'-8"	117.00
9'-9" to 10'-4"	117.00	9'-9" to 10'-4"	122.00
10'-5" to 11'-0"	122.00	10'-5" to 11'-0"	127.00

EXTRAS

WOOD		COLOR	
BALSA & REDWOOD CENTER	$3.00	SOLID OR TINT	$5.00
BALSA CENTER (Per Inch)	2.50	RAILS OR CENTER (Tape Off)	8.00
REDWOOD (Straight)	5.00	ADDITIONAL STRIPES.. Each	2.00
REDWOOD (Curving)	7.00		
REDWOOD (Crossing)	9.00		
LAMINATED WOOD SKEGS	5.00		

TRADE INS ARE VALUED ACCORDING TO THEIR CONDITION
TAX WILL BE ADDED TO ABOVE PRICES

Ole Custom Surfboards, Seal Beach, California, Price List. Circa early 1960s. Courtesy of Buck Labadie/Artstuff. $100-150

Dave Sweet Custom Boards, Santa Monica, California, Decal. Peter and Cathy Noble, Monterey, California. $80-120

Dave Sweet Surfboards, Santa Monica, California, Business Card. Peter and Cathy Noble, Monterey, California. $40-60

Ole Custom Surfboards Decal. Peter and Cathy Noble, Monterey, California. $60-90

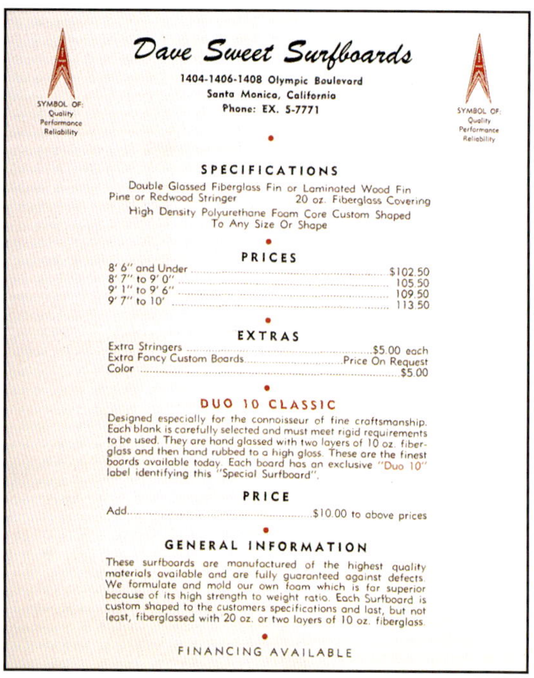

Dave Sweet Surfboards

1404-1406-1408 Olympic Boulevard
Santa Monica, California
Phone: EX. 5-7771

SYMBOL OF: Quality Performance Reliability

SPECIFICATIONS

Double Glassed Fiberglass Fin or Laminated Wood Fin
Pine or Redwood Stringer — 20 oz. Fiberglass Covering
High Density Polyurethane Foam Core Custom Shaped To Any Size Or Shape

PRICES

8' 6" and Under	$102.50
8' 7" to 9' 0"	105.50
9' 1" to 9' 6"	109.50
9' 7" to 10'	113.50

EXTRAS

Extra Stringers	$5.00 each
Extra Fancy Custom Boards	Price On Request
Color	$5.00

DUO 10 CLASSIC

Designed especially for the connoisseur of fine craftsmanship. Each blank is carefully selected and must meet rigid requirements to be used. They are hand glassed with two layers of 10 oz. fiberglass and then hand rubbed to a high gloss. These are the finest boards available today. Each board has an exclusive "Duo 10" label identifying this "Special Surfboard".

PRICE

Add.............$10.00 to above prices

GENERAL INFORMATION

These surfboards are manufactured of the highest quality materials available and are fully guaranteed against defects. We formulate and mold our own foam which is far superior because of its high strength to weight ratio. Each Surfboard is custom shaped to the customers specifications and last, but not least, fiberglassed with 20 oz. or two layers of 10 oz. fiberglass.

FINANCING AVAILABLE

Ole Custom Surfboards, Seal Beach, California, Price List. Circa early 1960s. Courtesy of Buck Labadie/Artstuff. $80-120

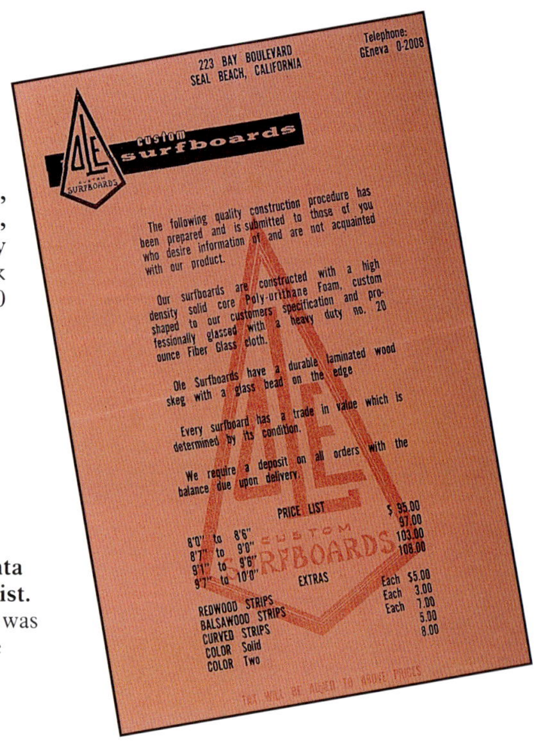

223 BAY BOULEVARD
SEAL BEACH, CALIFORNIA

Telephone:
GEneva 0-2008

custom surfboards

The following quality construction procedure has been prepared and is submitted to those of you who desire information of and are not acquainted with our product.

Our surfboards are constructed with a high density solid core Poly-urithane Foam, custom shaped to our customers specification and professionally glassed with a heavy duty no. 20 ounce Fiber Glass cloth.

Ole Surfboards have a durable laminated wood skeg with a glass bead on the edge

Every surfboard has a trade in value which is determined by its condition.

We require a deposit on all orders with the balance due upon delivery.

PRICE LIST

8'0" to 8'6"	$ 95.00
8'7" to 9'0"	97.00
9'1" to 9'6"	103.00
9'7" to 10'0"	108.00

EXTRAS

REDWOOD STRIPS	Each	$5.00
BALSAWOOD STRIPS	Each	3.00
CURVED STRIPS	Each	7.00
COLOR Solid		5.00
COLOR Two		8.00

Dave Sweet Surfboards, Santa Monica, California, Price List. Circa mid-1960s. Dave Sweet was one of the first shapers to use foam. Mauna Kea Galleries, Kamuela, Hawaii. $120-180

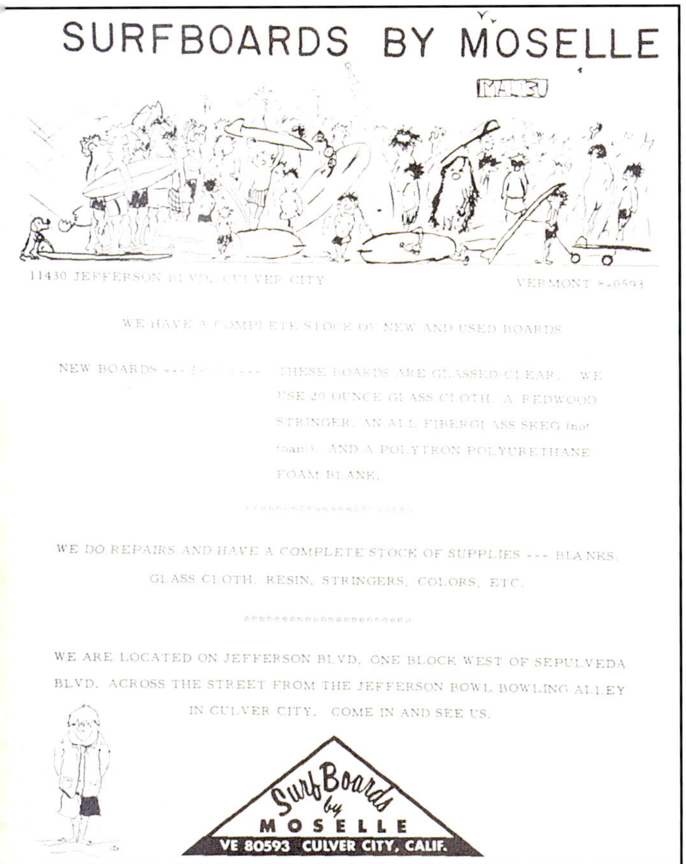
SURFBOARDS BY MOSELLE

11430 JEFFERSON BLVD., CULVER CITY — VERMONT 8-0593

WE HAVE A COMPLETE STOCK OF NEW AND USED BOARDS

NEW BOARDS --- [illegible] --- THESE BOARDS ARE GLASSED CLEAR. WE USE 20 OUNCE GLASS CLOTH, A REDWOOD STRINGER, AN ALL FIBERGLASS SKEG (not foam), AND A POLYTRON POLYURETHANE FOAM BLANK.

WE DO REPAIRS AND HAVE A COMPLETE STOCK OF SUPPLIES --- BLANKS, GLASS CLOTH, RESIN, STRINGERS, COLORS, ETC.

WE ARE LOCATED ON JEFFERSON BLVD. ONE BLOCK WEST OF SEPULVEDA BLVD. ACROSS THE STREET FROM THE JEFFERSON BOWL BOWLING ALLEY IN CULVER CITY. COME IN AND SEE US.

SurfBoards by MOSELLE

VE 80593 CULVER CITY, CALIF.

Surfboards by Moselle Price List. Circa early 1960s. Peter and Cathy Noble, Monterey, California. $100-150

Surf Boards by Moselle, Culver City, California, Business Card. Peter and Cathy Noble, Monterey, California. $60-90

SURFBOARDS From THE SKAG

56 HERMOSA AVE.
HERMOSA BEACH, CALIFORNIA

WALT SLIKE — JIM WELLS, JR.

FR 6-2975 — FR 4-9474

Surfboards from the Scag, Hermosa Beach, California. Price list card. Courtesy of Buck Labadie/Artstuff. $100-150

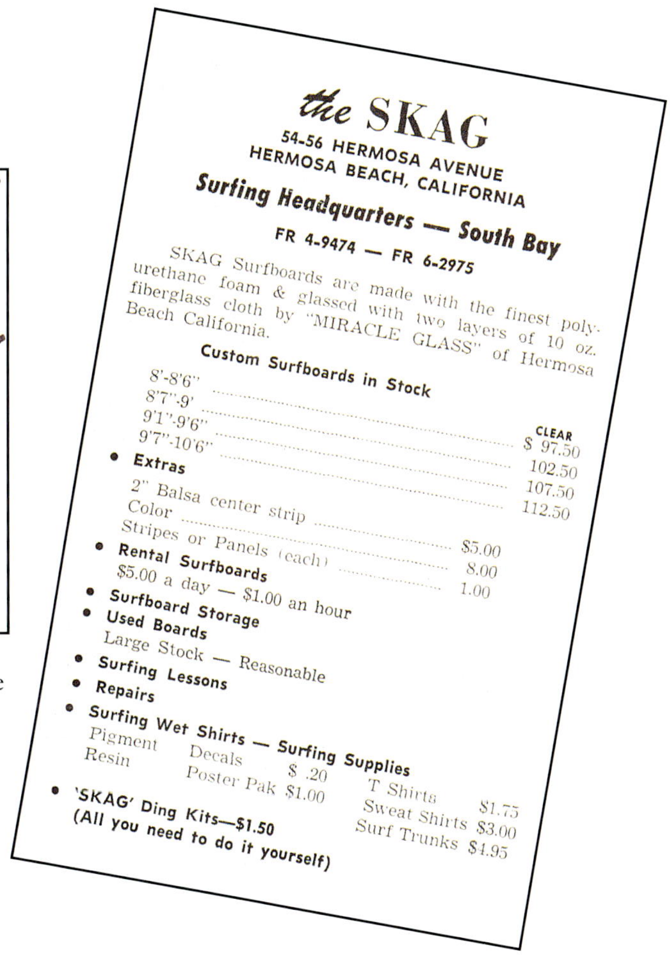
the SKAG

54-56 HERMOSA AVENUE
HERMOSA BEACH, CALIFORNIA

Surfing Headquarters — South Bay

FR 4-9474 — FR 6-2975

SKAG Surfboards are made with the finest polyurethane foam & glassed with two layers of 10 oz. fiberglass cloth by "MIRACLE GLASS" of Hermosa Beach California.

Custom Surfboards in Stock

	CLEAR
8'-8'6"	$ 97.50
8'7"-9'	102.50
9'1"-9'6"	107.50
9'7"-10'6"	112.50

- Extras
  - 2" Balsa center strip $5.00
  - Color 8.00
  - Stripes or Panels (each) 1.00
- Rental Surfboards
  - $5.00 a day — $1.00 an hour
- Surfboard Storage
- Used Boards
  - Large Stock — Reasonable
- Surfing Lessons
- Repairs
- Surfing Wet Shirts — Surfing Supplies
  - Pigment, Resin
  - Decals $ .20, Poster Pak $1.00
  - T Shirts $1.75, Sweat Shirts $3.00, Surf Trunks $4.95
- 'SKAG' Ding Kits—$1.50 (All you need to do it yourself)

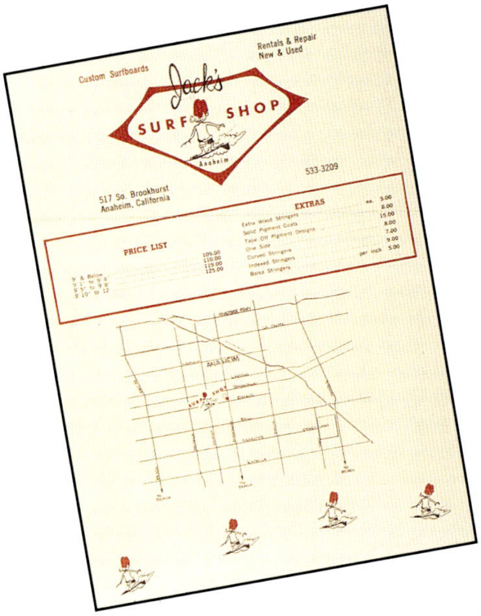

Jack's Surf Shop, Anaheim, California, Price List. Circa 1960s. Courtesy of Buck Labadie/Artstuff. $120-180

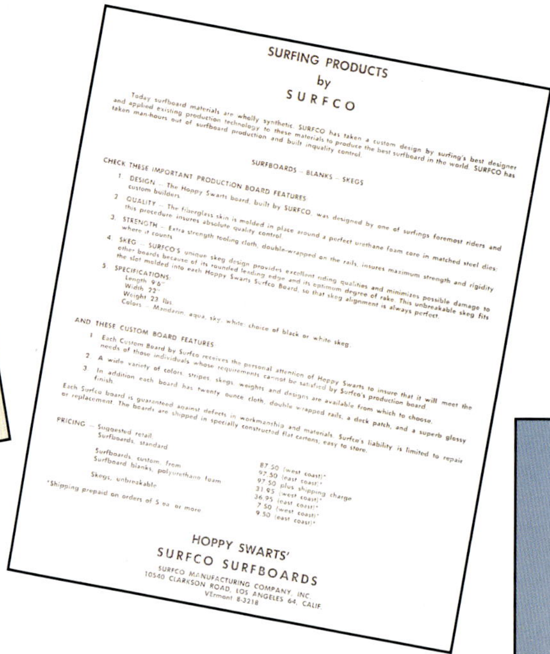

Hoppy Swarts Surfco Surfboards Price List. Circa early 1960s. Peter and Cathy Noble, Monterey, California. $100-150

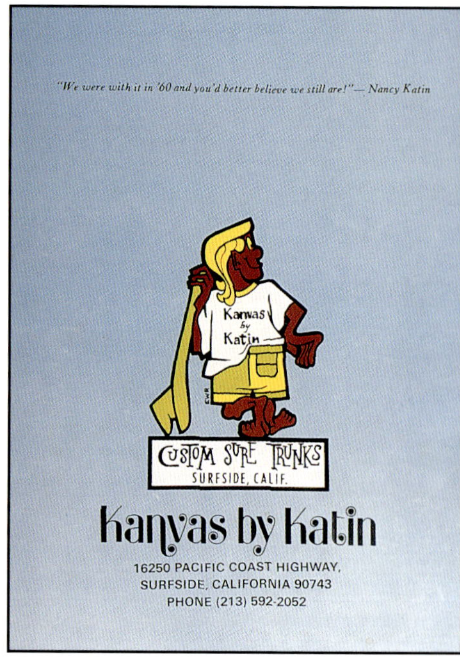

Vintage Advertisement. Mauna Kea Galleries, Kamuela, Hawaii.

Jack's Surf Shop, Anaheim, Decal. Peter and Cathy Noble, Monterey, California. $100-150

Jack's Surfboards, Huntington Beach, California, Decal. Peter and Cathy Noble, Monterey, California. $60-90

Kanvas by Katin, Custom Surf Trunks, Surfside, California, Decal. Peter and Cathy Noble, Monterey, California. $60-90

Buoy A person who floats around and never takes or attempts to ride a wave, often getting in the way of other surfers.

Allen Custom Surfboards, Decal. Courtesy of Buck Labadie/Artstuff. $60-90

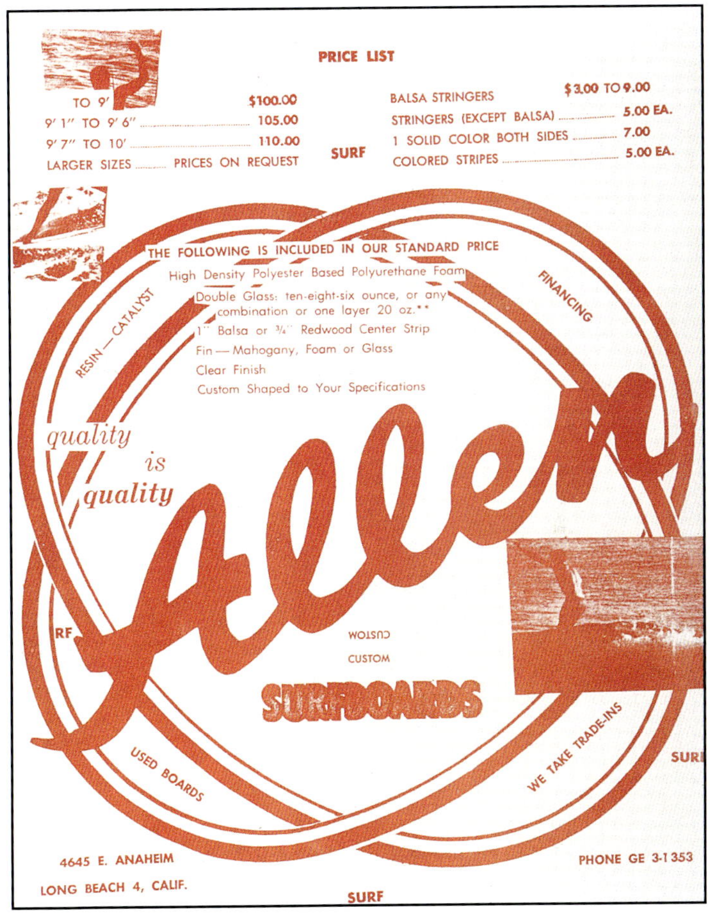

Custom Surfboards by Allen, Long Beach, California, Price List. Circa early 1960s. Courtesy of Buck Labadie/Artstuff. $120-180

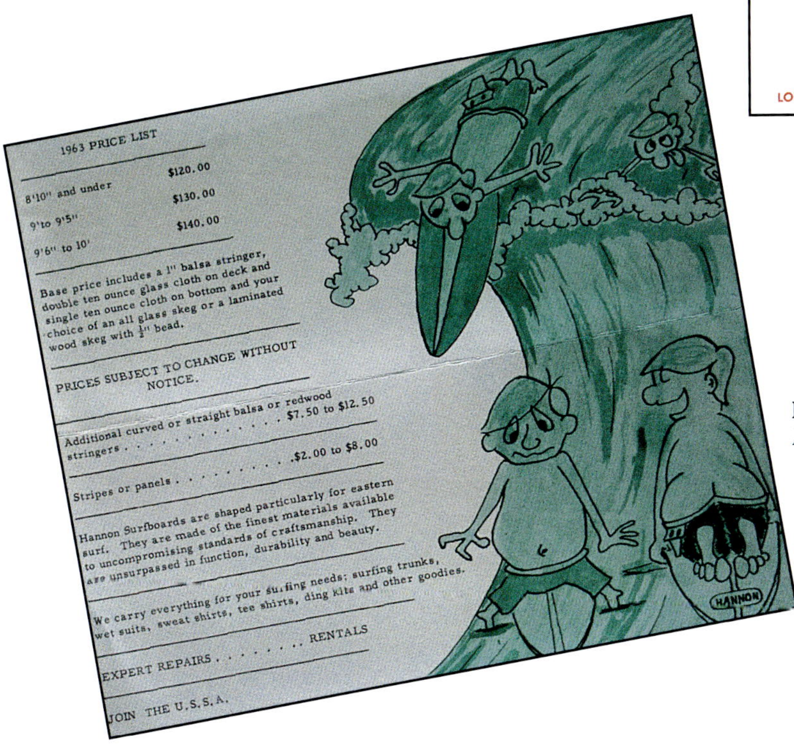

Hannon Price List. Circa 1963. Courtesy of Mark and Cindy Fragale. $120-180

Surfboard by Greek – Founded by Bob Barlen in 1962 in Huntington Beach, California, his entry into the surf scene was rather late. Soon becoming a powerful force in the industry, he created over 15 models, with his "Eliminator" being the most popular. With a wide network of dealers on the East Coast, Texas, Oregon, Puerto Rico and Hawaii, he shaped boards of Foss foam until 1968, when he switched to Walker. Among his many models were the Maui, Gun, East Coast Special, SS, and the Outlaw.

Eliminator by Greek Decal. Peter and Cathy Noble, Monterey, California. $80-120

Greek, The East Coast Special, Huntington Beach, California, Decal. Peter and Cathy Noble, Monterey, California. $80-120

Eliminator by Greek, 9'10". Single stringer, foam with redwood, Bob Bolin design, circa 1966. A true nose riding board, it also turned out to be popular with hot doggers. Eliminators were heavily produced for about two years and general examples are in poor condition due to their popularity. Peter and Cathy Noble, Monterey, California. $1,000-1,500

Liquidator by Greek, Huntington Beach, California, Decal. Peter and Cathy Noble, Monterey, California. $100-150

Surfboards by The Greek, Decal. Peter and Cathy Noble, Monterey, California. $60-90

Custom Surfboards by The Greek, Huntington Beach, California, Decal. Peter and Cathy Noble, Monterey, California. $60-90

East Coast Eliminator by Greek, Huntington Beach, California, 9'8". Single stringer, foam with redwood, circa mid-1960s. Unusual 'squirrel' or scooped tail. A very short-lived production. Courtesy of Mark and Cindy Fragale. $1,200-1,800

Gidget

"Gidget" is the real-life nickname of Kathy Kohner, a young surfer at Malibu in the mid-1950s. Called "Midget" by fellow surfers due to her size, she was angered by the comments and changed the nickname to "Gidget," which eventually stuck. In 1957, her father, Frederick Kohner, wrote a best-selling book about her adventures at Malibu, which was later adapted into the movie by the same name, giving surfing its first popular national exposure. The original film was shot at Secos, another Southern California surf spot, where Sandra Dee played the leading role with Mickey Munoz doing her stunt work. This was the start of a flurry of surf culture movies made by Hollywood, eventually putting the surfing psyche in the mainstream of popular American culture.

Gidget Decal. Peter and Cathy Noble, Monterey, California. $150-250

The Brute by Hannon, 9'9". Three stringer, foam with redwood and balsa, circa 1963. A rare example from a short-lived production of saddle boards. Courtesy of Mark and Cindy Fragale. $1,500-2,500

Surfboards by Jeffrey Dale, Santa Ana, 10'3". Wide single stringer, semi-gun, foam with redwood, fancy redwood fin and tailblock, circa mid-1960s. Allan Seymour, Pacific Coast Vintage Surf Auctions. $1,000-1,500

Girl Happy - **An MGM Film.** A promotional 8 x 10 glossy ©1965. Maunakea Galleries, Kamuela, Hawaii. $50-70

Ramsey-Jay, 10'2". Wide single stringer, foam with redwood, circa 1963. Allan Seymour, Pacific Coast Vintage Surf Auctions. $600-900

Flaherty Surfboards, Venice, California, Business Card. Courtesy of Buck Labadie/Artstuff. $60-90

Flaherty Decal. Peter and Cathy Noble, Monterey, California. $80-120

Flaherty, Santa Monica, California, 9'8". Wide t-bar stringer, foam with balsa, circa 1965. In the author's opinion, one of the finest line art logos representing the period. Peter and Cathy Noble, Monterey, California. $800-1,200

Morey-Pope Surf Shop – Founded by the team of Tom Morey (inventor of the Morey Boogie Board) and Karl Pope, their shop was located in Ventura, California. The uniqueness of their designs compared to other shops and shapers in the 1960s was their turned-down nose and rails. Their three most famous designs produced in the 1960s were the Snub, Blue Machine and Peck Penetrator. During the peak of the market in the 1960s, they turned out over 200 boards a week, all using Clark foam.

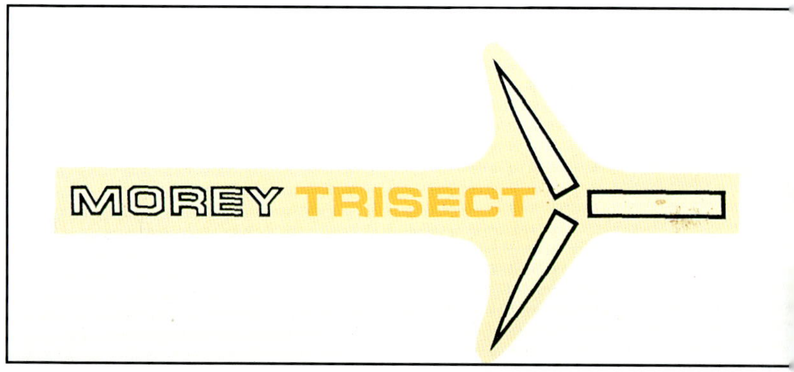

Morey Trisect. Peter and Cathy Noble, Monterey, California. $150-250

Morey, Pope & Company. Peter and Cathy Noble, Monterey, California. $25-35

Morey- Pope Blue Machine, 9'7". Wide t-bar stringer, foam with balsa, circa 1966-68. Optical psychedelic deck logo design reminiscent of the period. Hoffman Collection. $1,200-1,800

Surf Leash Connects the surfboard to a rider's ankle. Invented in 1969.

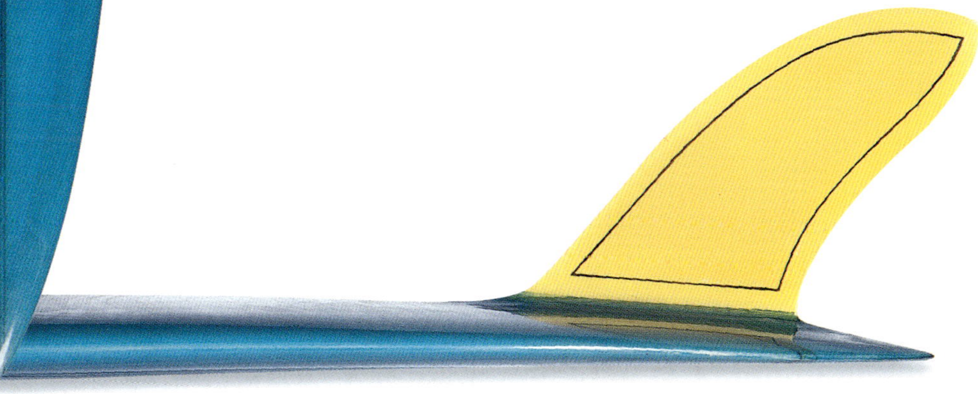

Lance Carson, 9'6". Three stringer, foam with redwood, circa 1967. There were only 25 of this famous nose-riding model produced. Peter and Cathy Noble, Monterey, California. $2,000-3,000

Fade A stalling maneuver allowing the surfer to slow down.

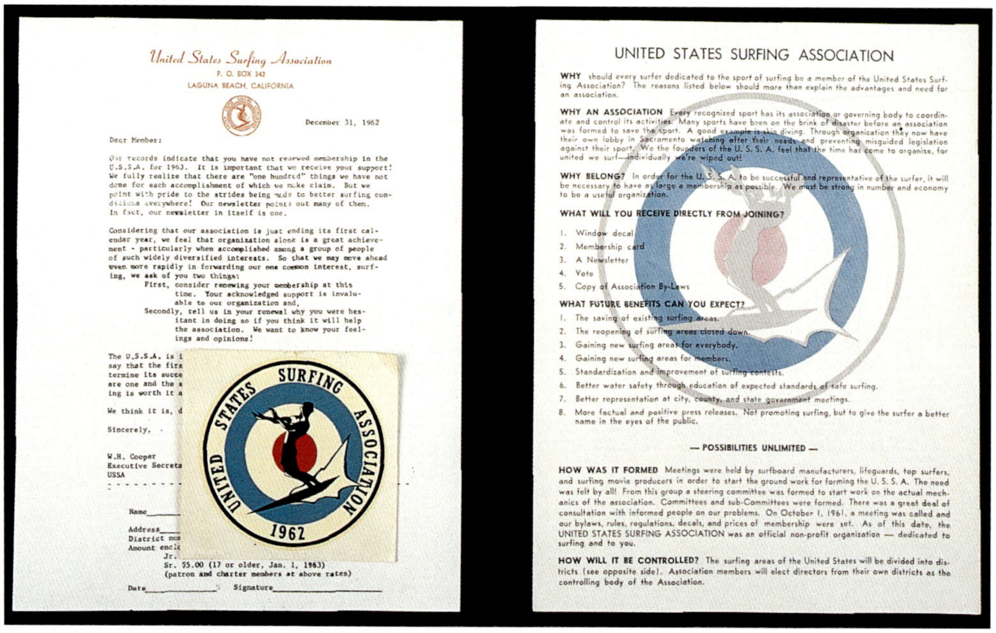

United States Surfing Association
P. O. BOX 342
LAGUNA BEACH, CALIFORNIA

December 31, 1962

Dear Member:

Our records indicate that you have not renewed membership in the U.S.S.A. for 1963. It is important that we receive your support! We fully realize that there are "one hundred" things we have not done for each accomplishment of which we make claim. But we point with pride to the strides being made to better surfing conditions everywhere! Our newsletter points out many of them. In fact, our newsletter in itself is one.

Considering that our association is just ending its first calendar year, we feel that organization alone is a great achievement - particularly when accomplished among a group of people of such widely diversified interests. So that we may move ahead even more rapidly in forwarding our one common interest, surfing, we ask of you two things:

First, consider renewing your membership at this time. Your acknowledged support is invaluable to our organization and,

Secondly, tell us in your renewal why you were hesitant in doing so if you think it will help the association. We want to know your feelings and opinions!

The U.S.S.A. is i
say that the firs
termine its succe
are one and the
ing is worth it a

We think it is, d

Sincerely,

W.H. Cooper
Executive Secreta
USSA

Name

Address
District nu
Amount encl
Jr.
Sr. $5.00 (17 or older, Jan. 1, 1963)
(patron and charter members at above rates)

Date Signature

UNITED STATES SURFING ASSOCIATION

WHY should every surfer dedicated to the sport of surfing be a member of the United States Surfing Association? The reasons listed below should more than explain the advantages and need for an association.

WHY AN ASSOCIATION Every recognized sport has its association or governing body to coordinate and control its activities. Many sports have been on the brink of disaster before an association was formed to save the sport. A good example is skin diving. Through organization they now have their own lobby in Sacramento watching after their needs and preventing misguided legislation against their sport. We the founders of the U. S. S. A. feel that the time has come to organize, for united we surf—individually we're wiped out!

WHY BELONG? In order for the U. S. S. A. to be successful and representative of the surfer, it will be necessary to have as large a membership as possible. We must be strong in number and economy to be a useful organization.

WHAT WILL YOU RECEIVE DIRECTLY FROM JOINING?

1. Window decal
2. Membership card
3. A Newsletter
4. Vote
5. Copy of Association By-Laws

WHAT FUTURE BENEFITS CAN YOU EXPECT?

1. The saving of existing surfing areas.
2. The reopening of surfing areas closed down.
3. Gaining new surfing areas for everybody.
4. Gaining new surfing areas for members.
5. Standardization and improvement of surfing contests.
6. Better water safety through education of expected standards of safe surfing.
7. Better representation at city, county, and state government meetings.
8. More factual and positive press releases. Not promoting surfing, but to give the surfer a better name in the eyes of the public.

— POSSIBILITIES UNLIMITED —

HOW WAS IT FORMED Meetings were held by surfboard manufacturers, lifeguards, top surfers, and surfing movie producers in order to start the ground work for forming the U. S. S. A. The need was felt by all! From this group a steering committee was formed to start work on the actual mechanics of the association. Committees and sub-Committees were formed. There was a great deal of consultation with informed people on our problems. On October 1, 1961, a meeting was called and our bylaws, rules, regulations, decals, and prices of membership were set. As of this date, the UNITED STATES SURFING ASSOCIATION was an official non-profit organization — dedicated to surfing and to you.

HOW WILL IT BE CONTROLLED? The surfing areas of the United States will be divided into districts (see opposite side). Association members will elect directors from their own districts as the controlling body of the Association.

United States Surfing Associaton Decal and Membership Letter. Circa 1962. Courtesy of Buck Labadie/Artstuff. $120-180

Del Cannon Surfboards, 9'8". Wide single stringer, foam with balsa, circa mid-1960s. Low production number 77. Allan Seymour, Pacific Coast Vintage Surf Auctions. As shown: $1,200-1,800. Average: $600-900

Newporter Championship Surfboards, 9'11". Foam with redwood nose and tailblock. Great cartoon logo. Allan Seymour, Pacific Coast Vintage Surf Auctions. $800-1,200

Inter-Island Surf Shop – Founded in 1961 by Mickey Lake and Joseph Kuala, their first shop was located in Kakako in Honolulu, where Mickey shaped the boards while Joseph did the glassing. Being the first surf shop to open in Hawaii, they opened at a time of transition where they first shaped boards of balsa, later turning to foam. Early on, they met Robert "Sparky" Shaffel, who later became the main shaper at Inter-Island and is credited with having invented the fiberglass fin. Mike Diffenderfer also became one of the principle shapers at Inter-Island, when, in 1964, the price of a nine-foot board was $134.50 and a ten-footer was $144.50. Inter-Island used Walker foam exclusively and, in 1965, with many surf shops opening in Hawaii, they decided to close their doors due to stiff competition and shape boards by custom order only. Currently, Inter-Island is producing boards with the principle shaper still being "Sparky" Shaffel.

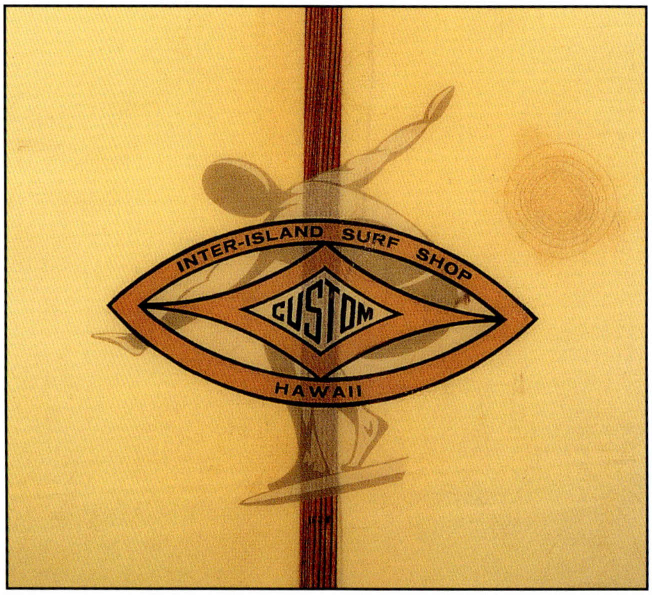

Inter-Island Surf Shop, Hawaii, 10'7". Single stringer, big wave gun, foam with redwood, circa 1964. Peter and Cathy Noble, Monterey, California. $3,000-5,000

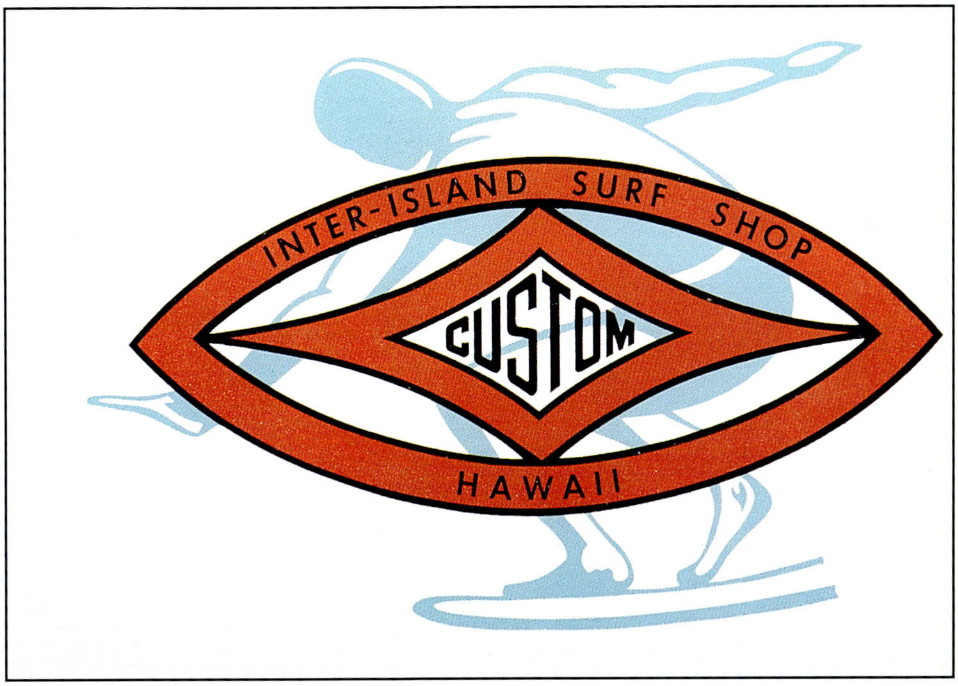

Custom Inter-Island Surf Shop, Hawaii, Decal. Peter and Cathy Noble, Monterey, California. $150-250

Mike Diffenderfer, 9'1". Single stringer, Hanalei gun, chambered balsa and redwood, circa 1969. Allan Seymour, Pacific Coast Vintage Surf Auctions. $3,000-5,000

Surfing Books

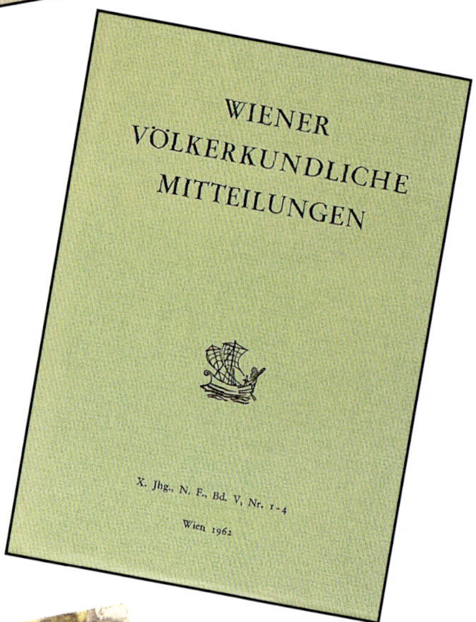

The prices listed below are for books with their original dust jackets in place (if so issued), and in good condition with no noticeable defects. Ex-library copies are worth considerably less. Autographed editions command a 50% to 100% premium. Exceptional mint condition copies are also considerably more valuable than the following listed prices.

All books courtesy of Mauna Kea Galleries, Kamuela, Hawaii.

Ball, John H. (Doc). *California Surfriders.* Los Angeles. 1946. $1,200-1800

Ball, John H. (Doc). *Scrapbook of Surfriding and Beach Stuff*, 1946. $1,200-1,800

Bartlett, Vernon and Maurice Bartlett. *You and Your Surfboard*, 1953, 24 pages. $200-300

Blake, Thomas. *Hawaiian Surf Riding, The Ancient and Royal Pastime*, Northland, 1961, and later published in 1963. $200-300

Blake, Thomas. *Hawaiian Surfboard*, Paradise of the Pacific Press, 1935, 95 pages. Issued bound in tapa cloth. Price is for good copies without insect damage. Add 100% more for copies with dust jackets, which are exceedingly rare and hard to find. $1,500-2,500

Bloomfield, John. *Know-how in the Surf*, Angus and Robertson, 1959, 205 pages. $150-250 Republished in 1960 and 1961. $100-150 Republished by Tuttle in 1965. $40-60

Brennan, Joe. *Duke of Hawaii*, Ballantine, 1968, 213 pages. $40-60

Cameron, Kirk and Jack Hanle. *The Surfer's Handbook*, Dell, 1968, 157 pages. $60-90

Cleary, William S. *Surfing: All the young wave hunters*, Signet, 1967, 126 pages. $60-90

Cook, Joseph J. and William J. Romeika. *Better Surfing for Boys*, Dodd Mead, 1967, 64 pages. $60-90 Revised and republished as *Better Surfing*, 1968, 94 pages. $40-60

Curlewis, Jean and Harold Gazneaux. *Sydney Surfing*, Art in Australia, 1929, 24 pages. $1,200-1,800

Dixon, Peter L. *The Complete Book of Surfing*, Coward-McCann, 1965, 220 pages. $40-60 Republished in 1966 by Longman's for the European market and by Ballantine. $60-90. Republished by Coward-McCann in 1967. $40-60 Republished by Ballantine in 1969. $30-50

Dixon, Peter L. *Men and Waves: A Treasury of Surfing*, Coward-McCann, 1966. $60-90 Republished by Ballantine in 1969. $50-70

Dixon, Peter L. *Men who Ride Mountains*, Bantam, 1969, 174 pages. $100-150

Dixon, Peter L. *Where the Surfers Are: A guide to the world's great surfing spots*, Coward-McCann, 1968, 234 pages. $50-70

Drummond, Ronald Blake. *The Art of Wave Riding*, Cloister, 1931, 26 pages. $800-1,200

Edwards, Phil and Bob Ottum. *You Should Have Been*

Here an Hour Ago: The stoked side of surfing, or how to hang ten through life and stay happy, Harper and Row, 1967, 178 pages. $200-300

Farrelly, Midget. *This Surfing Life*, Rigby, 1964, 138 pages. $100-150 Republished by Angus and Robertson in 1965 for the British market and by Tri-Ocean Books in 1965 for the American market. $100-150 Republished in 1967 by Arco under the title *This Surfing Life as Told to Craig McGregor* and in 1968 by Sphere Books under the title *How to Surf*. $60-90

Finney, Ben R. *Bulletin de le Societe des Etudes Oceaniennes*, 1959. $300-500

Finney, Ben R. *The Development and Diffusion of Modern Hawaiian Surfing*, 1960. $300-500

Finney, Ben R. *Hawaiian Surfing, A study of cultural change*, University of Hawaii, MS Thesis, 1959. $2,000-3,000 (Two copies are known to exist.)

Finney, Ben R. *The Surfing Community: Contrasting values between the local and California surfers in Hawaii.* One of the first articles ever written about localism, circa 1961. $300-500

Finney, Ben R. *Surfboarding in Oceania: its pre-European distribution*, Volkerkundliche Arbeitsgemeinschaft in der Anthropologischen Gesellschaft in Wien, 1959, 36 pages. $300-500

Finney, Ben R. *Surfing in Ancient Hawaii*, Journal of the Polynesian Society, 1959. $300-500

Finney, Ben R. *Wiener Volkerkundliche Mitteilungen*, 1962. $400-600

Finney, Ben R. and James D. Houston. *Surfing, The Sport of Kings*, Tuttle, 1966, 110 pages. $60-90 Published by Hugh Heartland in 1966 for the South African market. $100-150

Funnell, Ronald Spencer. *Surf-riding on the Atlantic Coast*, self-published, 1934, 36 pages. $600-900 Republished in 1953. $400-600

Grigg, Richard Wyman and Ron Church. *Surfer in Hawaii: A guide to surfing in the Hawaiian Islands*, John Severson, 1963, 64 pages. $150-250

Harris, Reginald S. *Heroes of the Surf, Fifty Years' History of Manly Life Saving Club*, 1961, 99 pages. $150-250

Hay, Harry. *Swimming and Surfing*, Jantzen, 1932, 12 pages. $800-1,200

Irwin, John Keith. *Surfers: A study of the growth of a deviant subculture*, University of California, MA thesis, 1965. $800-1,200

Johnson, Barry M. *Surf Fever*, Jacaranda, 1963, 34 pages. $200-300

Kahanamoku, Duke and Joe Brennan. *World of Surfing*, Grosset and Dunlap, 1968, 188 pages. $100-150

Kelly, John M., Jr. *Surf and Sea*, A. S. Barnes, 1965, 304 pages. $100-150

Klein, H. Arthur. *Surfing*, Lippincott, 1965, 238 pages. $60-90 Republished by Kaye Ward in 1967. $80-120

Klein, H. Arthur and Mina C. Klein, eds. *Surf's Up!*

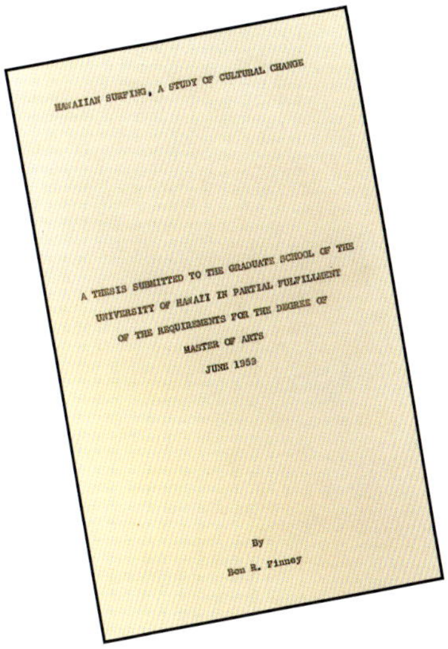

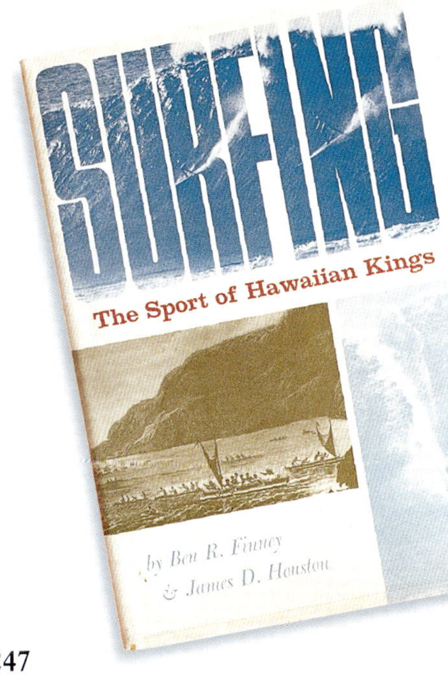

Klein, H. Arthur and Mina C. Klein, eds. *Surf's Up! An anthology of surfing*, Bobbs-Merrill, 1966, 223 pages. $80-120

Kuhns, Grant W. *On Surfing*, Tuttle, 1963, 119 pages. $80-120

Lowe, Arthur Milbourne. *Surfing, Surf-Shooting and Life Saving Pioneering*, 1958, 104 pages. $400-600

Masters, Ted. *Surfing Made Easy*, Masters-Graham, 1962, 66 pages. $200-300

Maxwell, C. Bede. *Surf: Australians against the sea*, Angus and Robertson,1949. $250-350

Muirhead, Desmond. *Surfing in Hawaii: A personal memoir with notes on California, Australia, Peru and other surfing countries*, Northland, 1962, 137 pages. $100-150

Olney, Ross R. *Kings of the Surf*, Putnam, 1962, 192 pages. $50-75

National Geographic. "Surf-boarders Capture California." National Geographic, September 1944. A scarce issue with the article by Doc Ball. $50-70

Olney, Ross R. *The Young Sportman's Guide to Surfing*, Nelson, 1965, 96 pages. Republished by Scholastic Book Service in 1968. $30-50

Patterson, Otto B. *Surf-riding Its Thrills and Techniques*, Tuttle, 1960, 150 pages. $100-150 Republished by Tuttle in 1966. $150-250

Phillip, George Blackmore. *Sixty Years of Recollections of Swimming and Surfing in the Eastern Suburbs*, self-published, 1939, 82 pages. $500-700 Republished in 1940 with 102 pages. $500-700

Pohl, Henry F. *Conquering the Surf: Lifesaving and surfboarding*, Hoffman-Harris, 1944, 45 pages. $400-600

Pollard, Jack, ed. *The Australian Surfrider*, Murray, 1963, 144 pages. $150-250 Republished in 1964. $80-120 Republished under the title *The Surfrider* in 1965. $60-90 Republished by Taplinger under the title *The Surfrider* in 1968. $50-70

Popular Mechanics. "How to Build Your Own Canoe, Kayak or Surfboard," Popular Mechanics, 1940, 14 pages. $100-150

Radlauer, Ed. *Surfing*, Bowmar, 1968, 32 pages. $40-60

St. Pierre, Brian. *The Fantastic Plastic Voyage: Across the South Pacific with surfers and a camera*, Coward-McCann, 1969, 253 pages. $100-150

Severson, John. *Great Surfing: Photos, stories, essays, reminiscences, and poems*, Doubleday, 1967, 159 pages. $80-120

Severson, John. *Modern Surfing Around the World*, Doubleday, 1964, 188 pages. $100-150

Shaw, Steven M. *A Surfboard Builder's Manual*, Products Unlimited, 1964, 62 pages, 2nd edition. $200-300 Presumably the first edition was published in 1963. $500-700

Slattery, Ray. *Grab the Belt*, Horowitz, 1963, 128 pages. $200-300

Spinner, Stephanie. *Water Skiing and Surfboarding*, Golden Press, 1968, 32 pages. $40-60

Stern, David H. and William S. Cleary. *Surfing Guide to Southern California*, Fitzpatrick, 1963, 272 pages. $100-150

Wagenvoord, James and Lynn Bailey. *How to Surf*, Collier Books, 1968, 93 pages. $40-60

Wilson, Doug E. *Learn to Surf*, European Surfing Co. Ltd., 1967, 33 pages. $200-300

Winders, John Robert. *Surf Life Saving in Queensland: An historical record of surf life saving in Queensland*, Surf Life Saving Association of Australia, 1969, 140 pages. $200-300

HAWAIIAN SPORT OF SURF PLAYING

Ancient Hawaiian Surf Glossary

ahua *n.* A place close to shore where a broken waves rises and breaks again. Also known as *kipapa* or *puao.*

alala *n.* A thin wooden surfboard, wide in the front and tapering toward the back, made of koa or breadfruit. Also called *omo.*

hamakuapoko *n.* A well-surfed Oahu location, literally "sky clouds of fragrance."

he'e *v.* To slide, to surf; to slip or flee.

he'e nalu 1) *v.* To ride a surfboard. 2) *n.* Surfing; literally "wave sliding." 3) *n.* Surf rider.

he'e pu'ewai *v.* To ride toward the mouth of a stream or up a stream.

he'e umauma *n.* bodysurfing.

hee *n.* 1) A flowing, as of liquid. 2) The menses. 3) A flight, as of a routed army. 4) The squid, so-called because of its slippery qualities.

hee *v.* 1) To melt; to run or flow, as a liquid. 2) To slip or glide along. 3) To ride on a surfboard. 4) To flee; to flee through fear.

heenalu *n. Hee* and *nalu*, the surf.

heihei nalu *n.* A surfboard race.

honua nalu *n.* The base of the breaker.

huia *n.* An especially high wave formed by the meeting of two crests, said to characterize the surf of Kaipaloaoa, Hawaii.

iki *n.* The collision of a returning wave with an incoming wave; this phrase may have been coined on the west side of Oahu, where these situations are common.

kaha *v.* To surf; to bodysurf.
kaha nalu *n.* Bodysurfing.
kahalaia *n.* The "site of four winds" at Hilo.
kakala *n.* The surf in which an *alaia* board is used; a curling wave.
kiko'o *n.* A twelve- to eighteen-foot surfboard that is hard to handle but good for surf that breaks roughly.
kioe *n.* A small surfboard.
kipapa *n.* 1) The prone riding position. 2) A place close to shore where a broken wave rises and breaks again.
kulana nalu *n.* The place where a surfer paddles to catch a wave; usually the most distant line of breakers.
lala 1) *v.* To surf diagonally to the wave front. 2) *n.* Diagonal surf. 3) *n.* A wave front; a wave to the right.
lala muku *n.* 1) A wave to the left. 2) The seaward side of a cresting wave.
lauloa *n.* One of two kinds of surf ridden (the other is *'ohu*); a long wave that crests and breaks from one end of the beach to the other.
lele wa'a *n.* Canoe leaping – that is, leaping from a canoe with a surfboard in order to ride the wave.
muku *n.* 1) The side of a wave near the crest. 2) The broken section of a wave. 3) A wave to the left. See *lala muku*.
nala ha'i lala *n.* A wave that breaks diagonally.
nalu 1) *v.* To form waves. 2) *n.* A wave; surf. 3) *adj.* Full of waves; wavy, as wood grain. Usage: *"Ke naluo nei ka moana."* "The ocean is full of waves."
nalu *adj.* Roaring; surfing; rolling in, as the surf of the sea.
nalu *n.* 1) The surf as it rolls in upon the beach; a sea; a wave; a billow. 2) The slimy liquid on the body of a newborn infant.
nalu *v.* 1) To be in doubt or suspense; to suspend one's judgement. 2) To speak secretly, or to speak to oneself; to think within oneself. 3) To talk together or confer concerning a thing. 4) To think; to search after any truth or fact.
nalu puki *n.* A wave that shoots high.
nalunalu *adj.* Rough; of sea with high waves; forming high waves.
no ka pakaka ale *v.* Gliding on the surf; probably refers mainly to canoe surfing.
nuumehalani *n.* A surf site on Oahu; mean "the heavenly site where you are alone."
'ohu *n.* One of two kinds of surf ridden (the other is *lauloa*); a low, small wave that rises without breaking but with enough strength to carry a board. Also called *opu'u*.
olo *n.* The long heavy surfboard reserved for chiefs.
omo *n. alaia.*
onaula-loa *n.* A wave of great length and endurance.
onini *n.* A surfboard used by experts, difficult to manage; a thick board made of *wiliwili*; perhaps the same as an *olo*.
opu'u *n.* A large surf, a swell.
owili *n.* A thick board of *wiliwili*; perhaps an *olo*.
pa-ha *n.* A surfboard.
papa he'e nalu *n.* A surfboard; literally, "a board for sliding waves." *Ha'awi papa he'e nalu*: To give a board with the understanding that it would be returned. Boards were apparently loaned rather than given.
po'o *n.* A Kauai location for many ancient surf competitions; means "to hollow out."
pu'ua *n.* A surfboard.
uo *n.* A Maui surf site; translates as "a nimble threading of a needle."

Surfboards:
Approximate Shapes and Sizes, after Finney

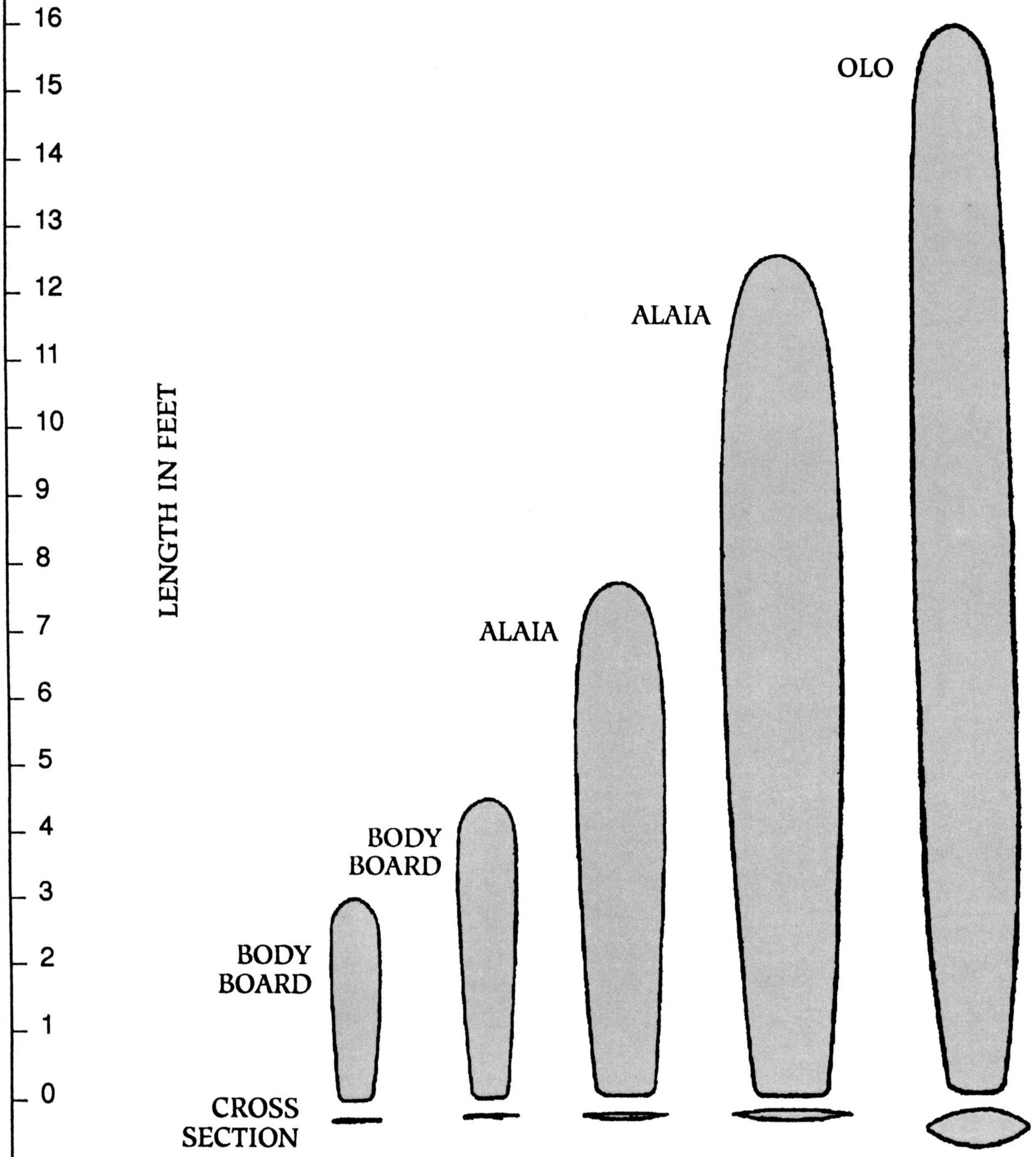

Bibliography

Ball, John H. (Doc). *California Surfriders.* Los Angeles. 1946.

Bingham, Hiram. *A Residence of Twenty-One Years in the Sandwich Islands,* New York. 1847

Blake, Thomas. *Hawaiian Surfboard.* Honolulu. 1935

Blake, Thomas. *Hawaiian Surfriding.* Flagstaff, Arizona. 1961.

Bloomfield, John. *Know How In The Surf.* Tokyo. 1965.

Cook, James. *A Voyage to the Pacific Ocean,* I-III, with atlas (vol. III by Lt. James King), London. 1784.

Dibble, Sheldon. *A History of The Sandwich Islands,* Honolulu. 1909.

Dixon, Peter. *Complete Book of Surfing.* New York. 1965.

Emory, Kenneth P. "Sports, Games, and Amusements," *Ancient Hawaiian Civilizations.* The Kamehameha Schools, Honolulu. 1933.

Finney, Ben. *Hawaiian Surfing, A Study in Cultural Change.* M.A. thesis in anthropology, University of Hawaii. 1959.

Finney, Ben. "Surfboarding in Oceania: its Pre-European Distribution," *Wiener Voelkerkundliche Mitteilungen,* II, 23-36. Vienna. 1959.

Finney, Ben. "Surfing in Ancient Hawaii," *Journal of the Polynesian Society,* LXVIII, 327-347. Wellington. 1959.

Finney, Ben. "The Development and Diffusion of Modern Hawaiian Surfing," *Journal of the Polynesian Society,* LXIX, 315-331. Wellington. 1960.

Ford, Alexander Hume. "Riding the Surf in Hawaii," *Collier's National Weekly,* XLII, XXI, 17. 1909.

Ford, Alexander Hume. "Out-door Allurements," Thrum's *Hawaiian Annual,* 143-149. 1911.

Kelly, John. *Surf'n Sea.* New York. 1964.

Klein, Arthur. *Surfing.* New York. 1965.

London, Charmian. *Our Hawaii.* New York. 1922.

London, Jack. *The Cruise of The Snark.* New York. 1911.

London, Jack. "My Hawaiian Aloha," preface to Charmain London's *Our Hawaii,* 1-33. 1922.

Malo, David. *Hawaiian Antiquities,* BP, Bishop Museum, Spec. Pub 2, 2nd Ed. (trans. Nathaniel Emerson, 1898. First published 1903). Honolulu. 1951.

Morrison, James. *The Journal of James Morrison, Boatswain's Mate on The Bounty.* London. 1935.

Patterson, O. B. *Surfriding, Its Thrills and Techniques.* Tokyo. 1960.

Ryan, Sam. *1960's Surfboard Collector and Price Guide.* Leucadia, Calif. 1994.

Severson, John. *Modern Surfing Around the World.* New York. 1964.

Stearn, David, and William Cleary. *Surfing Guide to South California.* Malibu. 1963.

Thrum, Thomas G. "Hawaiian Surf Riding," *Hawaiian Almanac and Annual for 1896,* 106-113. Honolulu. 1896.

Twain, Mark. *Roughing It,* p. 525. New York. 1872.

Young, Nat. *The History of Surfing.* Revised Edition. Australia. 1994.

Bing Surfboards Promotional Photo taken at LaSerna High School in Whittier, California. Circa mid-1960s. Mauna Kea Galleries, Kamuela, Hawaii. $60-90

Index

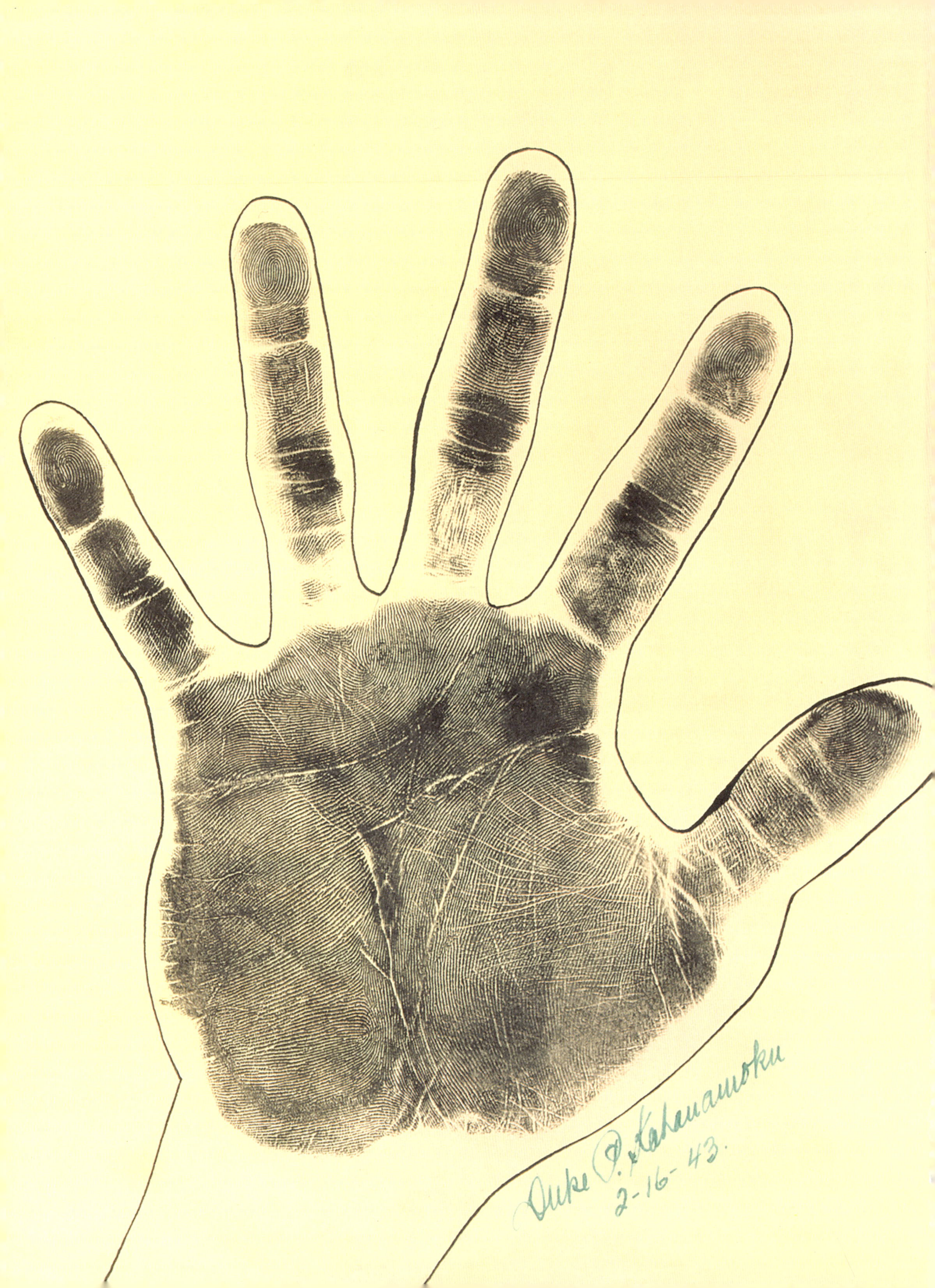
Duke P. Kahanamoku
2-16-43.